STRUGGLE ON THE NORTH SANTIAM

Struggle on the North Santiam

POWER AND COMMUNITY ON THE MARGINS
OF THE AMERICAN WEST

Bob H. Reinhardt

Oregon State University Press   Corvallis

Cataloging-in-publication data is available from the Library of Congress.

∞This paper meets the requirements of ANSI/NISO Z39.48-1992 (Permanence of Paper).

Oregon State University Press
121 The Valley Library
Corvallis OR 97331-4501
541-737-3166 • fax 541-737-3170
www.osupress.oregonstate.edu

To Evangelyn Fleetwood,
who preserved the North Santiam Canyon's history
with intelligence, wisdom, and love.

Contents

Acknowledgments

This book has been nearly fifteen years in the making. During that time, I have been blessed and lucky to receive support from many people—more than I can remember, I'm afraid! What follows is surely only a partial list, and I hope that the people I forget here will forgive me.

This project began as a paper and then master's thesis at the University of Oregon. Thanks to Dan Pope, Jeff Oster, Matt Dennis, and the late and marvelous Peggy Pascoe for their patient guidance. Thanks also to my graduate school colleagues and friends Ana Candela, Chris Brooks, Matt Conn, Elizabeth Medford, and Xiao Peng Shen.

At Oregon State University Press, Mary Elizabeth Braun invited me turn my thesis into a book and then supported the project even after she retired. I will always be grateful for her patience, enthusiasm, wisdom, and understanding. My thanks also to Kim Hogeland, who saw (and pushed, thankfully!) the book through to completion. I am grateful to everyone at Oregon State University Press, including the editorial board—thank you for your patience and support.

This project made only a brief appearance during my doctoral studies at the University of California, Davis, but I thank the people there who supported me and my intellectual development, including Chad Anderson, Jakub Benes, Shelley Brooks, Nate Carpenter, Andy Denning, Ari Kelman, Jordan Lauhon, Kathy Olmsted, Miles Powell, Eric Rauchway, Paul Richter, Alison Steiner, Alan Taylor, Chuck Walker, Clarence Walker, and Louis Warren.

At Boise State University, I have been blessed and lucky to work with wonderful students, faculty, administrators, and community members. I am especially grateful to Lisa Brady, Jennifer Stevens, and Emily Wakild for their support and suggestions for this project.

I am grateful to the staff and volunteers the various archives I visited for this project: the National Archives and Records Administration in Seattle, the Oregon Historical Society's Research Library (especially Scott Daniels), Oregon State University Special Collections and Archives Research Center (especially Chris Petersen),University of Oregon Special

Collections and University Archives, US Army Corps of the Engineers Libraries in Portland and Walla Walla, the Willamette Heritage Center (especially Kaylyn Mabey and Kylie Pine), and, more than anywhere else, the Canyon Life Museum in Mill City. Everyone at the Canyon Life Museum and the North Santiam Historical Society was incredibly help-ful, and I am especially grateful to Frances Thomas, Melody Munger, and, above all, the late Evangelyn Fleetwood, to whom this book is dedicated.

Frances, Melody, and Evangelyn also endured and critiqued portions and drafts of this project over the years, as have other audiences and read-ers, including: attendees of the conferences of the American Historical Association Pacific Coast Branch, the American Society for Environ-mental History, and the Western History Association; the anonymous reviewers for Oregon State University Press; my friends and colleagues at the Cascadia Environmental History Collaborative Retreat; and David Lewis, Myles and Sue McMillan, and Jim Quiring. I am so grateful for their feedback, which dramatically improved the manuscript. Any remaining problems and mistakes are mine alone.

Although this may be my book, many of the stories it contains are from the people of the North Santiam Canyon. My deepest thanks to everyone who so openly and generously shared their memories of their homes and communities.

Finally, I thank my friends and family, especially Leah, Liam, and Violet. Thank you for supporting me and this project over so many years and miles—in, out, and through the North Santiam Canyon.

Introduction

Next to a well-traveled highway on the margins of the American West, there is a place that seems easy to ignore. This particular place is the North Santiam Canyon, a fifty-one-mile stretch along Oregon's Highway 22 on the western side of the Cascade mountain range, surrounded by Douglas fir trees on the banks of the North Santiam River. It takes about an hour, depending on speed traps, to drive through the canyon. A few landmarks jump out to motorists: Mt. Jefferson to the east, occasionally peeking out over the treetops; two large dams (Detroit Dam and its regulating dam, Big Cliff) and their full reservoirs or empty reservoir beds, depending on the season; and always the North Santiam River, burbling, swirling, crashing, pooling, and tumbling alongside the highway. Houses and buildings are scattered along the roadside, sometimes gathered into villages and towns, and perceptive drivers might even notice the signs alerting them that they have entered or left behind one of these communities. But driving along at fifty-five miles per hour, one would be forgiven for not finding anything remarkable or memorable about the North Santiam Canyon, like so many other marginal places in the American West.

But those who slow down a little—even just to the forty-five-mile-per-hour limit posted in a few of the towns—will see more detail that suggests depth and complexity in the North Santiam Canyon. Those welcome signs have names on them such as Mill City and Gates, marking specific places with their own stories. Some of the signs are in the shape of circular saws and evoke the area's logging past, present, and future; a few signs include images of mountains and rivers, suggesting other ideas about the area's economy and identity. Higher on the hillsides away from the road, clear-cuts mar the view, but second- and third-growth stands peak out, as do patches of old-growth forest. Buildings more than a century old stand faded and dilapidated as well as repainted and renovated, occupied by residents of different means and interests who have their own sense of home in the canyon. And that's just the view from inside the car window. Stopping at a roadside restaurant such as Cedars Lounge in Detroit or Marion Forks Lodge offers not just a good sandwich or slice of pizza, but also selected stories about the area's past: paper menus with a map of Old Detroit, now submerged under the reservoir, from which Cedars Lounge was hauled up on a sled; paintings of Native peoples situated next to old maps and taxidermized animal heads, mounted on walls made of lumber produced in now-defunct mills not that far from Marion Forks Lodge. Intrepid and interested travelers might even stop for a while to visit the Canyon Life Museum in Mill City, where a floor studded with holes from loggers' boots supports exhibits on farming, mining, and more. In short, there is history in the North Santiam Canyon, as in other such places in the West.

Paying attention to that history leads to interesting questions about important events and themes in the history of the American West. Visitors might note repeated use of the name "Minto" and wonder why someone who never even lived in the area got his name on a mountain pass, park, road, and other landmarks. Others might have a vague (and generally correct) sense that the word "Santiam" has Native American origins and perhaps puzzle about what happened to those Native peoples. Railroad history buffs might stop in Mill City to see the old railroad bridge now used by pedestrians in the same spot that the Oregon Pacific Railroad crossed the river in 1888, supposedly on its way to becoming a transcontinental railroad—an aspiration that died in the upper canyon just a few years later. That projected route ran right through Marion Forks and Township 11, Range 7, where at the beginning of the twentieth century twelve false homestead claims led to the infamous Oregon Land Fraud Trials and the downfall—and death—of a US senator. If driving by Detroit Reservoir during the late fall or increasingly dry summers, passersby would certainly take note of the empty reservoir and stumps, but they would see no sign of the old town of Detroit that sat at the bottom of the reservoir and how "new" Detroit came to be in 1953. Seeing the vacant mill buildings in Idanha might remind some travelers that the North Santiam Canyon featured prominently in the old-growth forest controversies of the 1980s and 1990s, and a few might make the connection between the Yellow Ribbon Rallies of that time and the Save Our Lake (SOL) protests that occurred during the summer of 2001, when Detroit Reservoir went dry and the vulnerabilities of the tourism industry became apparent. In short, visitors might be surprised to learn that the North Santiam Canyon has been the site of interesting and important regional and national history.

To see, interpret, and make sense of the history of this place, and to suggest a path for studies of other such communities, this book focuses on power in the North Santiam Canyon. As long as people have lived in the region, they have sought to assert their autonomy. They have done so for myriad reasons: to control their homelands and cultures, as did the indigenous Santiam Kalapuyans and Molallans; to build their own farms and homes, like Euro-American families in the middle and late nineteenth century; and to profit from the area's resources, from miners in the nineteenth century and loggers in the twentieth century to tourism businesses in the twenty-first century. Their expressions of power have taken a variety of forms, from the resourcefulness of Depression-era subsistence hunting to loud demands for government assistance at the same time; from enthusiastic embrace of federal river development projects to passive acceptance or modest resistance to the same; from beautiful moments of family and community life to ugly expressions of xenophobia and racism. These efforts have shaped work, life, community, and lived experience, although local autonomy has always been structured and limited by powerful forces from beyond the area: citizens of larger urban areas in the Willamette Valley, capitalists from Portland and San Francisco and New York, national politicians and agents of the federal government, and, most importantly, distant and abstract market forces. In their responses to these external forces, people in the North Santiam Canyon have developed a narrative that celebrates local resiliency and independence while pitting a victimized "us" (local residents) versus a powerful "them" (outsiders, city folk, "the government"). That story has become a part of the identity of the North Santiam Canyon, where, as in so many other similar marginalized places in the American West, residents have in a multitude of ways, out of many motives, and to varying degrees of success tried to exercise limited power over their lives, their work, and their community.

UNDERSTANDING POWER IN THE WEST AND THE NORTH SANTIAM CANYON

This book draws on, builds upon, and departs from other histories of the American West that examine the workings of power on and within marginalized communities. Broad perspectives surveying the sweep of the region's history have explored the breadth and depth of external power exerted upon places like the North Santiam Canyon. In contrast to urban centers of wealth and power, small resource-dependent communities can seem like hapless, powerless victims of distant forces: distant politicians and entrenched government bureaucrats, cultural and social pressures emanating from urbane trendsetters, and global economic systems. In a famous 1934 essay for *Harper's*, Bernard DeVoto described the West as a "Plundered Province," an economic colony whose residents had been "looted, betrayed, [and] sold out" by ungrateful Easterners.[1] This direct interpretation was simplistic in laying blame solely on outsiders, but its focus on the influence of external forces has resonated with historians for decades, from the enthusiastic endorsement of Walter Prescott Webb to the thoughtful and complex analyses of Nancy Langston, Patricia Nelson Limerick, Earl Pomeroy, Hal Rothman, Richard White, Donald Worster, and others.[2] William Robbins has developed perhaps the most convincing and nuanced of these interpretations through histories written at different scales, from a history of a small Oregon coastal community to a broad survey of the entire American West.[3] As Robbins explains, the relationships of marginalized places to larger sources of power, "Isolated, with relatively small populations, and lacking significant influence in the trade and exchange relation, resource-dependent communities are by-products of industrial strategies and decisions made elsewhere."[4] From historical perspectives that appreciate the power of national and global forces, small communities like the North Santiam Canyon can seem relatively insignificant and powerless.

Things look a little different closer up. Historians studying marginal communities in the American West have explored how people in such communities have sought to assert their autonomy. These examinations of local power offer examples and paths that this book seeks to follow and extend. The first step on that path is to try to re-create a place's history and explain how and why that place changed over time; Richard White's *Land Use, Environment, and Social Change*, William deBuys's *Enchantment and Exploitation*, and William Willingham's *Starting Over* approach such description and analysis from the perspective of environmental change, evolving ideas about and uses of the land, and careful demographic study of the local population, respectively.[5] In exploring the myriad ways people respond to the overwhelming influence of a specific source of power, Brian Leech's *The City That Ate Itself* provides an excellent guide, showing how the residents of Butte, Montana, created community, endured hardship in the mines and in their homes, and at times actively resisted the power of the Anaconda Mining Company.[6]

Bonnie Christensen's history of tourism in Red Lodge, Montana, shows the multitude of ways in which Westerners have transformed their communities, their identities, and even themselves in an effort to confront the challenges of the transition from natural resource extraction to a tourism-based economy.[7] To make sense of the actual experience of life and work in a Western natural resource extraction community, James Feldman's engaging history of Sand Island, Wisconsin, demonstrates how local conditions, and the way local people understood and interacted with those conditions, shape exactly how "a peripheral economy work(s)."[8] Such on-the-ground perspectives explain a variety of ways in which people on the Western periphery have worked against and with external forces. Such an approach does not ignore or minimize the influence of outside forces, but it does show how the people subject to those forces have not sat back and watched things happen to them—they made things happen, too. By building on these analyses and focusing on local perspectives, choices, and actions, this book examines how residents of the canyon have responded to, interacted with, and even, rarely, gotten the better of external forces.

To explore those local perspectives, this book draws on both local archives and histories as well as regional and national sources. The North Santiam Historical Society (NSHS) has sought to preserve the area's past, collecting thousands of photographs, hundreds of personal recollections, dozens of boxes of documents, and a bank vault full of newspaper clippings, maps, and other ephemera. The NSHS maintains an archive of local newspapers, which provide an invaluable chronicle of events as well as express a local point of view that needs critical contextualization, as William Willingham explains.[9] The NSHS also maintains a number of local reminisces and narratives, from the oral histories recorded in *Just a Few of Our Memories* to the unpublished, three-hundred-plus-page manuscript of longtime resident and history buff John Lengacher. Others have written about aspects of the area's history, including Cara Kelly's master's thesis on precontact land-use patterns, Evangelyn Fleetwood's twenty-page time line of notable events, Jim Petersen's history of the Freres Lumber Company in Lyons, Jim Quiring's forthcoming book about the Little North Fork River, and the "autobiography of a place" about Niagara written by Lisa Chaldize, Melody Munger, and Debbie Corning.[10] These local perspectives and sources complement insights from other sources, including qualitative and quantitative information from the US Census, records from the US Army Corps of Engineers, urban newspapers and trade journals, and materials preserved by the Willamette Heritage Center in Salem and the Oregon Historical Society in Portland. Taken together and critically analyzed, these firsthand accounts and information reveal the many ways people in the North Santiam Canyon have sought to assert their autonomy in relationship to the world outside.

THE PATH THROUGH THE CANYON AND ITS HISTORY

The path through the North Santiam Canyon's history follows the routes that run into and through the area, especially Highway 22, a popular road

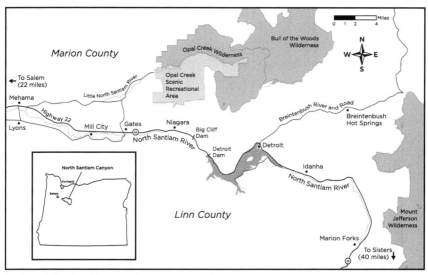

The North Santiam Canyon. Map illustrator: Edwin Xavier Pinedo.

connecting Oregon's Willamette Valley to central Oregon and beyond. The Willamette Valley is the center of state and regional economic, political, and cultural power: it is the location of the state's biggest cities (Portland in the north and Eugene in the south), most of the state's population, and the state capital in Salem. About twenty-two miles east of Salem on the highway, the North Santiam Canyon begins at the towns of Lyons and Mehama.[11] There, the gently sloped farmlands of the Willamette Valley transition into mountain terrain and dense Douglas fir forests, and the highway saddles up alongside the North Santiam River for a sixty-mile journey into the Cascade mountains. Continuing east along the river brings one into Mill City, the largest population center of the area with about eighteen hundred residents living on either side of the river, which divides Marion and Linn Counties. A few miles up the river, the steep hillsides briefly spread out into a valley and the town of Gates, the last part of the lower canyon.

After Gates, the walls close in again and travelers enter the upper canyon. Ten miles up Highway 22, Detroit Dam rises 463 feet above the river, backing up a reservoir with thirty-two miles of shoreline. The town of Detroit sits at the northeast end of the reservoir. Idanha comes next, about fifty miles from Salem; its two hundred residents and vacant mill buildings represent the last population center. A few miles later, travelers come to a few vacation homes, a fish hatchery, and a historic restaurant at Marion Forks. The highway then skips over the North Santiam River for another ten miles, when the river breaks east for its headwaters in the Cascade mountains. Highway 22 continues to the junction with Highway 20, which crests the Cascades at Santiam Pass and heads east toward central Oregon. Each village and town along the North Santiam River has its own specific history, and there are differences between the lower canyon closer to the Willamette Valley and the more isolated upper canyon. But in practice—here in this book and in the lived experience of people in the area—the communities of the North Santiam Canyon have more in common than not.

This analysis of the North Santiam Canyon breaks roughly into two halves. The first part covers the period prior to Euro American contact in the mid-nineteenth century up through the Great Depression. Chapter 1 begins with the first people to call the area home: the Santiam bands of the Molalla and Kalapuya peoples. These Native groups created a multitude of connections into and through the area, creating a sense of home that incorporated the canyon as a place in which to survive and thrive and as a corridor through which to move. Chapter 1 also describes the first Euro Americans in the area: fur trappers and miners, explorers and road build-ers, and the first Euro American families to resettle the area, so recently dispossessed from Kalapuyans and Molallans, in the nineteenth century. These newcomers initially used and conceived of the canyon as a path to other places, establishing connections to the outside world, especially federal land policy largesse, that made their enterprises possible. Chapter 2 narrates the construction of the Oregon Pacific Railroad into the North Santiam Canyon during the 1870s and 1880s, a development that opened up opportunities for local agency as well as external influence, both legal and not. Chapter 3 focuses on life, work, and community in the area under the shadow of the Hammond Lumber Company, which dominated the area from 1894 to 1934. Chapter 4 considers the Great Depression and connections to the outside world, which had made it vulnerable to the effects of the Depression, retracted during this period, and local residents responded by pursing both self-sufficiency and government support. The Great Depression period highlights the theme of the book's first section: people living in the canyon exercised autonomy and cultivated connec-tions to external forces, hoping that both local power and outside power could coexist and even reinforce each other.

The second part of the book shows more powerful and abstract outside forces coming to the canyon, and explores how residents increas-ingly responded with anxiety, alarm, and anger. Chapter 5 details two infrastructure projects built between 1934 and 1953 that fundamentally transformed the North Santiam Canyon and the region: Highway 22 and the Army Corps of Engineers' Detroit Dam. Although most local residents enthusiastically supported these changes and their promised economic development, a few people expressed reservations about how these technological wonders might transform—or even destroy—their homes and communities. Chapter 6 examines the timber economy and identity of a "timber community" that developed along the new highway from the 1940s through the 1980s, during which time timber workers and local timber companies sometimes conflicted but often cooperated with each other and among themselves, attracting at one time unwanted legal attention. Chapter 7 explains the development of a fiercely independent identity in the canyon at the end of the twentieth century. That identity crystalized during the old-growth controversies of the 1980s and 1990s, and it hardened into a more general canyon-versus-outsiders perspective at the beginning of the twenty-first century, when the vulnerabilities of the local tourism economy became increasingly obvious.

At the end of this journey through this place and its history, the book's epilogue considers the community that has emerged from the transformations and tumult of the second half of the twentieth century, reflecting on the possibilities for local autonomy in the twenty-first century. In looking toward this future, the people of the North Santiam Canyon, like other such marginal places in the community, have a deep reservoir of history from which to draw. That history contains frustrations, failures, and even foolish and destructive responses to external forces. But it contains power, too—the power of knowing that the residents of the North Santiam Canyon and places like it are real people making real decisions that have real consequences.

1
Making Homes, Profits, and Paths in the North Santiam Canyon

An archeological report conducted by the Smithsonian Institute in 1948 came to this conclusion regarding Native American settlement in the North Santiam Canyon: "It is the unanimous opinion of all who have done archeological survey work in the [North Santiam Canyon] that the combination of the steep terrain and the dense timber must have had a strong restrictive influence on the permanent habitation of the small Canyons which open into the main river valley."[1] True enough: steep hillsides, dense forests, and other environmental challenges can make it difficult to live in this place year-round. Yet from its earliest history as a human space beginning approximately six to ten thousand years ago, the North Santiam Canyon has been both a home and a transitory place. Native peoples—Kalapuyans in the west near the Willamette Valley, Molallans in the east toward the ridge of the Cascade Mountains, and from across the mountains to the east Wasco and other peoples of what would later be called Warm Springs Indians—used the North Santiam Canyon for its riches in fish, berries, and other foods and resources.[2] They established seasonal camps for fishing and food preservation, identified and cultivated the most productive huckleberry grounds, and developed a comprehensive network of trails for moving and trading. In these and other ways, Native peoples settled the canyon and incorporated it into their world and their sense of home. The area would also become a refuge—a relatively remote place that staved off the flood of Euro Americans who came to the Willamette Valley in the nineteenth century.

When Euro Americans began traveling up the North Santiam, they initially saw not a home, but a place from which to profit and through which to traverse. In the 1840s, trappers came and left when they had gathered their pelts; beginning in the 1850s, miners established seasonal residence, then took the ore and headed back to the towns and cities where they could sell their finds. Road surveyors from the Willamette Valley came in the late 1840s looking for a way through, not for a place to stay. Eventually, in the 1850s and 1860s, Euro Americans came with the intention to create homes and settle—more accurately *resettle* and colonize—lands in which Native peoples had already created homes.[3] Though their narratives and memories focused on independence and self-sufficiency, these resettler colonizers also depended on external forces, especially the federal government and the market, and they encouraged connections with the outside world.

SANTIAM PEOPLES AT HOME IN AND THROUGH THE CANYON

Despite the assertions of the 1948 Smithsonian report, Native peoples used and held dear the North Santiam Canyon. The Santiam bands of the Kalapuyan and the Molallan peoples knew well what the area had to offer: game, fish, plants, and a route through which goods, people, and power passed. Historians of these peoples, especially Santiam descendent and anthropologist David Lewis, have explored their life ways and connections to other Native groups.[4] Archeological work since the 1948 Smithsonian report reveals the breadth and depth of the Native presence in the area. By 2002, archaeologists had unearthed more than four hundred prehistoric sites and one hundred historic sites, with more discoveries every year.[5] Native peoples left evidence of their lives and work in a variety of ways, from projectile points and other tools to dozens of miles of trails crisscrossing the Cascade mountains. Though Native peoples may not have created the Smithsonian's idea of "permanent habitation," they certainly knew and defined the North Santiam Canyon as part of their home.

Native use and seasonal occupation of the area were shared between the Kalapuyans in the west in the lower elevations closer to the Willamette Valley, and Molallans in the east more proximate to the higher elevations of the Cascade mountains.[6] A long history of interactions between these and other peoples blurs any boundary lines in the North Santiam Canyon. At the beginning of the nineteenth century, the total Kalapuyan population numbered around eight thousand, according to Alquema, a Santiam Kalapuyan chief in the mid-nineteenth century.[7] Organized into small, loosely affiliated autonomous groups, the Kalapuyans spoke unique dialects and divided their time between permanent villages in the Willamette Valley and seasonal movement throughout the surrounding hills and mountains.

The Kalapuyan group on the western side of the North Santiam Canyon were known by Euro Americans as the "Santiam" after a local chief, whose name was also used by Euro Americans for the surrounding rivers.

Other Kalapuyan groups called the Santiam Kalapuyans *(an)hálpam*, meaning "the upland people" or the "upstreamers" for their location in relation to other Kalapuyan bands.[8] In these homelands east of the Willamette Valley, the Santiam Kalapuyans, like other Native peoples in Oregon and throughout the American West, developed complex and sophisticated cyclical subsistence and agricultural practices—their seasonal rounds—by which they not only survived but thrived.[9] During the colder and wet winter months, the Santiam Kalapuyan drew on preserved foods while living in lower-elevation villages consisting of multifamily houses and lodges. They looked forward to the early spring and the time they called *am pláatowaʰ*, "it [leaves] buds out," when they would begin their movement away from their villages to harvest a diverse array of foods, including acorns, *wapato*, and the bulbs of the camas plant. The Kalapuyans knew the places rich in these foods because they had cultivated their environments, especially by burning forest and field throughout the summer and fall. These practices created conditions that both encouraged the growth of food plants and eased the work of harvesting those foods. Their summer and fall seasonal rounds also took the Kalapuyans into the higher elevations of the North Santiam Canyon, where they hunted elk, deer, and other game and collected huckleberries, the location of which they knew well and passed down from generation to generation. With the late fall—October was *tin tan kwaʰ*, "leaves fall off"—and knowledge of the colder months to come, the Kalapuyans preserved game and other foods and returned to their winter villages. Through such sophisticated knowledge and deliberate practices, the Santiam Kalapuyan created a homeland stretching from the Willamette Valley into North Santiam Canyon.

Their neighbors to the east were the Molallans, whose territory stretched along the western side of the Cascades from Mt. Hood in the north to Mt. McLoughlin in the south.[10] The Molallans numbered fewer than the Kalapuyans—about three thousand at the beginning of the nineteenth century—and they had developed a seasonal round similar to that of the Kalapuyans.[11] During the colder winter months, Molallans stayed in villages closer to the Willamette Valley, but from spring through the fall, they made use of the abundance of the North Santiam Canyon. Traveling higher in the open areas of the mountains, the Molallans hunted more large game than the Kalapuyans and used various methods: bow and arrow, traps, disguises made of deer heads, and trained dogs. The Molallans also took fish, dug for camas, and gathered huckleberries: the name "Molalla" may be derived from *ulali*, "berry" in the Chinuk Wawa trade language used widely throughout the Pacific Northwest.[12]

The North Santiam Canyon had long brought Kalapuyans and Molallans into contact with each other. Though the Molallans and Kalapuyans spoke different languages, they shared a variety of relationships. Marriage bound the two peoples together, with wealthier members of both groups seeking to extend their influence through polygyny, including relationships with members of other tribes. The most notable of these unions was that between Santiam Kalpuyan chief Alquema and Margaret, daughter of Coastno, chief of the Santiam Molallans. Yet the relationship between the Molallans and Kalapuyans was not entirely amicable. In interviews conducted during the 1920s, the Kalapuyan John Hudson—son of Alquema and Margaret—remembered a story of fear among his people. He recalled that the Kalapuyans "would always be watchful there when they knew an owl was making noises in the nighttime. Or if a screech owl was talking in the darkness they would say, 'Wonder why it is doing like that? Maybe (foreign, non-Kalapuya) people are going (scouting) around.' They were always fearful when they heard an owl in the nighttime. They would say, 'Maybe it is a Molale who has made himself (like) an owl.' "[13] The ethnographer who recorded this interview, Melville Jacobs, asserted that Molallans had a reputation for taking slaves from Kalapuyans. This is entirely possible, as slaves represented wealth and power among Molallans—a practice Santiam Kalapuyans rejected, in contrast to some other Kalapuyan bands. Through slavery, marriage, and other interpersonal relationships, power moved between the Molallan and Kalapuyan people of the North Santiam Canyon.

Kalapuyans and Molallans were also connected to people, ideas, and trade goods from outside the Willamette Valley. A comprehensive network of trails along ridges and waterways crisscrossed the North Santiam Canyon and traversed the Cascades. Elders from the Warm Springs Reservation, which lies just over the mountains to the northeast of the canyon, detail a trail that followed the North Santiam River to its headwaters, passed by Mt. Jefferson into central Oregon, and then branched north up the Deschutes River and south along a major route called the Klamath Trail, toward Crater Lake.[14] To the west, another route ran along the base of the Cascades, providing a north-south connection for native peoples in the Willamette Valley and beyond.[15] It appears on the 1851 treaty map as the "supposed course of the Molalla trail of the Klamath," a reference to the Klamath people of southern Oregon, with whom Molallans shared linguistic and social customs and other close associations, including hunting elk and camping together in the Willamette Valley. During a February 1848 incident, for example,

Chief Coastno of the Santiam Molalla came to the defense of some Klamath people who had traveled north along the trail and whom Euro Americans sought to drive out.[16]

These trail networks facilitated the exchange of goods in and out of the North Santiam Canyon. Santiam Molallans possessed hide blankets from buffaloes found east of the Cascades.[17] Kalapuyans also wore buffalo robes and used other goods from the east, according to Alquema: "They say that some of those (wealthy) people had buffalo hides for their blankets. They purchased them far away in country to the east. They say they got their (better) blankets from there."[18] Archeological research has also unearthed goods that reveal relationships with people to the south and west, including whalebone clubs, knives, and implements similar to those used in Northern California and southern Oregon.[19] Most projectile points in the North Santiam Canyon were made of material from Obsidian Cliffs, a site at the western base of the North Sister mountain, dozens of miles away.[20] The North Santiam Canyon, then, was a place where Native peoples traveled and that they knew intimately as their home.

THE PERSISTENCE OF SANTIAM PEOPLES

In the early nineteenth century, newcomers from Europe and the United States began to appear in the homelands of the Kalapuyans and Molallans, but those interactions remained limited by Native choice. Initial contact came in 1812, when Douglas McKenzie of the Pacific Fur Company (John Jacob Astor's ill-fated global fur-trading scheme) met Kalapuyans during a foray up the Willamette River. Euro American reports of the Molalla did not appear until 1841, although the Santiam Molalla probably had earlier contact with Euro Americans, given their mobility and the amount of interaction between Kalapuyans and Molallans; furthermore, archaeological digs in Molallan lands have unearthed many European and Euro American goods.[21] In the first decades of the nineteenth century, the Pacific Fur Company and then the North West Company built trading and trapping posts in the Willamette Valley, but the Native peoples there initially frustrated efforts to incorporate them into the fur trade. William Wallace of the Pacific Fur Company dismissed the Kalapuyans as "totally ignorant of hunting Furs"; another fur trader, Alexander Henry of the Northwestern Company, said that the Kalapuyans "have no idea of the value of our goods."[22] Wallace and Henry meant these assessments as insults, but as Melinda Jetté observes, their rejection suggests the Kalapuyans' commitment to their traditional seasonal round and their existing trade relations with other Native peoples, including the Molallans.

Moreover, it demonstrates their desire to retain autonomy by limiting interactions with the newcomers.[23]

Native autonomy eroded over the next few decades as more newcomers arrived while disease decimated Native peoples. By the 1820s, the Kalapuyans had made what Melinda Jetté calls a "modest accommodation to the economics of the fur trade," conducting business with the newcomers and showing them hospitality and help in times of need. Other newcomers came not to trade but to take land and stay: retired North West Company employees and their Native wives, who started farms and families on the edge of Santiam Kalapuya territory, and, in far greater numbers and much more closely to Santiam country, the Americans who followed the establishment of a Methodist mission in the middle Willamette Valley in 1834. By 1850, there were more than two hundred Euro American households on the eastern side of the valley, encroaching into the North Santiam Canyon.[24] While the numbers of Euro Americans increased, Native populations dramatically and tragically decreased as a result of disease, including epidemics of malaria in the 1830s and measles in 1848. By the middle of the century, the precontact Native population in the Willamette Valley had been reduced by as much as ninety percent. That horror reached into the North Santiam Canyon: as of 1851, the Santiam Kalapuyans numbered 165 people and the Santiam Molallans just 65.[25]

By midcentury, the much-depleted Kalapuyans and Molallans agreed to treaty negotiations with the US government, while continuing to insist on control over their homelands. In June 1850, responding to demands of Euro Americans in the Willamette Valley that the federal government take control of native lands and distribute them to American settlers, Congress authorized a special treaty commission to negotiate with the Native peoples of the Willamette Valley.[26] The first of those negotiations began on April 16, 1851, at the American settlement at Champoeg. Though the agents sent by the government intended to move all Willamette Valley Native peoples east of the Cascades, the Santiam Kalapuyans, represented by Alquema, Sophan, and Tiacan, refused to leave their home. As Tiacan explained to the treaty commissioners, "their hearts were upon that piece of land, and they did not wich [sic] to leave it." Treaty negotiations with the Molallans began in May 1851, the month after Kalapuyan negotiations, and the Molallans likewise refused to leave their territory. "They had thought and counseled over it," recorded the interpreter, "and they did not wish to leave their country." In response to a question about how long they had lived here, Molallan principal chief Guai-Eck-e-te replied, "he did not know how long, but, he thought, from a short time after God made the world."

Despite the persistence of federal negotiators, the Santiam peoples refused to give up the land they knew and loved in the North Santiam Canyon. The Kalapuyan and Molallan negotiators well understood the demographic powers at work in the Willamette Valley. Crooked Finger of the Molalla noted that his people "were dieing [*sic*] off very fast," and the Kalapuyans lamented that "they had decreased to nothing, and in a short time the whites would have all their lands without their removing." The Santiam peoples consented to sell most of their lands to the American commissioners, but they refused to move east of the Cascades. Alquema blasted the Americans' greed. "We have been willing to throw away the rest of our country, and reserve the land lying between the forks of the Santiam!" he exclaimed. "You thought it was too much, then we agreed to take only half of it . . . You thought it was too much!" The Kalapuyans were exasperated and insistent. "You want us still to take less, we can't do it, it is too small, it is tieing [*sic*] us up in too small a space." The Molallans, too, said they were willing to sell some territory, but they insisted on retaining their homelands in the North Santiam Canyon. Days upon days of negotiation would not budge them from that place, and the Americans finally relented. "Thinking it better not to urge or compel them to do it [move them east] against their wishes," as the negotiations' secretary recorded, the treaty commissioners accepted the demand of the Santiam Kalapuyans for a reservation west of the Cascades, along the southern bank of the North Santiam River; the Santiam Molallans retained their own reservation to the summit of the Cascades, east of the Kalapuyan reservation.

The Santiam peoples sought not only control over the North Santiam Canyon but also to limit and manage their interactions with the Euro American newcomers. Both the Kalapuyans and Molallans initially rejected the government's efforts to pay for their land with goods and supplies, instead insisting on cash payments. By controlling the medium of exchange, the Kalapuyans and Molallans could control the integration of the market economy into their traditional ways of cultivating the abundance around them, rather than completely adopting Euro American agriculture as the Americans wanted. When treaty commissioners asked whether "they wanted Plows and farming utensils generally," the Kalapuyans plainly stated "they did not." Nor did they want "teachers among you to teach your children," as offered by the federal government. Instead, the Kalapuyans and Molallans wanted to be left alone and to

Section of an 1851 map by Edward Starling and George Gibbs, showing the location of the reservations of the Santiam Kalapuyans and Santiam Molallans as agreed upon during the 1851 treaty negotiations. Courtesy of David Lewis.

engage with Euro Americans on Native terms—to use US government cash to buy what they wanted to complement and sustain their life ways.

On the issue of cash, as with the extent of their homelands, the Kalapuyans and Molallans compromised. The US government agreed to pay the Santiam Kalapuyans $500 in cash and $2,000 (as valued by the government) of goods such as blankets, shirts, and handkerchiefs yearly for twenty years. The Santiam Molallans were promised $200 cash and $800 of goods for the same amount of time. For this payment—totaling $10,000 cash and $40,000 in goods for the Santiam Kalapuyans, and $4,000 cash and $16,000 in goods for the Santiam Molalla—the US government took no less than one million acres of Native land in the Santiam country.

Despite this loss and the compromises, Kalapuyan and Molallan representatives saw the 1851 treaty as a source of hope. It would keep them in the North Santiam Canyon, a place so dear to them that, as Alquema explained when pushed by the treaty commissioners to move east of the Cascades, "it may be better for us [to move east], but our minds are made up. . . . We would rather be shot on it than to remove." Upon agreeing to the final terms that would reserve some of their home, Alquema exclaimed, "Yes! It is good [and] I agree to it." With permanent reservations away from Euro Americans and a reliable source of cash—plus some goods, which could be useful—the Kalapuyans and Molallans might keep their lives and livelihood.

But the Euro American newcomers could not tolerate even the small amount of land, cash, and cheap goods for which the Kalapuyans and Molallans had negotiated. Although authorized agents of the federal government signed the treaty documents, Congress never ratified the treaties of 1851.[27] Oregon's territorial governor Joseph Lane wanted all Native peoples moved east of the Cascades, echoing and encouraging the demands of the Euro American squatters filling the Willamette Valley. They could not support, and successfully lobbied against, the 1851 treaties through which the Santiam peoples had worked so hard to assert their autonomy. As Greg Whaley writes, "the Indians, knowingly or unknowingly, negotiated treaties that were not passable."[28] Federal negotiators returned to the Willamette Valley in January 1855 to treat with Kalapuyan and Molallan peoples in Dayton, Oregon. In the intervening years, Melinda Jetté notes, Euro American demands for Native lands had only increased, as did other "microtechniques of dispossession," such as hunting game and cultivating new crops that competed with the plants on which Native peoples relied.[29] Such pressures weakened the negotiating position of the Santiam peoples, whose populations had continued to decline. From the three chiefs who represented the Santiam Kalapuya in 1851—Tiacan, Alquema, and Sophan—only Alquema returned for the 1855 negotiations.[30] Santiam Molallans do not even appear in the 1855 negotiations; they were merged into the broader category of "Molalla." Rather than entering into treaties with separate tribes, negotiations took place between the US government and all remaining Indians in the Willamette Valley and surrounding areas, including every band of Kalapuyan and Molallan, from the Columbia River in the north to the origins of the Willamette River in the south, and from the coastal mountains in the west to the summit of the Cascades in the east.

These simplified negotiations resulted in the dispossession of Santiam lands in the North Santiam Canyon. The 1851 treaties had required patient negotiation between multiple parties bargaining from different positions of strength, resulting in a series of carefully calculated compromises that, most importantly, allowed the Santiam peoples to remain in their homelands. In contrast, the 1855 treaty dictated terms that overwhelmingly favored the US government and Euro American newcomers. The government promised a sum of $195,000, mostly in the forms of goods and services chosen by the government to "advance [the Native peoples] in civilization, for their moral improvement and education." The government would build houses and farms; it would buy stock, farming tools, seeds, and clothing; and it would pay for the services of a doctor, teacher, blacksmith, and "superintendent of farming operations." All of this would help Indians progress toward "civilization" by forcing them to adopt sedentary farming practices and abandon their seasonal rounds. It also meant giving up the North Santiam Canyon, which the US government took in the treaty of 1855, along with the rest of the Willamette Valley and western Cascades. The Santiam Kalapuyans and Molallans were forced to leave their huckleberry patches, hunting grounds, and trails in the canyon, and they moved to a small reservation in the Grand Ronde Valley on the western edge of the Willamette Valley.

Over the following decades, the Native presence in the canyon decreased, but the area remained part of their world. The Santiam Kalapuyans and Santiam Molallans, along with other western Oregon native peoples, created a new life at the Grand Ronde Indian Reservation beginning in 1856 and eventually as part of the Confederated Tribes of Grand Ronde (established in 1983).[31] The North Santiam Canyon still remained a part of their home, retained through stories and memories as well as the history recorded in the 1851 treaty betrayal. In the twentieth century, Grand Ronde peoples left the reservation for farm work in the Willamette Valley and, according to David Lewis, to work in the woods and mills of the North Santiam Canyon.[32] The area was also visited and used by Native peoples of the Warm Springs Reservation, established in 1855 and located east of Mt. Jefferson. Elders of the Warm Springs peoples remember traveling as young children with their families across the Cascades to the huckleberry patches in Grizzly Flats, Marion Lake, and Marion Basin, and taking trips to the confluence of the Breitenbush River and North Santiam River—now the site of Detroit—where they gathered fish and gambled with visiting Klamath peoples.[33] Lowell Fleetwood, a longtime resident of Mill City, remembers Native people using old fish-drying racks and selling some of their salmon and huckleberries to the Euro Americans in the area.[34] The Native presence is hard to see when driving along Highway 22 in the twenty-first century. But that highway runs along well-trod paths blazed by Kalapuya, Molalla, and other Native peoples who traveled into and through the canyon, incorporating it into their sense of home and connecting it to the world beyond.

TRAPPERS AND MINERS SEND NATURE TO MARKET

While Santiam Kalapuyans and Molallans made the North Santiam Canyon part of their home, Europeans and Euro Americans initially saw not a place in which to live and thrive, but a place from which to profit. Furs and then precious minerals drew transient profiteers to participate in the resource exploitation typical of the American West, as many historians of the region have examined.[35] Although fur trapping and mining were relatively short-lived as active industries, they took an important place in local lore. Among local historians and longtime residents of the North Santiam Canyon, the most widely circulated fur-trapping story is that of three unnamed French Canadians who arrived in 1844, gathered furs for less than a year, and then moved on in 1845, when the area was "trapped out."[36] An apocryphal story, perhaps, but the area was certainly part of the larger fur trade in the nineteenth century. Peter Skene Ogden, an agent of the Hudson's Bay Company (HBC) that dominated the fur trade in the Pacific Northwest, crossed the Cascades from east to west in 1826 "by one of the middle passes, probably that at the head of the Santiam River," although his journals are not entirely clear on the geography.[37] Joseph Gervais, a Willamette Valley trapper, trader, and farmer, reported that in the late summers of the 1830s, he and his family traveled through the North Santiam Canyon to the eastern side of the Cascades, where they would "trap and hunt before the rainy season was near." Before returning to the Willamette Valley via the canyon, Gervais sold his furs to a trader who took them to Fort Vancouver on the Columbia River, the great trading post and emporium of the HBC.[38] Such stories—legendary and historical—both contribute to and draw heavily on romantic narratives about independent and hardy souls braving the wilderness in pursuit of profit and adventure.[39]

These fur trappers and traders integrated the canyon into a larger global system driven by powerful market and political forces. Ogden, Gervais, and the three unnamed French Canadians came to the area at the behest of business interests in London, Boston, and other Western metropolises. There, the rage for beaver-pelt hats and other fashion trends created a sprawling industry that reached into nearly every fur-bearing stream system in North America. The riches of the fur trade were also bound up with geopolitical considerations in the Pacific Northwest. The apocryphal three French Canadian trappers arrived toward the end of the implementation of the HBC's "fur desert" policy, which began in 1824. Jealous of the region's furs and anxious about Americans competing with British interests in the area, the HBC directed its agents, employees, and contractors to trap and otherwise kill so many beaver as to drive the animal to extinction, in the hope that Americans would lose interest in the Oregon country.[40] In short, the North Santiam Canyon, like other fur-bearing areas in the Pacific Northwest, was on the front line of a battle between British and American imperialists in the mid-nineteenth century. Although the policy may have frustrated American fur trappers, it certainly did not stop American settlers from pouring into the Willamette Valley and pressuring the United States to take possession of all the Oregon country. When the United States and Great Britain finally agreed in 1846 to set the US-Canada border at the 49th parallel and the HBC began its retreat northward, the fur trade in Oregon was already receding into history. The North Santiam Canyon, meanwhile, had become part of the American empire and permanently connected to international economic forces.

Not long after fur trappers left, prospectors and miners arrived, attracted to real and rumored flecks of gold, silver, and other minerals that offered the possibility of profit. Although mining in the canyon remained limited compared to other Western gold rushes like those in California in 1849 or southern Oregon in 1852, it brought similar processes and forces: hyperventilating excitement that attracted a rush of small prospectors who were soon displaced by larger, more heavily capitalized mining operations.[41] Mining took place in the streams, hills, and mountains to the north and south of the North Santiam River. The earliest report of prospecting comes from 1854, when five men traveled to Mt. Jefferson in a failed attempt to strike it rich.[42] Prospectors filed mining claims as early as 1860, but the first documented discovery of gold in the area came in 1863 in what would become known as the Quartzville district, about twenty miles south of the present town of Gates.[43] Jeremiah Briggs was the first to establish a claim in this area, but other prospectors soon joined him, finding small quantities of silver as well as gold. Other hopeful prospectors made their way north to mine along the Little North Fork (a tributary of the North Santiam) and established claims along the stream banks. They followed promising reports like that printed in 1864 in Sacramento's *The Daily Bulletin*, which described rock specimens from the Santiam bearing "gold [that] is thick set in . . . in several places I saw half-a-dozen fibres an inch long." The *Bulletin*'s correspondent continued, "from these indications I am afraid this country will soon become too rich for a poor man to lie in," and warning that the area would soon be afflicted by the runaway speculation and hyperinflation that so often accompanied mining booms.[44]

Such promises attracted waves of miners into the 1880s and 1890s, but the big mining boom never came. Prospectors established mines with hopeful names such as the Crown, Silver King, and Bonanza.[45] Placer mines that sorted valuable minerals from surface diggings yielded modest results. An 1897 article in the *Dayton Herald* newspaper reported that placer miners "appear well pleased with their mines." But some of those miners had ambitions to dig deeper: "they talk of putting in a hydraulic plant on each one of the claims."[46] By then, extensive digging and tunneling operations already provided quicker access to the diluted ore of the region, and more intensive operations eclipsed the small placer mines. By 1889, tunnels as long as 270 feet had been driven into the mountainsides. But the mines did not give up the easy profits that had been hoped for, and by the end of the century, many prospectors had turned their gaze to more promising and exciting digs elsewhere. Mining in the canyon had been a brief and limited affair that enriched few; as one resident says, "[It] was just enough to keep them [prospectors and miners] interested."[47]

Mining depended on connections to the outside world, and during its short history, mining helped develop and expand these relationships. Most prospectors from the Willamette Valley traveled on a rough road that led to the confluence of the Little North Fork and the North Santiam River. From there, miners chose their path: northeast along the Little North Fork into that mining area, or southeast over the hills toward Quartzville. These rough trails became well-worn paths and even roads; by 1878, a daily stage route ran the twenty miles between Gates and Quartzville, facilitating and encouraging the development of mining.[48] Other paths led into the mining regions of the North Santiam Canyon; Jeremiah Briggs made his way from the south by following the South Santiam River to Quartzville Creek and then proceeding northeast. Over such paths, trails, and proto-roads, miners traveled into the canyon, carrying supplies, food, and information secured from Albany, Salem, and Portland. If the miners were lucky, they returned to the Willamette Valley with gold, silver, and other minerals that would eventually be incorporated into international commodities markets.

Though the area's mines did not produce spectacular profits, they provided enough gold and silver to attract the interest of external investors. Capital came mostly from the Willamette Valley and spurred the growth of a number of externally owned claims and mines. In 1897, H. D. Ponnay of Portland, representing forty-four other Portland-based investors, reported pulling forty-five dollars' worth of gold in "2 1/2 days of labor by them in washing it from the dirt," and the group planned to shift from placer mining to more intensive operations, including a smelter in what had become known as "Mineral Harbor" along the Little North Fork. Outside capital funded other substantial mining operations; most notably, the Albany and Lawler mines.[49] In 1895, the Albany mine employed fifty to sixty men at two dollars daily, running two shifts a day, seven days a week. The Lawler mine ran a similar schedule but with a slightly smaller group of wage laborers, hiring between forty and fifty men. The intensive digging and blasting of these and other mines quickly liquidated the valuable ore, and by 1900, miners accounted for only three percent of the workforce.[50]

Although external capital and market forces drove miners and their tools into the North Santiam Canyon, the actual experience of mining depended on the actions and perceptions of people trying their luck at this difficult work. The journal of a small party from Willamette University in Salem that visited the area in 1864 gives some sense of what it was like to try to prospect in the North Santiam country.[51] The group started off in high spirits, "destined for the Santiam gold," hiking dozens of miles along trails of various quality and safety up the North Santiam River and then the Little North Fork. The area's beauty struck them with awe. "The country around [is] most grand and sublime in the scenery," wrote the journal's author, who later in the trip was astonished by the "mountain laurel now in bloom . . . its beauty would surpass any of the most beautiful flowers in the City of Salem." But most of the journal relates the challenges and frustrations of the trip. They lost supplies when crossing back and forth across the river, the fish would not bite, and their packs were too heavy. They suffered discomfort, from stomach sickness and "pains in my hip" to general exhaustion, becoming "very thirsty our breath is horse and legs trembly." As for striking it rich, the party had little luck. They found "quartz all day long along the gultch" but no gold. After less than a week, the party turned back, happy to report "no limbs broken" and "satisfied to escape from those wild and solitary regions."

Few small prospectors became rich in the North Santiam mining country, but some survived even after the large operations shut down. In 1975, a man by the name of Dewey Bevier still held and worked a claim in Quartzville, and mining operations on the Little North Fork continued well into the 1980s.[52] Such efforts represented a way that people in the North Santiam Canyon sought to leverage their connections to the outside world to their advantage. The market forces that drew external capital also attracted small placer miners. The wagon roads on which ore from the Lawler and Albany mines traveled also bore the weight of independent prospectors who succeeded Jeremiah Briggs. The very act of survival by these miners exercised their power, as they found ways to get their supplies, travel to the Willamette Valley, and sell the minerals they had worked so hard to carve out of the canyon.

Though the choices made by miners and prospectors influenced their daily lives, their options were limited by their connections to outside forces. Even the most independent of prospectors was intimately connected to and ultimately dependent on market forces out of their control. Miners needed food, axes, picks, tents, and other supplies that they could only get from the outside world. The ore that took so much labor to extract from the hills was worthless unless it was sent through the market in exchange for cash, goods, and services. As the scale of mining increased and larger companies claimed more land and resources, it became difficult for small operations to compete. To confront this challenge, some of these local operations sought the investment of external capital, thereby further increasing their dependency on outside forces. Like the fur trappers before them, miners and prospectors heeded the demands of international economic forces, and their choices and actions bound the canyon to those outside forces.

EXPLORERS AND TRAILBLAZERS

While fur trappers and then miners pursued profit along trails and paths, the growing population of Euro Americans in the Willamette Valley longed for easier ways to travel through the canyon and over the Cascades. Until 1846, nearly all emigrants from the Oregon Trail crossed the Cascade Range by floating down the Columbia River from The Dalles, then traveling through Oregon City and into the Willamette Valley. The desire for easier and more direct routes led to interest in different passages across the Cascades, including the paths through the North Santiam Canyon associated with Peter Skene Ogden and Joseph Gervais in the 1820s and 1830s. This abstract interest became much more concrete in 1845, when a party of westward bound settlers wandered around the east side of the Cascades, desperately searching for a way to the Willamette Valley. They had left the Oregon Trail at Fort Boise to follow the unemployed fur trapper Stephen Meek, who promised to take them directly west over the Cascades, a route that may have taken them through the North Santiam Canyon. But Meek lost his way and the emigrants' trust in eastern Oregon. His misguided party eventually blundered their way north along the Deschutes River to rejoin the Oregon Trail at The Dalles, but not before at least two dozen people died.

Meek had tragically failed, but the idea of building a wagon pass over the middle of the Cascades through the North Santiam Canyon continued to motivate Euro Americans in the Willamette Valley. The first attempt to establish a wagon pass through the canyon came the year after Meek's failure. Reports about the tragedy provoked Willamette Valley residents to pursue a new route over the mountains.[53] A public meeting in Salem in 1846 selected a committee of six, including Joseph Gervais, to travel up the North Santiam River and further explore the route previously described and used by Gervais and other fur trappers. This first exploration turned out to be a failure; the route was simply too rugged, and the committee pronounced it unusable for wagon travel. The attention of Willamette Valley residents turned to a more southerly route from Albany east up the South Santiam River and over the Cascades at what is now Santiam Pass. This became the route of the Willamette Valley and Cascade Mountain Wagon Road, built between 1861 and 1868 and used primarily for transporting livestock to and from the open ranges of central Oregon.[54] Meanwhile, a road through the North Santiam Canyon and over a more northerly pass remained undeveloped.

Undeveloped but not unknown. Certainly, the Native peoples of the Santiam knew of the routes over the Cascades and along the North Santiam River, and that knowledge had passed on to some Euro Americans. The Methodist missionary Josiah Parrish, who came to Oregon in 1840, reported that the Molalla had taught him about the pass. As noted above, Joseph Gervais had reported his own travels over the Cascades through the North Santiam Canyon. Other fur trappers and traders traced that route, informed by their interactions with the Native peoples on whom they depended for trade relations and marriage arrangements. Stephen Meek may have been aiming for the North Santiam thanks to his interactions with Native peoples and fur trappers who traveled that way.[55] Knowledge about the route up the North Santiam had spread in the 1850s and 1860s to the point that the area became a health refuge for people who sought relief and recreation in the pure mountain air.[56] So, even though the 1846 expedition had failed to find a suitable wagon route through the North Santiam Canyon, people knew that there had to be a way.

The man who brought together all these reports, and who would eventually claim and get credit for finding a path through the North Santiam Canyon and over the Cascades, was John Minto.[57] Born in England in 1822, Minto emigrated to Oregon at the age of twenty, married Martha Ann Morrison, and settled in the middle Willamette Valley. He developed orchards and a thriving Merino wool business and served in a variety of public positions in the Salem area, including four terms as a state legislator. Personal tragedy prompted John Minto's first interest in the North Santiam Canyon. In 1867, the Mintos' eighth child died just eight days after birth, and Martha Ann nearly died as well. On doctor's orders, Minto took his family into the North Santiam Canyon seeking "higher altitude as a means of safety." For the next six years, the Mintos summered in the North Santiam Canyon, and Minto became known as an expert on the area. He took a particularly active interest—obsession, even—in finding and publicizing a pass over the Cascades. As one of his memorializers wrote, "Mr. Minto would have preferred the honor of discovering an advantageous mountain passageway for egress from and ingress to the Willamette Valley . . . than the honors of a membership in Congress."[58] Minto found just that passageway through the North Santiam Canyon.

In October 1873, two hunters looking for game in the upper canyon reported to Minto that they had seen valleys leading all the way up to Mt. Jefferson. Minto followed these rumors into the canyon, and after a twelve-day journey to the upper reaches of the North Santiam River, he returned to Salem and "reported a deep valley apparently almost dividing the range."[59] Minto persuaded Marion County commissioners to authorize a small road-finding expedition, which Minto led, submitting a report in August 1874 that laid out a wagon road along the North Santiam River, over the Cascades through a "narrow cut or pass lying across the summit ridge" and then down into central Oregon. This report eventually led to a six-foot-wide stock road that reached the Detroit-Idanha area in 1878 and passed over the Cascades in 1879.[60] Another member of Minto's party filed incorporation papers for the "Astoria-Salem-Winnemucca Railroad," an ambitious idea for a railroad from northwest Oregon to northern Nevada that never got past the promotional stage. Minto was frustrated with the lack of development of his route, so when in 1880 he learned of the possibility of a slightly lower elevation and easier pass, he convinced Marion County commissioners to fund another expedition. Minto confirmed the existence of this other pass at an "easy grade for railroad purposes," reporting back to a new Willamette Valley railroad company, the Oregon Pacific Railroad, which followed Minto's path, as discussed in chapter 2. It would be decades before Minto's path became a highway crossing the Cascades, but the pass—forever to be known as Minto Pass—had been found.

Minto had put his name on the canyon, but there were some in the area who challenged his story, asserting their own role in, and even control over, the route and pass. Ephraim Henness, who lived in the North Santiam Canyon from 1854 until his death in 1949, hotly disputed Minto's claims. The Hennesses were among the earliest Euro American families to make their homes in the upper North Santiam Canyon. Throughout his life, Henness maintained that he and his father, Thomas, found the pass. In an interview for the local newspaper in 1929, Henness claimed that "he and his father . . . left Mill City June 1st, 1873, with packs on their backs, and headed for the Jefferson park country." After a week of hiking along paths well worn by the native Santiam peoples, they came to the summit of the pass, "being the first white men that ever made the trip up the Santiam River."[61] This journey in June 1873 would have put the Hennesses at the summit four months before Minto's explorations later that autumn. Henness furthermore maintained that he led Minto's second trip up the pass in the summer of 1874, although Minto did not include Henness's name in his report to the county.[62] Minto, in fact, did not mention Henness at all in his histories of the pass's "discovery." In Minto's telling, his own tenacity and determination—in addition to his political connections and not a little self-promotion—produced the paths, roads, and eventually railroad that gave the Willamette Valley access to the North Santiam Canyon and over the Cascades. But the story of the pass's discovery looks a little different from inside the canyon.

The fight between John Minto and Ephraim Henness is an early symbol of the canyon's small influence relative to that of outsiders. Despite Henness's adamant protestations that he and his father found the pass first, John Minto got credit for the discovery of what is still known as Minto Pass. Minto's name is also attached to other landmarks in the area, including a lake and a US Forest Service trail that leads to the pass. Minto also claimed the privilege of naming a number of other local landmarks, including Breitenbush Creek, Pamelia Creek, Independence Valley, Gatch Falls, and Marion Lake. So explained Minto in a 1903 article published in the *Oregon Historical Quarterly*, "Minto Pass: Its History, and an Indian Tradition," one of Minto's many publications that burnished his reputation and his claims to establishing a route over the Cascades. As for Henness, a post office on the North Santiam took the family name in 1879 but closed four years later. Beyond its limited notoriety in the canyon, the Henness name is virtually unknown.

Henness represents an irony that would become part of local history and identity: an eagerness to establish connections with the outside world combined with frustration at how outsiders would use those connections. That Minto's name is attached to the pass seems appropriate. From the beginning, outsiders were the ones pushing for a road with ambitious plans to serve their own interests, from bringing in more Euro Americans from the East to moving livestock from the valley over the mountains to central Oregon. Nevertheless, people who would eventually identify themselves as canyon residents and locals also participated in the development of this connection. Henness groused about not getting credit for finding the pass, but he was happy that route existed. After all, he boasted of having not only discovered the pass, but also leading Minto on the 1874 expedition that eventually brought in the railroad. Henness and others in the canyon wanted connections to the valley and beyond, but they resented how outsiders claimed those connections in ways that pushed locals aside.

RESETTLING THE CANYON

The first Euro Americans to make their homes in the North Santiam Canyon arrived well before routes through the area had been established. They arrived before the miners began blasting away at the hills and just a few years after the fur traders left their traps and trails behind. They came even before the treaty negotiations of 1851 and 1855, while the North Santiam Canyon was still Native land. In 1850, responding to the demands of Euro American squatters who wanted to legitimize their illegal takings of Native lands, the US Congress passed the Oregon Donation Land Claim Act, which gave 320 acres of land to any single man over the age of eighteen, or 640 acres to any married couple. Twelve years later, Congress passed the Homestead Act, which halved the amount of land a person could claim. Supported and encouraged by the federal government, Euro American families began trickling into the North Santiam Canyon's few prairies, which the Santiam and Molalla peoples had only recently signed away. These Euro American resettlers cultivated their own communities, while at the same time relying on and developing connections to the world outside.

Federal land policies combined with family and kinship networks to bring Euro American colonization to the North Santiam Canyon.[63] Just east of present-day Lyons, John Fox helped establish the farming community of Fox Valley in 1852 and was soon joined by others, including the family of John Bright Potter, a wagonmaker from Missouri who arrived with his wife and three children in 1853 and filed a Donation Land Claim in 1855.[64] Farther west, near present-day Mehama, the Stout family—Sarah, Ephraim, and their five children—arrived in the spring of 1853 after traveling by wagon train from Iowa. One of their children was Jane Stout, who had married Thomas J. Henness before leaving Iowa; they brought their own seven children, including a son they named Ephraim who would later challenge John Minto. Farther east in 1862, King Cross and Hazard Smith used the Homestead Act to claim land on a prairie—King's Prairie—south of the river near present-day Gates.[65] The Hennesses, looking for opportunities farther up the canyon, bought out Smith's claim in 1864. In 1874, two women staked important claims in the area: Mary Gates, who with her husband Albert settled on 80 acres of land in what would become Gates, and Sarah Elizabeth Hensley, who claimed 160 acres on the future site of Mill City, where she built a cabin with her son Newton.[66] The 1880 census counted 512 people in the North Santiam Canyon, their small farms and homesteads knitted together by kinship and legitimized by the federal government.[67]

These first Euro American newcomers made great efforts toward improving their quality of life, often by drawing on abundant resources that Native peoples had cultivated just a few decades before. In Fox Valley and Mehama, more than ninety percent of the population worked on farms in 1880.[68] The ample game of the Elkhorn area, north of Gates, was a welcome addition to the settlers' diet, as were the numerous berry bushes throughout the region. Minnie Smith McCarty of Gates later remembered, "We never suffered for food." The family made sure that the "smokehouse was always filled with smoke and salted wild game and our pantry filled with dried and canned berries." The Smith matriarch worked hard and with resourcefulness, as Minnie recalled: "Mother had but few jars in which to can so she used to can berries in long necked bottles, poking each berry in with a stick, corking and sealing with wax. When winter came, she opened the bottle by breaking off the neck." Game taken from the forests offered more food and supplies, with "Bear grease and elk fat . . . used for making tallow candles, and we were never without the best of meats as there were no game laws in those days."[69] Stories of these years include other kinds of resourcefulness. Minnie McCarty recalled how the family secured a sewing machine with which they made gloves from tanned elk skins. Charles Kelly, a third-generation resident, remembers his grandparents as the archetypical independent farmers: "All they ever needed were coffee and salt and sugar. They raised everything else; ate whatever they could raise."[70] Such memories rarely reflect on how such resourcefulness drew on resources once used so effectively by Native peoples, instead focusing on Euro American resiliency, determination, and other themes from popular—and incomplete—narratives and myths of the American frontier.[71]

Although their descendants spoke with pride about their families' self-sufficiency and independence, these early Euro American resettlers actively encouraged the development of transportation and market connections to the outside world. The road-building efforts of outsiders were of particular interest to residents, as such paths made living in the area a viable proposition. Prior to the construction of these roads, it was too difficult for some settlers to stay. Sarah Elizabeth Hensley, the first settler of the Mill City area, left after a few years because Mehama, the nearest supply post, was only accessible by foot or horseback over rough trails.[72] Those who stayed made every effort possible to build better connections to the outside world. In Mehama, Louis Stout ran a ferry across the river, connecting Marion and Linn Counties and facilitating travel from the north side of the river down to the Albany area. Farther up the canyon, the Smith and Henness families crossed the river by means of a dug-out canoe; similar makeshift methods of river transport were used in Gates until the construction of a covered bridge in 1887.[73]

As transportation and market connections between the canyon and the Willamette Valley increased, so did the ways that residents connected their local economy to outside markets. In the Gates area, T. J. Henness built a tannery for elk skins, which were then sewn into gloves by his wife and daughters for sale in valley markets such as Albany.[74] Ephraim Stout's mill in Mehama not only produced rough lumber for local residents, but also specialized in cedar lumber shipped down to Salem.[75] The valley was also the intended destination for products from local farms, particularly the dairies of the Fox Valley area, which provided milk for processors such as the Mt. Angel Creamery thirty miles away.[76] Even as they continued to rely on their own resourcefulness, residents sought to develop external economic connections in an effort to improve their quality of life.

For these first Euro Americans living in the canyon, cultivating local community and building external connections were not contradictory processes; they were complementary and in fact mutually constitutive and necessary. Residents sought to create local institutions to serve local interests while also integrating the area to the Willamette Valley and beyond. Post offices provided desperately desired and needed communication with the outside world. The first post office in the area was established in Fox Valley in 1874; three years later, the Mehama Post Office began service.[77] Another post office opened in present-day Gates in 1882. Canyon residents also took a particularly active interest in schools, first in Fox Valley and Mehama (established 1855 and 1866, respectively) and then farther up the canyon at King's Prairie by 1872.[78] Other community institutions developed during these decades, including a cemetery in Fox Valley (1859) and a Sunday school for community religious education (1872). In 1876, Mehama became the canyon's first platted and county-recorded town, and two years later, Mehama had its own voting precinct, with sixty-five registered voters.[79] Forty-three of those voted for Republican Cornelius C. Beekman in the 1878 gubernatorial race, which Democrat William Wallace Thayer won by just a few dozen votes. From polls and post offices to schools and churches, residents simultaneously committed to connections to the outside world even as they expressed their own choices inside the canyon.

Euro American emigration brought good voting citizens, institution builders, and more complicated elements to local communities. In 1871, brothers William and Charles Thomas took up a homestead claim of eighty acres on the far eastern side of King's Prairie, on the south side of the wagon road to the mining districts in Quartzville.[80] Born in Missouri in the 1830s—either one or five years apart, depending on what they told different census takers—the Thomas brothers developed a checkered reputation.[81] In many ways, they participated in canyon life like other residents, tending to their farm, taking occasional odd jobs as day laborers, and guiding miners headed to Quartzville. But John Lengacher, a longtime local resident and chronicler, wrote that William and Charles "would attend dances, gamble, drink, and create problems." Among those "problems": accusations of cattle poisonings, a bar fight that ended with Charles shooting and killing another man, and an unsuccessful assassination attempt against Charles, who was allegedly shot by one of his own nephews. A vigilante committee tried to run William and Charles out of the canyon, but without success. They sojourned briefly in the Detroit area, where they participated in more mischief of a federal nature (see chap. 2). By 1910, William and Charles had returned to the Gates area, where they lived out the rest of their days, a thorn in the side of locals who considered themselves more respectable. In the Thomas brothers, the canyon had its first villains, an obligatory part of the frontier myth. The Thomas brothers were problems born and raised elsewhere, but they were very much a part of the communities forming in the area.

The Historical Atlas Map of Marion & Linn Counties, Oregon, published by a San Francisco company in 1878, showed how much the North Santiam Canyon had transformed in just a few decades. The Native presence had been displaced by names like Stout, Henness, and other Euro Americans who claimed the land as their own. These resettlers established farms, schools, post offices, and more. In Mehama, the

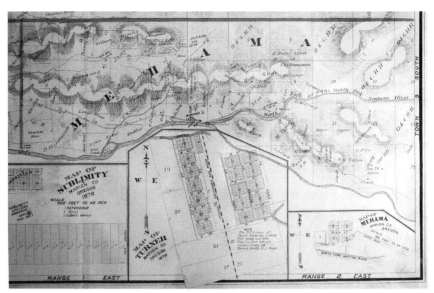

This 1878 map of the Lower North Santiam Canyon and the insert for Mehama reflects the spread of Euro Americans and the displacement of Native peoples from the area. From Edgar Williams & Co. and Marion County Historical Society, Historical Atlas Map of Marion & Linn Counties, Oregon, 1878 (Salem, OR: Marion County Historical Society, 1976, 48-49 [reprinted 2004]. Courtesy of Willamette Heritage Center.

Atlas explained, "the population is about forty. The village has a school-house, blacksmith shop, and a hotel and ferry." The area connected to the Willamette Valley and beyond by means of wagon roads, ferries, mail service, and market links. These connections remained rough, but they were growing and developing fast, providing residents with access to the outside world. Those connections also exposed local residents to outside forces. The 1878 *Atlas* shows thousands of acres granted to the Oregon & California Railroad, which used the sales of such land to fund the slow construction of a line down the Willamette Valley. But by then another railroad company—the Oregon Pacific—had plans to build its own trans-continental line running through the North Santiam Canyon. The area had drawn the attention and investment of railroad men and capitalists from the Willamette Valley and far beyond. Their interest—encouraged by locals—would bring to the area exciting opportunities and enormous challenges for the exercise of local autonomy.

2

Railroad, Fraud, and Complicity in the Canyon

On November 29, 1888, a locomotive crossed the North Santiam River in Mill City, bringing rail service for the first time to the heart of the North Santiam Canyon. It had been a long time coming. The railroad's chief dreamer, "Colonel" T. Egenton Hogg, had been scheming to build a railroad into and through the area since 1871, and local residents had supported the project through its many fits and starts. Neither residents nor Hogg would get exactly what they hoped for. Hogg's railroad would never cross the Cascades, thanks to financial malfeasance and stubborn geography. Canyon residents' dreams of widespread wealth and prosperity would also go unfilled, although the villages and towns along the North Santiam River grew quickly. More importantly, the railroad developed economic, political, and cultural connections that fundamentally altered the relationships of power between the North Santiam Canyon and the world outside. The railroad brought opportunities for the exercise of local power, as residents used the new connection to improve their living conditions and develop as communities. They also found ways to profit, from serving tourists to real estate speculation—legal and not. Though residents welcomed and capitalized on the changes brought by the railroad, their actions also encouraged the presence and influence of outside economic and political forces.

OUTSIDERS BUILD A RAILROAD

The railroad that snaked its way alongside the North Santiam River in the late nineteenth century was largely the brainchild of Thomas Egenton Hogg. Born in Baltimore in 1828, Hogg first came to Oregon in 1871 in part to leave behind memories of an odd career serving the Confederacy. His most notable success was the seizure in 1863 of a Union steamship, a task the Confederate leadership had not authorized. The act nevertheless impressed the Confederate Navy, which ordered Hogg—now sworn in as an acting master—to capture the Union ship *San Salvador* and take it

32

to California to raid Union shipping lines. Hogg apparently could not keep his task secret; the US consuls in both Panama and Havana notified the *San Salvador*'s captain, who foiled the plot and captured Hogg and his fellow pirates. The Union Navy charged and found Hogg guilty of treason and sentenced him to death. A lenient judge reduced the sentence to life in prison, and he spent the rest of the war at Alcatraz and then San Quentin. Upon his release in May 1866, Hogg gave himself the title of colonel, dropped his first name, and went north to Oregon to sell a dream: a new east–west railway that would connect Oregon to the rest of the country.[1]

Hogg's dream mixed ambitious boosterism with geographic fantasy. His plan specifically called for the new line, eventually christened the Oregon Pacific Railroad, to begin in Yaquina City, on the central Oregon coast, and terminate in Boise City, Idaho, where it would meet up with an expected extension of the Chicago and Northwestern Railroad. Moving east from Yaquina, the railroad would cross the coastal mountain range east of the small town of Nashville and then proceed to the Willamette Valley through Corvallis and Albany. Here it would connect not only with three existing north–south railroads, but also with various stern-wheel riverboats on the Willamette River. The railroad's 1880 prospectus detailed the rest of the journey: "Passing eastward, this line opens up access to unequaled timber and lumber supplies on the western foot-hills of the Cascade range," pointing to the railroad's real eventual purpose: exploitation of the Douglas fir forests in the North Santiam Canyon and beyond. The prospectus became increasingly fanciful, referring to the "rich adjacent agricultural districts"—of which there were hardly any in the North Santiam Canyon—and promising an "unrivaled pass through the Cascade mountains at the foot of Mount Jefferson," which ignored the steep and rugged terrain that such a path would have to take. Undeterred by actual geography, Hogg's prospectus boasted that the "route [is] a necessity to any connecting line seeking an outlet to the Pacific coast south of the Columbia river, and its course eastward, through the rich valleys and over the fertile plains of central and eastern Oregon." The Oregon and Pacific would, in short, transform the West and become "the natural connection for any new line from the east."[2]

In such extraordinary claims, Hogg had plenty of company among other railroad boosters in the West in the last quarter of the nineteenth century. From San Francisco to Spokane, dreamers and schemers like Leland Stanford of the Central Pacific, Thomas Durant of the Union Pacific, Ben Holladay of the Oregon and California, and Jay Cooke and

Henry Villard of the Northern Pacific swindled the American public with their plans—sometimes successfully, but often not, as Richard White as persuasively argued—to build transcontinental railroads.[3] Although Stanford, Durant, and their ilk would have resented association with such an upstart as Hogg, they shared important traits. They had few qualms about distorting and manipulating their companies' finances, often driving their enterprises to ruin, as Hogg's case would eventually demonstrate. They also had a flair for dramatic and extravagant claims, particularly when speaking to investors and newspaper reporters. Standing before an audience in Corvallis in 1881, Hogg claimed that his railroad would cross the Cascades and reach Boise City—more than five hundred miles away—"within two and half years," despite the railroad from Yaquina not yet having made the fifty-mile journey to Corvallis four years after ground was broken. But although their promises and prospectuses seem absurd, railroad men like Hogg understood that railroads could surmount peaks, cross canyons, and travel at speeds that would utterly transform American society, culture, and politics. As historians such as William Cronon and Katherine Morrisey have shown, railroads fundamentally rearranged relationships between people and their environments, creating new "mental territories" that connected people, ideas, goods, and capital across vast distances.[4] Hogg, like the railroad barons he aspired to emulate, believed his railroad could create a new geographic and economic reality.

Through such a monumental transformation, Hogg promised to bring the world to Oregon and profits to his investors. The railroad would facilitate commerce and exploit the region's natural resources, gathering together "inexhaustible sources of wealth in her fields, forests, fisheries, and mines—which, when developed, will be the marvel of our time." The Oregon and Pacific would move that exploited wealth to Yaquina Bay, "the only central, adequate and available harbor," connecting Oregon to national and global markets by means of both "steamships plying to and from San Francisco, but also to European grain ships of the deepest draught." The new railway would also open up passenger transportation, establishing a "direct railway connection with the east [that] shall place [Oregon's] capitol within six days' journey from New York and her centres of population, manufacture, and production; nearer to San Francisco by one-half the time now required for the transit." For those still not convinced, Hogg closed his prospectus with a modest reassurance: "The company hazards nothing in declaring the Oregon Pacific railroad enterprise to be one of the best, safest and most profitable ever presented to the public."[5]

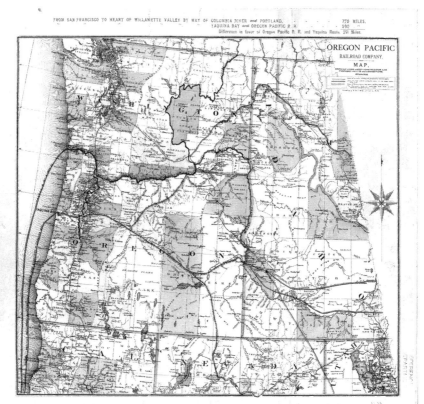

This undated (ca. 1885) map of the Oregon Pacific Railway's anticipated routes shows the new geography imagined by the railroad's supporters, whereby trains and steamers would connect the North Santiam Canyon to Boise, Idaho, the Oregon coast, San Francisco, and beyond. Item G4241.P3 1885.O73, Oregon Historical Society.

The glowing prospectus projected far too much confidence in the railway, which traced a complicated route to ultimate failure. Work began in 1871, when Hogg and some associates secured title to the Corvallis & Yaquina Military Road Company, as well as part of the Willamette Valley & Cascade Wagon Road.[6] The lands from these wagon roads, along with grants from the state, gave Hogg both a path for his railroad and collateral with which to attract investors and secure their support. In 1872, Hogg incorporated the Corvallis and Yaquina Bay Railroad Company, which failed to make any headway, and then followed that venture with the Willamette Valley and Coast Railroad Company, incorporated in 1874. This second company began grading the route for the line, but the process was slow and expensive, and the Willamette Valley and Coast Railroad failed to lay any track. Hogg then made his bold proposal in 1880 for the Oregon Pacific Railroad in an effort to secure more investors. This third attempt drew more attention and capital, and in July 1881, construction of the Corvallis-Yaquina branch began. The first branch was completed by 1885, and in 1887, the Oregon Pacific Railroad ran freight and passengers between Albany and Corvallis, then on to Yaquina and from there, via steamship, to San Francisco. It had taken more than thirteen years for Hogg's dream of a grand railroad to crawl from Yaquina Bay on the central Oregon coast to the eastern side of the Willamette River in Albany. Hogg's destination of Boise City was still five hundred miles away, on a path running through the North Santiam Canyon.

Hogg's grandiose promises and his railroad would terminate in the canyon. From Albany, the Oregon Pacific turned to the northeast and hugged the western edge of the Cascade foothills, passing through the village of Shelburn on its way to the southern bank of the North Santiam River. In early November 1888, the Oregon Pacific entered the North Santiam Canyon in the new town of Lyons, and on November 29, 1888—just a year after arriving in Albany—Hogg's railroad "leaped the North Santiam and landed in Marion County about 12 p.m. today," as the *Oregon Statesman* reported.[7] Then the real work began. So far, the Oregon Pacific had traveled 119 miles, crossed two major rivers (the Willamette and North Santiam), and summited one mountain pass in the Coast Range. But that pass—the town of Summit marks the spot—sat at an elevation of just 700 feet, and the Oregon Pacific's route mostly traversed the flat land of the Willamette Valley.

Now, from an elevation of 843 feet in Mill City, the Oregon Pacific would have to gain another 4,000 feet in less than 60 miles, all the while clinging to the precipitous bank of the North Santiam River. These realities dashed Hogg's dreams. While grading continued apace and nearly reached the summit of the Cascades, the laying of rail ties and tracks fell behind schedule before grinding to a halt in December 1889. Eight years earlier, Hogg had promised that he needed less than a year for the Oregon Pacific to reach "a point east of the Cascade Mountains." But in 1889, the Oregon Pacific got as far as it would go: near present-day Idanha, about 30 miles from the Santiam Pass and 457 miles short of its original destination in Idaho.

Even as his dream died, Hogg continued to play the role of railroad tycoon, projecting confidence in his ambition, practicing financial slights-of-hand, and rejecting the reality unfolding around him. While construction in the North Santiam Canyon halted, Hogg made flamboyant displays of wealth in Albany, where, as a Portland newspaper reported in October 1889, he invested in "city water works, Magnolia flouring mill, eight city lots and 47 acres of suburban land, the total value being $150,000."[8] Just a few months later, the Oregon Pacific defaulted on its interest. Creditors started hovering, and the company went into receivership in October 1890, a harbinger of a broader economic depression that hit the country in earnest beginning in 1893.[9] Hogg left Oregon but managed to get himself appointed as receiver, and over the next two years he made myriad attempts of varying degrees of legality to raise money, regain control of the company, and restart construction. All failed. The county sheriff tried to sell the company but also failed, despite slashing the price from $1 million in January 1892 to $200,000 in December 1893. By that time, a judge had removed Hogg from the receivership, saying that Hogg "neglected the duties of his trust,"[10] and the country spiraled into a financial crisis that decimated railroad values. The Oregon Pacific sold in 1895 for the fire sale price of $100,000, most of which went to taxes and legal fees. Hogg, meanwhile, made his way to Philadelphia, where he died of a stroke in 1898.

The Oregon Pacific Railroad and its successors exposed the North Santiam Canyon to enormous influence from external forces. The financial dealings of the company made it clear just who was in charge of and stood to benefit from the railroad. While Colonel Hogg spoke of public benefits, he was even more attentive to his investors, most of whom came from the East Coast. The Oregon Pacific's potential and promises attracted prominent nineteenth-century industrialists and railroad speculators. They included F. W. Rhinelander (president of the Milwaukee, Lake Shore and Western Railroad), Joseph Wharton (co-founder of Bethlehem Steel), and John Insley Blair, who owned (among many other railroad properties) the Chicago and Northwestern Railroad, which the Oregon Pacific was supposed to meet in Boise City for its transcontinental connection.[11] Hogg promised his investors an enormous return. The 1880 prospectus estimated over $2 million in revenue during the first year compared to just over $1 million in expenses, leaving around $900,000 "available for dividends on stock (over 21 per cent on $3,900,000 [the initial investment sought by Hogg])."[12]

As the Oregon Pacific imploded from 1890 to 1894, investors focused on protecting their assets. Disgusted with Hogg's mismanagement and justifiably suspicious that Hogg would use his receivership to renege on financial obligations to bondholders, John Blair and Joseph Wharton led an effort to take Hogg to court in January 1892. They sought to prevent a proposed sale of the railroad for $1 million, which they deemed far below the Oregon Pacific's value and, more importantly, inadequate to pay back the railroad's outstanding debts and obligations. They succeeded in this effort, as well as in having Hogg removed as receiver. It was a pyrrhic victory. In December 1893, the Blair and Wharton bondholders group put in their own low-ball bid of $200,000—which was $800,000 less than the sale they had prevented two years before—only to see the court reject their offer and the railroad sold off for just $100,000 the next year. Out of that, Blair, Wharton, and other investors received just $4,000—adding insult to financial injury.

Workers on the Oregon Pacific, however, could claim no victory at all. While Hogg, Blair, Wharton, and the others squabbled and plotted ways to recoup their investment, the railroad workers were still waiting for their paychecks. When the state finally wrested the Oregon Pacific from Hogg's grip, the company owed workers $127,000.[13] Eventually, some of these paychecks would be delivered. Others were less lucky. Members of the Henness family in Gates were some of those Hogg and his eastern investors left out in the cold. Lincoln Henness estimated that Hogg owed over $10,000 for the supply line he, his brother, and his father had run for the railroad crews in the Detroit-Idanha area.[14] In the end as in its beginning, the Oregon Pacific's financial considerations and priorities lay outside the North Santiam Canyon.

OUTSIDE PROFITEERS AND FRAUDS

The construction of the Oregon Pacific encouraged in the canyon a typically Western form of profiteering: land speculation and fraud. As Patricia Limerick writes, "If Hollywood wanted to capture the emotional center of Western history, its movies would be about real estate."[15] Americans of all types in the nineteenth and early twentieth centuries tried to get rich by claiming, legally or otherwise, Western farmland, timberland, and railroad land. The announcement of the Oregon Pacific's plans attracted outsiders who hoped to capitalize on cheaply secured and potentially profitable land near the railroad's path. Among these speculators was John D. Daly, a Corvallis-based newspaper editor, Republican politician, and the US surveyor general of Oregon until his death in 1907. Daly moved from California in 1878 to Yaquina Bay, where Colonel Hogg's grand plans for the Oregon Pacific were starting to take shape. Daly followed the Oregon Pacific's tracks to Corvallis and Hogg's promises to the North Santiam Canyon. When Hogg's railroad failed, Daly told the *Corvallis Gazette* that he would find a way to get the railroad across the mountains. That plan fell through, but Daly maintained a claim next to the Minto/Henness Trail near the confluence of Marion Creek and the North Santiam River, right along the projected path of the railroad—a valuable piece of real estate, if the railroad ever arrived. That never happened, and Daly died in 1907 under mysterious circumstances.[16] He was hardly alone in seeing profitable opportunities along the Oregon Pacific's planned path through the North Santiam Canyon.

Land speculation quickly gave way to land scams, which flourished in the last decades of the nineteenth century. The federal government's General Land Office lacked the capacity (and sometimes the will) to ensure the legitimacy of claims made under public domain disposal laws such as the Homestead Act, leaving the laws ripe for abuse.[17] Portlander Stephen A. Douglas Puter led the most infamous of these frauds in Oregon. Puter had been engaging in such schemes since he was an eighteen-year-old axman in Humboldt County, California. As he learned logging and lumbering, he also developed his talents in land fraud. That classic American form of entrepreneurship became his specialty once he moved to Oregon in 1888, the same year the Oregon Pacific crossed the North Santiam River in Mill City. After pulling off scams in Lane and Tillamook Counties, Puter set his sights on the rich Douglas fir stands of the North Santiam Canyon.

Along with his girlfriend and business partner Emma Watson, and their co-conspirator Horace G. McKinley, Puter put together a scheme that led to the Oregon land fraud trials of 1903-10.[18] The basic idea of the scam was simple: file fraudulent homestead claims in remote places and sell those valuable claims to timber companies. In practice, that meant lies and accomplices, as Puter explained: "We concluded to make a lot of homestead filings there, under the pretense that it was being done by settlers who had long been residents of the township." To make the claims, Puter enlisted both acquaintances and strangers to whom he then "furnish[ed] money with which to make final proof and cover their incidental expenses, and as soon as final proof was made, to have them deed the land to us at a price agreed upon in advance."[19] Puter and his partners then planned to sell the deeded land to timber companies for a nice profit—Puter believed he could get at least five dollars an acre for 160-acre claims that cost no more than twenty-five dollars in fees.[20]

The Oregon Land Fraud Trials centered on 1,920 acres in Township 11 South, Range 7 East, Willamette Meridian, in the heavily forested area where Marion, Minto, and Bruno Creeks drain into the North Santiam River, near the present-day cabins, restaurant, and fish hatchery at Marion Forks. At the time, only the Minto (or should it be Henness?) Trail provided access to this remote and rugged country. That was part of the attraction for Puter, who believed that "the prospects of Governmental inquiry concerning entries were exceedingly remote."[21] Additionally, that area had been slated for inclusion in the 7,000-acre Cascade Forest Reserve, created in 1893 by President Grover Cleveland under the authority the 1891 Forest Reserve Act.[22] That law had given the president of the United States the power to set aside federal forest lands with the goal of managing and protecting those forests from depletion and abuse.[23] Existing claims in the proposed reserve were all the more valuable, because by the "lieu-land" provisions of the 1897 Forest Management Act, such claims could be exchanged for an equal amount of federal timber land elsewhere—land with more merchantable trees located closer to existing railroads and mill facilities, and therefore more valuable.

Finding a buyer for fraudulent claims was easy enough. Puter had a previous relationship with Minneapolis lumberman Charles Axel Smith, who would eagerly accept the fraudulent land claims.[24] But getting started with the plan—"our idea was to locate as many persons as possible in that township"—was a little trickier, as there were few people who actually lived anywhere near Township 11 South, Range 7 East. Nevertheless, in October 1900, Puter arranged for twelve homestead claims, filed by ten people (two people filed twice using false names) appearing at two different land offices to help hide the fraud. None of the claimants actually lived in the canyon; Frank H. Walgamot, for example, worked as a dentist in Portland.[25] Nor had the claimants even seen the land on which they were supposedly building homes.[26] Puter then set about securing final proof of these claims, contacting—and bribing—a number of government agents and politicians, from local forest superintendents to US Senator John H. Mitchell of Oregon. After a visit to Washington, DC, Puter finally arranged the property transfer, selling the land to C. A. Smith for $10,080.[27] Puter's expenses for filing fees and payments to the claimants amounted to $3,800. Puter had spent an approximately $4,100 on bribes, leaving less than $2,000—not quite the $9,300 he had initially anticipated, but a tidy (and illegal) profit nonetheless.

This elaborate plan fell apart 1902, when federal agents sent by the US secretary of the interior learned of Puter's scheme while investigating a separate land scam. A federal grand jury convicted Puter of fraud in November 1904. Puter immediately turned state's evidence and provided testimony and additional witnesses against Senator Mitchell. In July 1905, another federal grand jury found Mitchell guilty of accepting Puter's bribe. Mitchell told his secretary that "all I ever got was some little checks" and took his case to the US Supreme Court, but he died in

December 1905 while awaiting his appeal. In the meantime, Puter had slipped from captivity, showing up in Boston and then in California, where he was captured and returned to Portland in March 1906 to serve a two-year sentence in the Multnomah County jail.

While imprisoned, Puter wrote an exposé detailing his activities and the workings of land speculation and schemes. Calling himself the "King of the Oregon Land Frauds," Puter styled the salacious account, *Looters of the Public Domain*, as a tell-all confession, a way to recover his honor, and a means by which to identify the crooks at the top. As Puter wrote, "I wish to lay particular stress upon the well-accepted fact that those 'higher up' were eager to crucify the 11-7 gang [referring to the township/range in the canyon where the scam took place] upon any kind of legal cross in the hope that the sacrificial offering would atone for the stains of their own sins."[28] In this, Puter appealed to Progressive Era sentiments that targeted corruption, inefficiency, and (occasionally) behemoth corporations.[29] It worked. President Theodore Roosevelt granted him a pardon, and Puter walked out of jail in January 1908. He ended up back in California, where he got involved in land-claim schemes of questionable legality.[30] His book remained to bear witness to the manipulation, profiteering, and outside influence borne in on the railroad.

Puter, McKinley, Wharton, Blair, and the outsiders they worked with and represented failed to go as far as they had hoped in extracting wealth from the canyon. In this, they had failed as much as Hogg. But their efforts reveal the extent to which the railroad introduced external influence. From Portland to New York, investors, government officials, and members of the general public who had never even thought about the mountains east of Salem could now imagine the possibilities for profit, wealth, and fraud in previously remote places like Gates and Detroit. The North Santiam Canyon, through the Oregon Pacific and its successors, had become even more connected to the world downstream. And that is just the way some local residents wanted it.

LOCAL PROFITEERS AND FRAUDS

The people of the North Santiam Canyon did not reject the influence of the railroad and possibilities for profit it brought. Communities along the projected route joined Hogg in his railroad fever, eager to secure the economic benefits of new connections with the outside world. Citizens of Benton and Linn Counties raised $35,000 in 1878-79 to attract the railroad through their area, and Albany residents collected an additional $40,000 to subsidize construction.[31] In the North Santiam Canyon, residents expressed similar enthusiasm for the railroad, and some donated their own land to the company in an effort to speed along its construction. The name of Gates comes from just such a donation. Don Smith, one of the first Euro Americans to settle in the upper canyon, refused to donate his land to the railroad, instead demanding $450 payment. Fearful that such a rebuke would halt construction, Mary Gates gave the railroad some of her land for construction of a turning "Y" and station, and in return the railroad company named the station Gatesville.[32] Similarly, James Lyon donated part of his homestead on the western edge of the canyon to the railroad right-of-way; the town of Lyons was platted soon thereafter by James, his wife Emma, and James's brother Henry. The local newspaper summarized the hopes of Mrs. Gates, the Lyons family, and other residents: "As soon as the [railroad] is built over the mountains we expect to make this the largest city between Albany and Boise City."[33]

North Santiam Canyon residents found many ways to exercise power and seize economic opportunities offered by the construction of the Oregon Pacific. The Oregon Pacific needed railroad ties, and the Douglas fir forests of the North Santiam Canyon offered plenty of raw material and willing suppliers. J. D. Hiatt and Gyp Myeres of Lyons built a sawmill for the purpose of cutting railroad ties; so did Samuel Myer, farther up the canyon in an area that would become known as Niagara. The Oregon Pacific's agents found plenty of people willing to sign contracts to supply the railroad with the ties it needed to wind up the North Santiam.[34] The prospect of cutting trees, first for railroad ties sold to the Oregon Pacific and later for shipping, attracted new entrepreneurs, too. In 1887, four businessmen from the Willamette Valley came to the canyon and incorporated the Santiam Lumbering Company—the mill that gave Mill City its name.[35]

The construction of the railroad brought other economic opportunities. Most of the men who built the railroad came from far beyond the canyon, including China and Italy.[36] Residents with a longer tenure in the area found other ways to profit from the railroad. The Henness family ran a supply line for Oregon Pacific construction crews, but railroad workers also needed food, and the Smith family of Gates responded. Minnie Smith McCarty of Gates recalls that "We were called on to feed the railroad workers," and they had to be flexible and ready to serve, "from one to 200 men, mostly Italians." The Smith family was well prepared for this task, keeping "a large 50-gallon iron soup kettle on a fire in the yard for cooking potatoes and fried meat and made gravy on two kitchen stoves." Running this business required an understanding of the nature of railroad work, for "many [workers] had no money, but their leader explained that they would pay when they returned after working." Unlike the Hennesses' betrayal by Hogg and Oregon Pacific investors, the Smith family's faith in the railroad workers was repaid, according to Minnie. "My father [Don Smith] kept no books, but always was convinced that every one of them returned."[37]

Railroad workers also needed lodging, and entrepreneurial residents quickly met that need. Mary Gates profited from her donation of land to the railroad by building a hotel, the Pioneer House, that was home to many of the rail workers employed during construction. Even after construction on the Oregon Pacific ended, the railroad continued to bring in guests looking for lodging. In 1889, the Santiam Lumbering Company in Mill City built a hotel of its own, the Cliff House.[38] Farther west, James and Mehama Smith founded the Mehama House hotel in 1893, which welcomed three to four guests every few days between 1893 and 1903. The Mehama House offered room, board, and games of solitaire to travelers from as close as Mill City and Stayton to as far away as Canada and Ireland.[39]

People were not just traveling in and out of the canyon on the railroad; they were coming to stay and settle. In addition to Gates and Lyons, other villages sprouted up in anticipation of and response to the Oregon Pacific's arrival, with names like Green Basin, Berry, and Detroit appearing on maps of the Oregon Pacific route. Mill City would become the largest town, driven by the Santiam Lumbering Company's booming mill. These communities were home to a variety of businesses. The Smith family in Gates also operated a mercantile, and there were two other general stores in Gates as well as a shoe store. A little farther up the line and river, Niagara was home to a couple of saloons, a store, and three hotels at its peak, in addition to a sawmill pumping out railroad ties.[40] Even Detroit, which was so sparsely populated and remote that S. A. D. Puter believed his land scams would go unnoticed, had its own store, built in anticipation of the railroad.

In addition to such entrepreneurial efforts, some residents engaged in more ambitious financial undertakings, particularly in real estate. As in other places throughout the West, the promise of a railroad brought plenty of investors—or speculators, depending on one's perspective. Some of those investors were local. In Mill City, Sarah Elizabeth Hensley profited from the railroad's arrival. Hensley first came to the area in 1874 but left after being "starved out" by the rough supply trail at the time. She returned to Mill City with the railroad in 1888 and became an important real estate figure in the community. She sold twenty acres of land to the Santiam Lumbering Company as well as various lots throughout Mill City.[41]

Farther up the river, a few residents made their own illegal financial dealings. In the winter of 1901, while Stephen Puter's gang of fraudsters filed false homestead claims in the Marion Forks area, a legitimate canyon homesteader named John A. W. Heidecke decided to get in on the game. Forty-four years old and recently married, Heidecke held a 160-acre homestead near Pamelia Creek in the township directly north of Puter's fraud. Heidecke filed his claim in 1894 and was well connected in the village of Detroit; he worked as a common laborer in one of the many mills that sprang up with the railroad.[42] When Heidecke caught wind of the scam in Township 11-7, he sensed an opportunity to cash in on his connections and knowledge of the area. Tracking Puter and McKinley down in Albany, Heidecke confronted the hucksters and, in Puter's words, "hinted that unless he [Heidecke] could get something out of it he would report the matter to the Commissioner of the General Land Office." Heidecke, in other words, blackmailed Puter. "The upshot," explained Puter, "was that McKinley [Puter's partner] settled with Heidecke by paying him $50, for which amount he agreed to keep his mouth shut."[43] Thus began John Heidecke's brief life of crime and fame.

Heidecke became a central player in the Oregon land frauds. When the federal government began looking into the validity of Puter's homesteading claims, Heidecke eagerly partnered with Puter to deceive the special investigator C. E. Loomis with a special "tour" of Township 11-7 that would confirm the homestead claims. Waving aside Puter's detailed instructions for this deception, Heidecke told Puter to "leave it to me." After welcoming Loomis with a generous serving of alcohol, Heidecke guided the investigator around the area, showing cabins that supposedly proved the homestead claims but were actually unused structures that did not even lie within the specified claims. When Heidecke ran short of the twelve cabins he was supposed to show, he circled back around, guiding the government agent to the rear and sides of structures they had already seen, as though these were different buildings— a fine deception that Loomis was all too eager to accept, as he had also been bribed by Puter.[44] Loomis returned to Salem and filed a favorable report confirming the fraudulent claims, upon which Heidecke received another $250 from Puter, along with $110 that Puter had paid Heidecke in advance of the tour. Adding in the initial $50 blackmail, Heidecke had to that point pocketed $410 for playing along with Puter's scam.

As the government became increasingly suspicious of the Puter land claims, it dispatched another investigator to the canyon: Captain Salmon B. Ormsby, superintendent of the Cascade Forest Reserve. As with the first investigation, Puter tried to ensure a favorable report, bribing Ormsby's son and sending word to Heidecke to put on a repeat performance of his homestead tour. Heidecke agreed and then promptly took his own approach to the deception. Superintendent Ormsby arrived in Detroit in January 1902, just a month after the birth of Heidecke's first child, a daughter named Helen. Heidecke was not eager to leave the newborn and mother alone to go traipsing about the woods. Instead of taking Ormsby on the full tour, Heidecke started off with the superintendent, but then, as he later testified, "pretended to be sick, and returned to Detroit." Heidecke seems to have understood that Ormsby was already primed to sign off on the claims, so why go through the trouble of hiking through the dead of winter? Ormsby was in fact eager to approve the claims, and implored Heidecke to sign another affidavit. Heidecke refused, holding out for a better deal, which he promptly got when Ormsby promised to get Heidecke appointed as a forest ranger—a fine opportunity at steady employment for the new father. Heidecke signed the affidavit, deposited another $250 bank draft from Puter, and took up his new job as a forest ranger.[45]

The government caught up with Heidecke during the Oregon land fraud trials, but even then, the wily mountaineer demonstrated cunning equal to and even surpassing Stephen Puter. Knowing that the game was up, Heidecke "turned traitor" and "joined forces with the Government," as Puter noted with aggravation. As the "star witness," Heidecke helped the prosecution put together the puzzle pieces of the fraud, explaining the homestead tours, false affidavits, and bribes. He also revealed a few extra payments he received without Puter's knowledge—fifteen dollars from Loomis and another twenty dollars for the Ormsby charade. Under vigorous cross-examination, Heidecke "was on the verge of collapse," according to Puter—an excellent performance by Heidecke, who was excused from the stand and escaped prosecution, unlike Puter.

Although he avoided jail, Heidecke's life in the canyon was over. He lost his position as forest ranger, sold his homestead, and moved to the Willamette Valley with his wife Georgeanna to live with her sister and two brothers in Polk County. Heidecke died in February 1931, a month after the birth of his second grandson. Nine years later, in a fitting coda to the story, Heidecke's homestead on Pamelia Creek reverted to possession of the federal government and was later purchased by Frank Potter, then manager of the Mill City Manufacturing Company lumber mill. In a process similar to that employed by S. A. D. Puter (but legal and less profitable) Potter swapped the land for timber in an adjoining section—a slightly ironic fate for land that once belonged to the canyon's main figure in the great Oregon land fraud trials.

Heidecke played the main role, but other residents actively participated in the Puter fraud. During special investigator Loomis's tour, Heidecke introduced the special investigator to Charles and William Thomas, brothers infamous for their association with assassinations and cattle poisonings, whom a vigilante committee had chased out of Gates ten years before. Now in their seventies, the Thomas brothers lived in Detroit as underemployed teamsters, and they agreed to take ten dollars each for swearing to the truth of Heidecke's false affidavits. Heidecke also got a helping hand from Lewis Jacobs, a German immigrant who ran a store and hotel in Detroit and was known as "Accommodating Jakey" thanks to his willingness to sign "any old paper that might be presented to him." Jacobs did just that for Special Agent Loomis, swearing that Puter's fictitious pioneers "had come to Detroit for supplies . . . and I have frequently seen [one of the homesteaders] upon such occasions."[46] Jacobs left the area before the Oregon land fraud trials even began, leaving behind his reputation as an accomplice to fraud. He moved his family to Klamath Falls, where he lived until 1932 as a store owner, railroad promoter, real estate investor, and respected "pioneer, merchant, and capitalist," as his obituary read.[47] Other Detroiters with less prominent roles stuck around to help Puter. As the government's dragnet started to close in, some "confederates at Detroit" funneled information to Puter, and during the trial, Puter's legal defense team "arranged to have witnesses on hand from Detroit." In short, while Stephen Puter became infamous as the self-titled "King of the Oregon Land Fraud," the con never would have happened without Heidecke, the Thomas brothers, "Accommodating Jakey," and other willing local accomplices hoping to turn the situation to their advantage.

Some other residents seem to have also taken advantage of—while perhaps not breaking—public domain land-claim laws. In the few months before and after Puter's gang of ten fraudsters filed for 1,920 acres of land in Township 11 South, Range 7 East, thirty-four other people filed claims for 5,280 acres in that same area.[48] Most of these claimants' names do not appear in the census records from the canyon in 1900, but there are a few: Sebastian Delby, William Horn, William McLaughlin, Robert and Dora Pierce, Truman Pritts, Don Carlos Smith, and James Taylor. Other claims were filed by people whose family names would later become closely associated with the area, such as Frederick Bruckman, whose son Merle would open Bruckman's Breitenbush Springs resort in the Detroit area in the 1920s (see chap. 5). Most of these claims seem at first glance to be legitimate, although some raise suspicion. Don Carlos Smith, for example, "reconveyed" his homestead in the Marion Forks area to the federal government in exchange for potentially lucrative mining property in Township 15 South, Range 3 East—precisely the process followed by Puter and his gang.

These speculative efforts share a broader similarity with John Heidecke's cunning collaboration with Puter, Sarah Hensley's real estate investments in Mill City, and the Smith family's entrepreneurial activities in Gates. All suggest how people in the North Santiam Canyon, as shrewdly as any outsider, seized economic opportunities brought by the railroad. Far from hapless hicks and ignorant bystanders, residents knew well the myriad ways, legal and otherwise, they might benefit from the railroad and its connections to the world outside. The railroad had promised profit to that outside world—farmers in the Willamette Valley, investors in San Francisco and New York— but local people leveraged the railroad for their own economic purposes. In their creative manipulations, investments, and entrepreneurship, people in the canyon turned Hogg's aborted dream into their own "successful failure," as one historian characterized the Oregon Pacific Railroad.[49]

LOCALS BUILD COMMUNITY AND CONNECTIONS

People in the canyon celebrated the railroad and the connections it brought for reasons beyond profit. They saw an opportunity to cultivate community while also further integrating with the world downstream. Residents embraced the railroad on its arrival, incorporating it into the fiber of daily life. Mill City residents Charles and Mary Kelly recall that "When the train arrived from Albany, almost the entire town would be there to meet it. . . . It was the 'main event' of the day."[50] In 1895, that "main event" started at 3:30 p.m., when a Corvallis and Eastern second-class train of freight and passengers arrived in Lyons. The train then made its way up to Mill City, Gates, Minto, Niagara, Halstead, and Detroit, stayed overnight, and returned to the Willamette Valley the next day.[51] By 1915, the railroad's new owner, the Southern Pacific, added a few more stops—Gooch, west of Mill City; Berry and Breitenbush, west of Detroit; and Hoover, east of Detroit—while also shaving a few minutes off the trip.[52]

This undated (ca. 1895) photo shows a Corvallis & Eastern Railroad train in Mill City with lumber ready to ship out to external markets (left) as workers, passengers, and freight arrive (right). From "Mill City Views," photo book 127, page 28, image 116, Canyon Life Museum.

The importance of the train's daily comings and goings shines through clearly in turn-of-the-century photographs portraying the impressive engines and cars steaming into Mill City, welcomed by crowds of people. The trains brought ideas, goods, and people into and out of the area, as the Kellys summarized: "Residents could get their mail, orders of supplies, and greet the passengers all in one trip to town." In addition to using scheduled trains run by the Oregon Pacific and its successors, energetic and brave residents also piloted their own manually powered handcarts down the tracks.[53] The track belonged to the railroad company, but local residents used it to integrate the canyon's communities and connect them to the world outside.

In conjunction with and following the construction of the railroad, residents pushed for even more connections to the outside world. Post offices continued to be the main source of information, and as the population increased, new offices sprang up at nearly every bend of the river. In 1888, Mill City got its first post office with postmaster John A. Shaw, one of the owners of Santiam Lumbering Company.[54] Detroit and Idanha also built their first post offices during the early years of the railroad, in 1893 and 1895, respectively. Other post offices went in at now-forgotten settlements such as Minto, Berry, and Green Basin. Niagara established its own post office in 1893; "Ripley's Believe It Or Not" featured it as the world's smallest post office, with just one row of six boxes inside a six-by-eight-foot building. By the end of the nineteenth century, these post offices offered communication both within and beyond the canyon, simultaneously connecting local communities with each other and to the world outside.

The railroad inspired another way to communicate and build community: newspapers. The area's first newspaper appeared on May 8, 1891, when S. G. Dorris published the first issue of the *Mill City Gazette*.[55] The paper covered local events, from social calls to the latest news about the Oregon Pacific's fate, as well as news from Oregon, the United States, and beyond. In so doing, the *Gazette* hoped to help build a vibrant community: "Let's all put our shoulders to the wheel and give a strong hard push and pull together," urged Dorris in the paper's first issue, "and we will see the results in a short time that will exceed our most sanguine expectations."[56]

The *Gazette* also sent news to several Willamette Valley papers, including the *Evening Capital Journal* of Salem and the *State Rights Democrat* of Albany, which republished reports of interest from the *Gazette*, especially concerning the Oregon Pacific railroad. The valley papers seemed equally interested in a quarrel that broke out between the *Gazette* and a competing newspaper that appeared in 1892, the *Santiam Lumberman*, published upriver from Mill City in Green Basin. The *Santiam Lumberman* supposedly represented the interests of the upper canyon; in response, the *Gazette's* new editor O. A. Cheney established another newspaper, the *Detroit Weekly Freeman*, published even farther up the canyon. The competition didn't last long; the *Freeman* and *Lumberman* ran for less than a year, while the *Gazette* would run until 1912. But even that short contest, and certainly the *Gazette's* longer publication, demonstrated some of the depth and complexity of building a community tied through communication channels to the outside world.

Along with transporting lumber, goods, and local residents, the railroad also increased tourism. Visitors from Salem, Portland, and beyond would travel on the railroad to hike, camp, and enjoy the fishing in the North Santiam River and the many lakes throughout the area. Mt. Jefferson attracted the interest of mountaineers and hikers, eager to summit the second-highest peak in Oregon and happy to be sped toward their challenge on the comfort of the railroad and the developing tourism infrastructure in the canyon. In 1915, for example, Lucy Lewis, a librarian from the Oregon Agricultural College in Corvallis, traveled with a group of friends and amateur mountaineers from Albany to Detroit, walked to

Hoover, and then spent nearly two weeks camping and exploring around Mt. Jefferson, recording in detail their adventures and delight with the Cascades. After demonstrating to their satisfaction their ability to survive and thrive in the wild, the group returned to Detroit, relieved to find not only the train that would return them to the valley, but also other modern conveniences, as Lewis recorded: "Never was there a dinner so satisfying and so completely devoured as that one at the Detroit hotel."[57]

Other visitors engaged the services of local guides, such as John Outerson, who ran a store, pack train, and guide service in Detroit. Greeting customers at the Detroit train station, Outerson would outfit the visitors and prepare the pack animals with "speed and skill . . . [that] bordered on the magical," as one canyon resident recalled.[58] The visitors and Outerson (or other local guides) then trotted or walked into various locations in the upper canyon, like Pamelia Lake, twenty-five miles southeast of Detroit, where they would camp and fish for a few days before returning to Detroit for the trip back to the Willamette Valley and beyond. Residents were quick to utilize the railroad as a means to bring in tourists, and they eagerly developed this connection with the outside world.

As tourism became important to the local economy, it also became part of the canyon's identity. The proprietors of businesses catering to tourists projected an image focused on what the area offered to outsiders. An 1895 article in the Salem *Capital Journal* newspaper enthused about the eagerness of the Mehama House hotel to "entertain the traveler, trout fisher, summer tourist, sportsman and wheelman at the charming mountain resort." In addition to comfortable accommodations, the Mehama House promised its guests "delicious and substantial viands to appease the appetites that are only acquired in that mountain atmosphere, at the forks of the Santiam."

Tourism businesses were not the only ones boasting of the unique traveler- and tourist-friendly environment of the North Santiam. In its first issue, the *Mill City Gazette* defined the canyon by its beauty and what it offered the tourist. The North Santiam River "makes it an ideal place for the deciples [sic] of 'Isaac Walton,'" misspelling the name of the famous father of fly-fishing. Fishermen could "lure the speckled beauty from the pellucid depths, and coming prepared with spears of gighooks and feeling so disposed secure plenty of fine salmon and salmon trout."[59] The area beckoned other sportsmen, who would find that "by going a short distance into the hills deer, bear, and elk can be found in abundance and any party that could desire more game than such as exist in this near vicinity is surely hard to please and had better go to the Wilds of Africa

A group of well-dressed tourists poses for a photograph in Detroit, ready to embark on a guided expedition of the surrounding lakes and mountains. Undated photo (ca. 1915) from "Old Detroit," photo book, page 16, image 45, Canyon Life Museum.

and hunt the wild elephant and boar." This was the image coming out of the canyon: a place of adventure and wonder, ready and eager to host visitors and take their dollars.

The railroad engine that crossed the North Santiam River in November 1888 brought the hopes and dreams of both outside forces and local residents. Hogg and his fellow investors dreamed of incredible profits passing along the rail line, moving freight and passengers from one side of the Cascades to the other. Although the railroad failed to achieve that complete connection, it increased external influence, offering outsiders profits of varying legitimacy and size, as the Oregon land frauds reveal in colorful detail. But residents were not simply observers in the development of the railroad and the changes it brought to the area. People in the canyon actively encouraged the construction of the railroad and integrated it into their community. They also found myriad ways to profit from that connection, from the Smith family's businesses in Gates and Sarah Elizabeth Hensley's Mill City real estate investments to the illegal schemes of John Heidecke's Detroit land fraud gang.

Canyon residents clearly found and cultivated opportunities through the railroad and the external power that it bore. But the choices they made were limited by market forces, external capital, and, perhaps not so obviously, a mentality of boosterism that veiled the potential negative consequences of their actions. The people of the North Santiam Canyon were imbued with a faith that further connections with the outside world would ultimately result in increased power for the community. When the *Mill City Gazette* declared that Mill City would become the "largest city between Albany and Boise City," it was expressing more than just a hope—it was a firm belief that the railroad would bring with it prosperity and power. This faith, which permeated small towns throughout the West, hid from residents the reality of diminishing options that resulted from centering their affairs on the railroad, market forces, and other connections to the outside world. That dependency became abundantly clear in the first decades of the twentieth century, when the canyon became part of, and beholden to, a vast timber empire.

3
Living and Working around the Hammond Lumber Company

The year 1920 was an important one for Clifton and Euphelia Morrow of Mill City. They bought their house on Third Street, Clifton joined the Masons and started a small business raising chickens, and Euphelia nearly died from a monthlong illness. It was also the year that Clifton took a job in the Mill City operations of the Hammond Lumber Company, the most powerful company in the North Santiam Canyon's history. From 1894 to 1934, A. B. Hammond, a San Francisco timber man, controlled most aspects of work and life in the canyon. He owned the railroad, the biggest mill, most of the logging operations, a hotel, a store, and many other businesses. Despite Hammond's pervasive influence, people like Clifton Morrow exercised independence and asserted autonomy in their own lives. Some eagerly cooperated with the company out of pride and in pursuit of wages and profit while others resisted Hammond indirectly, developing their own versions of what James Scott has called the "weapons of the weak" and "arts of resistance."[1] Reactions against Hammond also became ugly. Virulent racism manifested in various ways, partially in response to the influx of "foreign" workers Hammond's industries brought in. In their responses to and interactions with the Hammond Lumber Company, local residents shaped their lives while at the same time acting within the constraints of a system that favored outside forces. The story of the North Santiam Canyon's relationship to the Hammond Lumber Company demonstrates how locals used, benefitted from, and bristled against connections to the outside world.

A. B. HAMMOND: KING OF THE CANYON

Andrew Benoni Hammond would eventually become one of the most important capitalists on the West Coast, owner of numerous railroads and chief of one of the largest timber companies in the West. But in 1876, at age twenty-eight, Hammond was just beginning his exploits in Missoula, Montana, where he was partner in the mercantile of Eddy, Hammond, and Company.[2] His first major investment opportunity came in 1881, when Hammond's company secured the enormous Northern Pacific Railroad contract for railroad ties, trestles, and buildings—twenty-one million board feet of timber. As a biographer wrote, this investment "elevated [Hammond and partners] from typical frontier merchants to men of wealth."[3] Within sixteen years, Hammond would own most of Missoula, including the downtown business blocks, the First National Bank of Missoula, the Missoula Mercantile Company, the Missoula Street Railway company, and the *Missoulian* newspaper.

The combination of rheumatism, cold Montana winters, and a capitalist's appetite for bigger investments led A. B. Hammond out of Missoula and into the Pacific coast states. His first target was T. Egenton Hogg's failed Oregon Pacific Railroad, which Hammond and his partner Edward Bonner bought in December 1894. They spent $100,000, which the existing receiver of the company judged to be $300,000 less than the value of the railroad as scrap.[4]

The railroad, which Hammond dubbed the Corvallis and Eastern Railroad, provided access for the Hammond Lumber Company to enter the North Santiam Canyon. Having considerable experience in the Montana lumber trade, and aware of the opportunity for profit in that field, Hammond next set his sights on the Santiam Lumbering Company. The company had become a fixture in Mill City since its establishment in 1887, operating not only three separate milling facilities, but also a hotel and general store. The worldwide depression of 1893, however, brought hard times throughout the country, and on July 10, 1893, the Santiam Lumbering Company "ordered that on account of a depression in the Lumber Sales and stringency of money it was deemed best to close down the mill until such time as in the judgment of the directors it would justify running."[5]

The directors never did run the mills again. Whereas the Panic of 1893 spelled disaster for the Santiam Lumbering Company, it meant opportunity for A. B. Hammond.[6] On May 5, 1899, the company sold its complete holdings to W. W. Curtiss, acting on behalf of A. B. Hammond, who incorporated the business as Curtiss Lumber Company (the mills changed their name to Hammond Lumber Company in 1912). Like his purchase of the Oregon Pacific Railroad, Hammond got the Santiam Lumbering Company for a steal: just $25,000 for three mills, several businesses in Mill City, and thousands of acres of timberland.[7] Within the span of five years, A. B. Hammond had established control of the canyon's main industry and its only railroad, becoming the central figure of power along the North Santiam River. As the industry journal *Columbia River and Oregon Timberman* noted in 1900, "Mr. Hammond is identified with the Curtiss Lumbering Company, and this company virtually controls the entire situation."[8]

With mastery over transportation and industry in the canyon, Hammond quickly and dramatically enlarged his control over timberland in the area. Following the example of Frederick Weyerhaeuser and other lumbermen in the Pacific Northwest, Hammond bought as much land as he could.[9] Six months after Hammond's purchase of the Santiam Lumbering Company, the *Pacific Lumber Trade Journal* reported that Hammond's "Curtiss Lumber Co . . . have been making extensive investments in timber land in Marion County; their holdings at this time being fully 2,300 acres."[10] That figure would increase exponentially over the next decade, as Hammond and his agents gobbled up timberland. Like other timber barons of the time, Hammond secured these holdings through various means: incremental and dramatic, legitimate and illegitimate. For instance, in 1906, the *Timberman* trade journal reported on a recent Hammond purchase of 5,120 acres, completely on the level and in the public eye.[11] But at the same time, Hammond was working with S. A. D. Puter and other agents involved in the Oregon land fraud to secure thousands more acres in the North Santiam Canyon. Hammond successfully avoided not only prosecution but also any public association with Puter and the Oregon land fraud trials.[12]

By the time the Curtiss Lumber Company name was officially retired in favor of Hammond Lumber Company in 1912, the business owned 29,236 acres of canyon timberland, encompassing nearly eight hundred million board feet of timber.[13] To help finance this spending spree (as well as fund his extensive operations elsewhere on the West Coast), Hammond relieved himself of the burdens of running a railroad. In 1907, he sold the Corvallis and Eastern to the Southern Pacific Railway for $1.4 million, a handsome profit from his $100,000 investment thirteen years earlier. By June 1929, Hammond owned 52,480 acres of timberland holding more than two billion board feet of timber.[14]

Profits from the railroad sale not only financed the purchase of land and raw material but also funded major investments in milling facilities, equipment, and technology in an effort to increase capacity and production. The Hammond Lumber Company built a warehouse in 1906 with storage in the ground floor and an opera house / auditorium in the upper floor.[15] The company store burned down in 1907 and was rebuilt—this time with bricks instead of wood—in 1908. Hammond continually made investments in electric power, starting with a twenty-kilowatt generator that was in use by 1910 to light the mill and the managers' houses.[16] In 1926, the company installed an eight-hundred-kilowatt generator "to operate various electrified units, and the shingle mill which is to be entirely operated by electricity," according to the local paper.[17] Sixteen more electric motors went into service the following year, as did a new chipper and bark plant to process the leftovers from the saw, planing, and shingle mills.[18]

The extraction of timber from the forests changed dramatically during the Hammond years as well. In 1900, the company had one Lidgerwood "steam donkey," a relatively primitive device stationed at the entrance to a stand of timber that would drag logs down to the main Corvallis and Eastern railroad and a few miles of additional spur lines. Twenty-nine years later, the company owned two state-of-the-art Lidgerwood tower skidders, massive structures that stood one hundred feet high, with steel cables strung throughout the air, wrapping their tentacles around logs and dragging them to the Southern Pacific main railroad and dozens of miles of Hammond-owned spur lines reaching into the forests.[19] A 1929 appraisal calculated the total replacement value of Hammond Lumber Company property in Mill City alone at nearly $1.5 million, not including the Lidgerwoods, spur tracks, and other Hammond equipment scattered throughout the canyon.[20]

These extensive timber holdings and intensive production operations required hundreds of workers. High climbers, fallers, buckers, and other logging laborers chopped down massive old-growth trees in the canyon's steep and deep forests, sending them down to the sawyers, mill wrights, filers, and many other millworkers cutting and shipping out millions of board feet of processed timber from industrial operations in Mill City. This work was both as romantic and brave as celebrated by popular writers such as Stewart Holbrook and as dangerous and exploitative as revealed by historians including Steven Beda and Erik Loomis.[21] The process of turning a tree into lumber began at a logging camp, a temporary town where the loggers slept, ate, and lived while cutting trees in the surrounding area. Some of these camps had names, such as Hall's Camp (now submerged under Detroit Lake), but most were known only by a number, like Camp 17, the site of present-day Detroit, or Camp 11, which would later become part of Idanha. These were deliberately crude and transitory places, although some camps had electric lighting and showers in the cabins, as well as mess houses complete with kitchen and dining hall facilities.[22]

When the loggers had cut all of the trees within reach of the camp—or when the company decided the camp was not efficient enough—the camp was taken apart and moved to another location to begin the process again. Hammond Lumber Company operated at least twenty-six different logging camps in the North Santiam Canyon, running as many camps at a time as the company could afford and the market could handle.[23] As Hammond expanded its timber holdings and added more camps, the number of logging camp workers in the area increased rapidly: the 1900 census counted 67 logging laborers; in 1920, 189 people were working in logging camps, and just six years later, Hammond employed 441 people at camps in the North Santiam Canyon.[24]

Most men who weren't working for the Hammond Lumber Company in the forests were working for Hammond in the Mill City, by far the primary timber processor in the area. The Hammond Lumber Company's mill facilities dominated the Mill City landscape. From the modest buildings and infrastructure he acquired from the Santiam Lumbering Company in 1899, Hammond had by 1929 developed a sprawling industrial complex in Mill City. The company's operations included three mills (the main mill, a planing mill, and a shingle mill); machine shops; a wood-waste burner; lumber-drying kilns; a monorail for moving timber throughout the facilities; and log ponds, flumes, gates, and dams for holding the raw material pouring out of Hammond's lumber camps.[25]

When the lumber market boomed and Hammond's facilities buzzed with activity, work was not hard to find. New arrivals drawn to Mill City by reports of Hammond's growth went directly to the mill for employment, as did Charles Powelson, who told the local newspaper that upon his arrival at the turn of the century he "camped by the river side, walked across the crude bridge to the mill and applied for a job," which he promptly received.[26] In the first decades of the twentieth century, employment in the mills grew as rapidly as in the forests and logging camps: from approximately 60 in 1900, the number of millworkers jumped to 230 in 1920, and at its peak in the late 1920s, Hammond's mills in the canyon employed around 500 people.[27]

With more land, more timber, more facilities, and more workers, the Hammond Lumber Company rapidly increased production. Pacific Northwest timber industry trade journals tracked Hammond's spectacular growth in the canyon: 50,000 board feet per day produced in 1900; 80,000 in 1903; 100,000 in 1905; 325,000 in 1916.[28] In March 1928 alone, Hammond's operations shipped a record 5,600,000 board feet of processed timber.[29] Mill City's local newspaper, the *Mill City Logue*,

Undated photograph of a Hammond Lumber Company planing mill crew. From "Hammond Lumber Company," photo book 104, page 21, image 71, Canyon Life Museum.

started at the peak of Hammond's operations in 1926 and often featured triumphant headlines such as "Another Record Established: Mill Makes Record Shipment" and "Large Export Lumber Shipment Moves."[30]

In addition to operating the mill and the logging camps, Hammond also controlled most other facets of life in Mill City and the surrounding communities. The Hammond Company Store was the biggest merchant in the area, selling a diverse line of products, according to a 1927 newspaper advertisement:

> Hammond Lumber Company Store . . . Dealer In Groceries and Food Stuff, Cigars, Tobacco, Stationary, Soap, Hardware, Pipe, Stoves, Rangers, Watches, Clocks, Silverware, Candy, Electric Goods, Auto Supplies, Tires, Tubers, Powder Brick, Crockery, Dry Goods, Nylons, Shoes, Men's Furnishings, Drugs, Seeds and Feeds, Furniture and Paints at Reasonable Prices.[31]

Most everything people needed or wanted could be found at the store, and in some cases, items had to come from Hammond. "You had to buy your wood [for wood stoves, construction, etc.] from him," recalled Stanley Chance of Mill City, "He owned 87% of the land."[32] The company also developed more than five thousand acres of cattle grazing land by planting grass seed in logged off areas that the company then burned over.[33] The company built a slaughterhouse and freezing facility, used the beef in its logging camps, and sold meat in the Hammond Store, where porterhouse steak was fifteen cents a pound. But as a longtime resident remembers, "Sometimes you'd get meat that you couldn't shoot through it, hardly, it was so tough."[34]

The list of Hammond's possessions and influence in the canyon goes on and on: railway station and post office, dentist's office, confectionery store, smokehouse, dozens of residential houses, and more. Hammond paid for the doctor that brought people into the world, treated them in illness and injury, and saw them through their deaths, after which they found their final resting place in a cemetery owned by Hammond Lumber Company. Hammond did not practice the kind of direct, paternalistic control of true company towns like DuPont, Washington; Potlatch, Idaho; or Valzetz, Oregon. Mill City was instead what Linda Carlson calls a "company-dominated town."[35] But that domination was comprehensive and all-encompassing, as German immigrant Otto Witt summarizes: "The life and activities in Mill City, and in fact the whole Santiam Canyon, was centered around the mill."[36] Andrew B. Hammond, who lived five hundred miles away in San Francisco and rarely visited Mill City, created the context within which canyon residents were born, worked, lived, and died.

WORKING IN HAMMOND'S CANYON

Working in this context brought both opportunities and challenges for canyon residents, as the journal of Clifton C. Morrow reveals.[37] Between 1919 and 1923, Morrow recorded the spectrum of his economic activities, from working as a brakeman on one of Hammond's logging trains to raising and selling leghorn hens and their eggs. His journal reveals the complexity of making a living during the Hammond years: wages and hours were modest, the work was dangerous and inconsistent, and Hammond's influence could be oppressive. Like his neighbors in Mill City and elsewhere along the North Santiam River, Clifton Morrow responded to these opportunities and challenges accordingly, creatively shaping his working life as best he could within the shadow of the Hammond Lumber Company's power.

With so many enterprises, from logging camps and sawmills to the confectionary store and medical offices, Hammond salaries and wages ranged widely. In 1915, a common laborer at Hammond's Mill City operations earned sixteen cents an hour, or $1.28 to $1.60 per day, depending on how long the mill ran that day.[38] As a point of comparison, unskilled workers at the Thomas Kay Woolen Mill, a major manufacturer in the Willamette Valley, made twenty cents an hour.[39] Most of the time, the Hammond mills in Mill City ran a single eight-and-a-half- to nine-hour shift, six days a week, although there were occasional ten-hour shifts when the supply of raw logs piled up and the market could handle increased production. More skilled or dangerous work usually brought higher wages. For instance, on June 24, 1919, Clifton Morrow "went to work for Hammond Lumber Company braking on the log train." This dangerous work could lead to dismemberment (of fingers and other appendages pinched while coupling cars) or even death, as brakemen were thrown from the train while carefully but quickly running across the tops of cars to apply the brakes. But it also paid $4.80 a day, nearly four times as much as a common laborer in Hammond's mills.

In exchange for these wages, Hammond's workers risked their bodies and their lives. Working conditions in the forests and mills were always dangerous and sometimes deadly. Clifton Morrow lived to the age of sixty-seven, but he witnessed plenty of early death in the forests. On August 4, 1919, Morrow saw a car full of logs run over a Hammond employee. The man's legs were instantly severed, and he died the next morning. Three days later, a hook tender named George Allen died in Hammond Logging Camp 14 when a tree fell on him. Nine days after Allen's death, and just two months after starting work for Hammond, Morrow quit his job as a brakeman and went to work for Gooch Lumber and Shingle, a smaller independent mill. Like other timber workers, Morrow knew well the dangers of working in the forests, but two deaths in three days was simply too much. He later came back to Hammond, working not up in the forests but in the company's Mill City facilities, where his journal records no deaths—just the four broken ribs he sustained while oiling mill machinery, which kept him out of work for eight days.

Unreliable and inconsistent employment also afflicted timber workers. Logging camps would sometimes shut down for days or even months at a time, thanks to the vicissitudes of the weather or the boom-bust nature of timber production, a common problem for resource extraction industries in the American West.[40] Camp 6 burned down in a wildfire in August 1911; Camp 14 closed in March 1923 because of "waist-deep" snow; and Hammond shut down Camp 17 for more than a month in 1928 "on account of a surplus of logs"—basically, a glut of raw timber.[41] As in the logging camps, employment in the mills also fluctuated. Mills would shut down owing to poor weather, a lack of sufficient log supply, over-production and the difficulty in securing sufficient railroad cars to ship all the processed timber out of the canyon, or for reasons that remained mysterious to Hammond workers.[42] Between July 1919 and January 1923, Clifton Morrow recorded nine unplanned work stoppages, including a spring snowstorm in April 1920 that dumped two feet of snow and shut down Camp 14, and two mill closures in January 1923, once "on account of being out of logs" and then five days later "on account of high water." Morrow also endured a three-month mill closure in 1921, when the lumber market busted: wholesale prices for lumber in the United States fell by more than half, and Douglas fir production in Oregon dropped by sixty-five percent from the previous year.[43] During that three-month closure, Morrow worked for just twenty-seven days, feeling acutely at home the booms and busts of distant markets.

Despite the inconsistency of work, vulnerability to market swings, and other hazards, many Hammond employees and canyon residents developed a sense of pride in their work. The company cultivated this pride by providing occasional bonuses and perks for employees. Pro-duction records in the mills resulted in rewards. In March 1916, the mill produced 325,000 board feet per day, and workers received a ten percent advance on wages.[44] Lesser accomplishments at the mill came with smaller rewards: workers got a cigar when production went over 200,000 board feet in a day. For some people, the Hammond Lumber Company's pres-ence was a source of pride. The 1916 Mill City School yearbook boasted that the Hammond mill "is the largest institution of its kind in the Wil-lamette Valley south of Portland. No mill in the state is better equipped and but few on the coast are adapted to make lumber for the finest retail businesses."[45] From this perspective, to work for Hammond and to live in the canyon was to be a part of something remarkable.

Others had a different view. Despite Hammond's occasional generos-ity and the economic opportunities brought by his company, a distaste and even disgust for the omnipotent absentee capitalist festered in some corners of the canyon. About those free cigars, former employee Stanley Chance said, "Big deal! They'd get cigars out of the store that hadn't sold. They were dry: you couldn't even chew them!"[46] The list of complaints about the company, and timber work in general, went well beyond dry cigars. Some residents expressed displeasure with what they saw as the company's monopolistic and destructive logging practices, adopting Progressive Era ideas and language about conservation and scientific for-estry.[47] In 1907, Ephraim Henness wrote to his old foe, John Minto, who as Marion County judge advocated for dispersed private ownership of timberland. "You may be assured that I agree with you in regard to placing all the vacant land . . . in the hands of the people and not in the hands of the large timber monopolies," Henness wrote, accusing "The Curtiss Co. [the first name of the Hammond Lumber Company] [of] wasting enough wood every year to keep Portland supplied."[48] From grumbling about cheap rewards to exploring anti-monopolist conservationism, people expressed different frustrations with Hammond.

Other concerns dealt with the household economy—specifically, how much of the family income went to Hammond's stores. Clifton Morrow kept careful track of his account balances, and the "Hammond Lbrs Comp. Store" always got a big share of his paycheck. For example, in September 1919, Morrow owed the Hammond store $39.62, which worked out to more than a quarter of his monthly pay from Gooch Shingle. But at least as a Gooch employee, Morrow was not forced to buy from Hammond's store, whereas Hammond employees felt an obligation to do so. Rilla Schaeffer arrived with her husband in 1925 and remembers the perils of taking business elsewhere: "We never tried buying our groceries anywhere but from Hammond . . . I know of neighbors that did go out and purchase elsewhere and they said they were discharged because of this."[49] Leora Stevens and her husband arrived in 1920, and she had similar memories of Hammond's retribution: "Oh yes, all employees in mills or whatever were supposed to charge the groceries so the boss could check on where they were trading. One month we had only an $8.00 charge and were put on the carpet."[50] Such complaints and concerns rarely went public, when they were entertained at all; Clifton Morrow's journal does not register any explicit complaints about Hammond. If the company would put someone "on the carpet" for not buying at his stores, the consequences of public criticism could be equally dire.

Residents also acted in ways that challenged the supremacy of the Hammond Lumber Company. A number of independent mills operated during 1900-1930, directly competing with Hammond's mill for the logs coming out of the area. Most were short-lived, such as the Santiam Lumber Company of Lyons, which operated for just over a year before fire destroyed it in 1916. But some outfits lasted much longer, such as Gooch Lumber and Shingle, established by Fred Gooch in 1907. Located just three miles west of Hammond's Mill City operations, Gooch competed directly with Hammond by producing produced both dimensional lumber and shingles, which Fred's daughter, Sylvia, remembers as "beautiful first grade lumber."[51] Such independent operations offered opportunities to some loggers and millworkers, who could and would take their labor to higher wages and better working conditions. Clifton Morrow did just that when he left his job as a Hammond brakeman after watching two friends die. Morrow moved to Gooch Lumber and Shingle, where he worked numerous jobs, from running the sawdust conveyer to tending the engine room. He started at $4.40 a day and was making $4.80 for an eight-hour day seven months later, when he quit Gooch to go back to work for Hammond. Canyon residents like Morrow could turn such competition for workers to their advantage when the lumber industry was booming, a common practice among timber workers in the American West.[52]

Hammond's other operations also met with competition from ambitious canyon businessmen. In 1925, Floyd Fleetwood opened a pool hall, restaurant, and confectionary, where, as his son remembered it, Floyd sold "beer, soda pop, cigarettes, tobacco and cigars; he sold marbles; he sold mouth harps; he sold billfolds; he sold cigarette lighters. Up in the window—he would buy in season these huge great big oranges and he'd just dump the whole box in there."[53] Louis Rada, an Austrian immigrant who arrived in Mill City in 1920 with his family, built the Hill Top Store across the river from Hammond's store in 1927. Along with a grocery store that offered many of the same goods as the Hammond company store, Rada also offered home appliances, ran a barber shop, measured for suits made by J. B. Simpson tailors, and sold Chevrolet cars.[54] Rada paid for a brief weekly advertisement in the *Mill City Logue* that read, "We can save you money at the Hill Top Grocery. We deliver," an indirect but clear challenge to the Hammond store's offerings.

Clifton Morrow also had an independent economic streak beyond changing jobs when the opportunity arose. In March 1920, the same month that he returned to work for Hammond, Morrow invested in twenty-five leghorn baby chickens. Thus began Morrow's egg business, which helped supplement his family's income. He got pretty good at it, too. In January 1921, he recorded the sale of five dozen eggs at forty-three cents per dozen for $25.80, the equivalent of about five days of work in the mill, assuming the mill stayed open. Morrow exercised his economic power in other ways outside of Hammond's grip. He occasionally bought goods from non-Hammond shops in the canyon, and he spread his spending outside the canyon, too, choosing to get his shoes repaired in Salem ("new soles and heels. Bill paid $2.50"), getting his watch fixed in Portland, and buying twelve pairs of socks from "Chicpee Mills" in Cincinnati, Ohio ("C.O.D. $3.15 paid $3.20 by mistake," a five-cent error that obviously grated Morrow). In such choices about where to spend their money, how to supplement their paychecks, and even whether to work for Hammond at all, Morrow and other canyon residents sought to exercise some economic independence.

LIVING IN HAMMOND'S CANYON

While they worked for and within A. B. Hammond's empire, people in the North Santiam Canyon took an active role in determining the shape of their own lives by building communities. Like Clifton Morrow, many residents shaped their worlds by actively participating in a consumption-oriented lifestyle. Some of that was made possible by the opportunities offered by the Hammond Company's extensive operations, especially the company store, which offered an array of consumer items. Participating in a process that historians have more often associated with larger cities like Seattle and Chicago, people in the North Santiam Canyon eagerly snapped up consumer goods and the aspirational middle-class values and identity they represented.[55] Portraits taken by the Salem-based professional photographer Thomas Cronise provide striking insights into the image that people in the area sought to project.[56] The photographs show not only the variety of finery available for purchase in the Hammond Store, but also the pride people took in their appearance and their identity as both producers and consumers. For example, a photograph of Mill City resident Elizabeth Denny shows her in a beautiful white dress, sitting in a rocking chair next to a fireplace, reading a book—a picture of middle-class domesticity. Young Gladys Schroeder of Gates also had her photo taken with a book in her hands, sitting delicately on a fine chair. Many canyon families presented their children in their Sunday best; Elbert Brown posed his two small children in clean white dresses and tasteful jewelry.

This ritual in middle-class representation was not limited to Hammond's office workers, mill foremen, and storekeepers. Seven years before Louis Rada set up his independent Hill Stop Store, he worked as a common laborer in Hammond's mill. Rada set aside enough of his paycheck for a portrait of his daughters Barbra and Carolina dressed in beautiful white dresses and boots. William Councilman also worked as mill laborer in Mill City; in 1923, he and his wife Lottie had their eight-year-old daughter Wilma photographed in her Sunday best. Clifton Morrow, too, valued the image projected by a professional photograph. "Received my picture. Had it enlarged," Morrow wrote on October 16, 1919, while he was running the sawdust conveyer belt for Gooch Shingle.

Elizabeth Denny posed for this photograph by Salem-based photographer Thomas Cronise in 1912. Denny holds an open book in her lap while gazing thoughtfully into a "fire" (added during the development process). Photograph 0187G021 from the Thomas Cronise Collection, Oregon Historical Society.

For Morrow, Rada, and other families from different backgrounds, these carefully staged photographs offered the opportunity to create family keepsakes while projecting pride in one's middle-class identity.

Canyon residents eagerly exercised their "purchasing power" for more straightforward reasons: entertainment and fun.[57] The Morrow family used Clifton's paychecks and egg money to make life in the North Santiam Canyon more enjoyable and beautiful. They were a musical family: Euphelia took piano lessons from Audrey Trego in Mill City, and Clifton played a mandolin equipped with strings he purchased from Wills Music Company in Salem. The Morrow family also liked to travel. Euphelia and niece Eva traveled to Salem for the Oregon State Fair in September 1919 and to Portland during the July Fourth holiday of 1920. Meanwhile, Clifton took a six-day trip up to Marion Lake for some hiking and fishing. In February 1923, Clifton traveled more than seventy miles to Harrisburg to buy a Chevrolet touring car, which the family drove to Salt Lake City that summer. Through these kinds of purchases, the Morrows and other residents converted their valuable Hammond wages into precious experiences and memories.

Even as they labored hard in Hammond's forests and mills, canyon residents found plenty of ways to enjoy themselves. Beyond travel and music, Clifton Morrow and his family enriched their lives through community. Clifton threw a surprise birthday party for Euphelia in 1920, and the family ate special meals of trimmed goose at Thanksgiving and Christmas, went fishing together on the North Santiam River, and frequently entertained their friends Edd and Edith. They often found entertainment in Mill City, too: Eva, for example, attended a basket social "given for the benefit of the church" and took in "a show in the opera house given by the school children." The opera house, Hammond Hall in Mill City, was a hub for socializing. Here Hammond hosted and charged admission for everything from boxing matches to "dancing, [a] roller rink, basketball, community plays, road shows and movies every Saturday night," as one former Mill City resident reminisces.[58] Residents participated in social activities of all types, from community dances to more sophisticated events, like the 1927 art exhibition advertised in the local paper: "Display Greatest Work of Old and Modern Artists Today and Saturday at Hammond Hall."[59] A different kind of artwork decorated the walls of the Hill Brothers' Pool Hall. A portrait of a nude woman set against a skyline of Douglas fir trees set a tone of erotic repose as loggers and millworkers found brief respite from the rigors of working for the company.[60]

Canyon residents particularly enjoyed themselves and came together as a community during holidays. At Thanksgiving, workers and families gathered for a community dinner, paid for by Hammond, with "enough turkeys and 'fixin's' to feed the whole town," as the local paper reminisced later, during the leaner days of the Great Depression.[61] After enjoying their traditional meal of goose for Thanksgiving in 1919, the Morrows "went over to the opera house for dinner" and "stayed for the afternoon show and dance in the evening." The Fourth of July was by far the most important holiday in the area. Although the Morrows preferred to use the long holiday weekend to travel—in 1921, for instance, they camped and fished upriver from Detroit—many other Mill City residents helped organized and participate in a holiday extravaganza, with music, historical reenactments, and dancing. Festivities began at five o'clock in the morning, when a local band ascended a Mill City hillside to blare out "The Star-Spangled Banner."[62]

These individual, familial, and community activities created a world outside of Hammond's direct control—part of what historians and sociologists call "civil society."[63] The canyon's civil society was further organized by "the multiplication of national bureaucratic structures": the efflorescence of churches, fraternal societies, and other civic organizations throughout the United States in the early twentieth century.[64] Mill City had Catholic, Church of Christ, and Presbyterian churches, drawing congregants from throughout the North Santiam Canyon. Clifton Morrow used his journal to record and reflect on Sunday services; on May 11, 1919, for instance, "Reverend Clark, Minister, Mill City" spoke on Revelations 3:14 and 2:20, admonishing his congregants against both "lukewarmness" and "sexual immorality." Residents also eagerly joined numerous fraternal and other civic organizations. Mill City's chapter of the ZCBJ (Zapadni Ceska Bratrska Jednota, a fraternal organization for Czech Americans), chartered in 1923, put on dances, plays, picnics, and more. Many of its members played in the Mill City Bohemian Brass Band, which performed in Hammond Hall. Clifton Morrow became an active member of the Mill City Masonic Lodge, being initiated into the society on April 17, 1920. Becoming a Mason was an important step in Morrow's life and required significant commitment; for instance, in February 1921, he and four other Masons "all went down to Stayton [eighteen miles away] to attend the Masonic Lodge. Got home at 2:30am." Other civic organizations included the Loyal Order of the Moose, the Knights of the Maccabees, the Boy Scouts, and the Women's Benefit Association, all of which established chapters in the area by 1930.[65]

The Independent Order of Odd Fellows (IOOF) most visibly manifested the diverse effort to create a semiautonomous civil society separate from Hammond. A fraternal mutual benefit society with roots in eighteenth-century England, the IOOF gained popularity throughout the United States and Canada after the Civil War. By 1910, the IOOF had more than one and a half million members in more than seventeen thousand lodges, far surpassing other mutual aid societies like the Loyal Order of Moose and the Fraternal Order of Eagles.[66] The organization had established chapters in Mill City and Gates by 1900, and the two chapters merged in 1907.

The IOOF offered its members a variety of benefits. Member dues and fees went toward funds for widows, orphans, education, disability, and funeral expenses. Injured members received at least two dollars per week for one year—provided that the "injury is not a result of intemperance or other vicious habits"—and the IOOF paid fifty dollars in funeral benefits "on the death of a brother in good standing."[67] Beyond such practical benefits, the IOOF and its women's auxiliary, the Daughters of Rebekah, offered residents opportunities for socialization, business contacts, and community.[68] Shortly after arriving in Mill City in 1920, Leora and Wilson Stevens made the strategic decision to join the Rebekah Lodge and Odd Fellows "so as to become acquainted and involved in the town's activities."[69] By 1915, the Odd Fellows had grown enough in significance (and wealth) to build their own meeting hall in Mill City. The hall hosted not only IOOF meetings, but also the local Masonic Lodge and Eastern Star chapters, as well as Floyd Fleetwood's pool hall, restaurant, and confectionary. The IOOF hall was, in short, the center of organized civil society.

The IOOF hall was also home to the local newspaper, the *Mill City Logue*, established in 1926, which symbolized the North Santiam Canyon's combination of economic dependency and spirit of autonomy. The *Logue* served as a reliable cheerleader and publicist for Hammond's operations, regularly reporting on the mill's improvements, expansions, and production records. The *Logue*'s editor understood that the paper's success depended on the success of Hammond's logging camps and mills, which drove economic activity and growth. Similarly, independent businesses, civic organizations, and other groups all relied on Hammond's operations: the jobs they provided, the wages they paid, and the workers and families they attracted to the area.

But even as Hammond's economic activities shaped their work and lives, canyon residents pushed to transcend those constraints. In the second issue of the paper, the *Logue*'s editor explained the endeavor: "The newspaper is a growth—a development made possible by the cooperative and receptive spirit of the people. It is the echo of the community's vision, a champion of the community's rights, and a direct avenue of the advancement of its civic conditions."[70] The leaders and members of churches, fraternal organizations, and other civic groups helped create that "cooperative and receptive spirit," and they shared the *Logue*'s vision for advancing "civic conditions" and "community's rights." The *Logue*, the IOOF hall, Louis Rada's Hill Top Store—while they all depended on the success of the Hammond Lumber Company, they also manifested a spirit of autonomy and created spaces within which canyon residents could exercise that autonomy.

DIVERSITY AND DIVISION IN HAMMOND'S CANYON

The "community" of which the *Logue*'s editor spoke so eloquently consisted of men and women from different backgrounds living and working in different situations, creating the conditions for both compromise and conflict. While their staged photographs projected an image of a shared

View of Mill City at the height of the Hammond Lumber Company's influence. The larger white building (right) is the Odd Fellow's hall, home to the local chapter of the Independent Order of Odd Fellows, the local newspaper, and other community organizations. From "Mill City Views," photo book 127, Canyon Life Museum.

middle-class identity, residents were practically divided by occupational differences. Falling, chopping, and shipping logs to the mills required experienced workers—foremen, engineers, head riggers, and the like—as well as laborers, woodchoppers, and other "unskilled" workers. The 1920 census counted an exact balance: 67 skilled and 67 unskilled workers in Hammond's Mill City and Breitenbush logging camps. Occupational differences were more extreme in Hammond's mill, where the 1920 census recorded 160 laborers, janitors, and sweepers working alongside 71 more experienced workers and taking orders from 15 foremen, superintendents, and managers.[71] Substantial wage gaps separated Hammond's employees, with managers and foreman taking home three to four times as much pay as common mill laborers and logging camp employees.[72]

While workers interacted in multiple shared spaces, including churches and civic organizations, occupational and wage differences produced different lives for these workers. Class differences manifested themselves in many ways, including the area's housing stock. In the spring of 1920, the Morrows bought a modest home, which the family valued at $700 ten years later—modest when compared to the town doctor's home, valued at $3,000 in 1930.[73] Walt Leisy remembers another way that class shaped the canyon landscape: "There was even a golf course up there at one time, for the executives of the mill."[74]

Such obvious differences between workers and executives could lead to unflattering impressions and interactions. Curtis Cline recalls that when Frederick Olin became superintendent of the mill, the promotion "went to their [Olin and his wife Jessie] heads pretty bad. . . . Mrs. Olin sent to Portland and got a dressmaker down there that come up here. . . . [Mr.] Olin went down to the tailor and he got a spike suit made and a plug hat."[75] The purpose of all this finery seemed clear to Cline: "They was going to show what a town boy could do, I guess." The Olins had made some indelicate decisions about how to spend their wealth, manifesting unseemly class divisions.

Gender as much as class shaped life in the canyon. Most people worked for Hammond, and almost all of Hammond's employees were men. But the community and its economy also relied on women's labor, both paid and unpaid. Rilla Schaeffer, for example, lived in Logging Camp 17 near present-day Detroit with her husband. Schaeffer gave birth to and raised a son, and she managed the household, including carefully calculating not only the amount of food the family needed when logging (and paychecks) stopped, but also how much they could spend to avoid crippling debt to Hammond's commissary.[76]

Women worked in the camps in other ways: Marie Cooper ran a hotel that hosted traveling merchants and railroad employees, Burnice Shields cleaned houses while raising her infant son, Mrs. Gower managed the commissary's accounts, Floy Ferguson worked as a stenographer, and the Bostrack sisters—Mollie, Caroline, and Mamie—all taught school in the Detroit area in 1920 while raising their younger brothers Johnny and Sherman.[77] Down in Mill City, women claimed numerous vocations, including hospital laundress, dressmaker, pipe organ musician, teacher, and "office girl" for the dentist.[78] As they did throughout American history, including in the extractive industries of the American West, women made things work in and outside of the canyon's logging camps and mills.[79]

The area also depended on the work and other contributions of people from diverse national and ethnic backgrounds. As historians have demonstrated, immigration fueled the industrialization and expansion of the American economy in the late nineteenth century and early twentieth century, and that was as true in Mill City as it was in New York.[80] Immigrant laborers had first come to the area during construction of the railroad in the 1880s, and as the Hammond Lumber Company began expanding its operations, modest ethnic communities developed. The 1910 census of the North Santiam Canyon counted 385 people born outside of the United States, almost fourteen percent of the population.

Ten years later, eighteen percent of residents had been born outside of the United States. Most were from Europe; in Mill City, for instance, 181 of the city's 292 foreign-born residents counted by the 1920 census hailed from twenty-five different European countries and regions.

When local contemporary accounts and residents' memories refer to "diversity," these are usually the immigrants they are talking about: Europeans preserving certain aspects of their cultural background while happily merging into mainstream American society. Arey Podrabsky speaks of the "Mill City Melting Pot" that welcomed Greeks who were "expert kite makers and fliers," Swedes who "were hard workers and renowned for their rugged toughness in the woods," and especially his own "ethnic Czechs," who formed the local chapter of the ZCBJ and the Mill City Bohemian Brass Band. Although the band took instructions in Czech and "their repertoire included polkas, waltzes, stirring marches, overtures, galopes, [and] schottisches," the Mill City Bohemian Brass Band "always, and I mean always," Podrabsky emphasizes, "[played] all the American patriotic songs." Performing patriotic music was "an absolute must," says Podrabsky, for the Czech immigrants to become fully American: "these new citizens felt a strong sense of loyalty to this great new country of freedom."[81] In such memories, European immigrants coupled amusement and entertainment with American patriotic fervor to create the "Mill City Melting Pot."

In the North Santiam Canyon, as elsewhere in the United States at the turn of the century, creating this melting pot involved the exclusion of other, nonwhite immigrants. Nationally, a variety of exclusionary processes, from legal mechanisms such as the Chinese Exclusion Act of 1882 to ideological traditions of xenophobic nativism, evolved and converged to create a shared identity—"whiteness of a different color," as Matthew Frye Jacobson has called it—among older Western European immigrants and more recent arrivals from Eastern and southern Europe.[82] In the North Santiam Canyon, that process took myriad forms, starting with the observation and essentialization of different kinds of difference. The 1920 census counted fourteen "Hindus"—Sikhs—and forty-seven Japanese residents, the largest single ethnic minority in the area.[83] In Arey Podrabsky's memories, such nonwhite foreigners added a curious, strange, and essentially foreign exoticism: the Sikhs wore turbans with "short silvery daggers" that they removed before their daily exercise routine of "various sizzling gyrations"; the Japanese men fished for steelhead "barefooted, laugh[ing] and yell[ing] while flailing wildly" while the "squealing women . . . beat [the fish] to death with a billy club . . .

laughing and chattering all the way."[84] From this perspective, the physical characteristics of the Sikh and Japanese were fundamentally different in type compared to the skills-based characteristics of the Swedes and Czechs, visibly distinguishing them from the nonwhite, non-European, assimilable immigrants from Europe who were eligible for the Mill City Melting Pot.

Contemporary accounts also found amusements in the otherness of these nonwhite groups, in one case seeing entertainment in their tragedy. After a flood in 1929, the local newspaper reported that "The Japanese colony . . . received a real thrill about two o'clock Wednesday morning when the head gate of the Hammond log pond washed out, a wall of water three feet high hitting the houses."[85] The families whose homes were damaged or destroyed by the flood certainly saw it as more than a "real thrill." The newspaper's approach in this case echoed broader exoticization of nonwhite others. At a 1926 Gates costume dance, for example, prizes were awarded to "Bob Martin of Stayton representing a Jewish character [and] Misses Mabel Stils and Rosalie Boatman representing negro mammies."[86] Like the Bohemian Brass Band's use of American patriotic tunes, such performances and stories of exotic nonwhite others served as both entertainment and a way to define who did and did not belong in the canyon.

Nonwhite residents found themselves excluded and attacked in more directly racist and insidious ways. The Mill City chapter of the Independent Order of Odd Fellows, like other civic groups and organizations, provided some practical benefits and helped integrate newcomers to the North Santiam Canyon community. But as the chapter's charter of 1900 made clear, only certain kinds of immigrants were eligible: "All candidates for initiation must be free white males."[87] The Mill City IOOF both followed the policies of the national IOOF—as well as other fraternal organizations—and revealed a widespread attitude of white supremacy in the canyon.

That attitude became increasingly aggressive in the 1920s, taking its most obvious form in the appearance of the Ku Klux Klan in the canyon. The Klan underwent a revival in the United States in the 1920s, spreading a particular brand of white Protestant American masculinity that attacked Jews, Catholics, "foreigners," and blacks.[88] For a brief moment, the 1920s Klan exercised remarkable political influence, especially in Oregon. Democrat Walter Pierce rose to the governorship in 1922 in part by courting Klan support; that same year, voters approved the Klan-backed Compulsory School Bill, which required all students to attend public schools—a direct attack on Catholic schools. By 1923, there were more than sixty Klaverns in Oregon, with members recruited through existing fraternal organizations, including the Scottish Rite Masons and the Odd Fellows.[89] Among those Oregon Klaverns was the Mill City chapter of the Klan, which held its meetings at the IOOF building.

The Mill City Klan hosted outside speakers to push the Klan's agenda, which included prohibiting teachers from wearing religious garb—another anti-Catholic measure, which the Oregon state legislature passed in 1923—along with laws prohibiting first-generation Japanese immigrants from purchasing or leasing land and allowing city governments to deny business licenses to Japanese immigrants, further advancing the Klan's anti-foreigner agenda. The Mill City Klan's guests included the Reverend Virgil Keller "Bearcat" Allison, a Protestant minister from Lebanon who traveled throughout Oregon evangelizing for the Klan. Allison visited the canyon at least twice, including to deliver a January 1927 lecture on "The Challenge of the Unclean." The *Mill City Logue* reported that "Rev. Allison is a forceful speaker and held the close attention of his audience for about an hour and a half." Having listened to Allison rail against "unclean" foreigners, attendees "sojourned to the I.O.O.F. Hall, where the ladies had prepared an appetizing lunch." Later that year, the IOOF hall hosted special guest Reverend Shaw of Stayton, who "for over an hour held the closest attention of the meeting while he talked on 'Why the KKK.'"[90] Offering a vision of white, Protestant Americanism (with distant but supposedly shared northern European heritage), the Klan found a receptive audience among the white residents gathered at the Mill City IOOF hall.

The Klan also found support from local Protestant congregations and ministers. During Reverend Shaw's visit in 1927, the "large crowd in attendance" joined in the singing of "The Star-Spangled Banner" and then listed to "music by the choir of the Church of Christ." That church's pastor, Reverend Bates, then "made a splendid talk on Americanism and Education," echoing the Klan's argument that parochial schools encouraged papism and discouraged patriotism. Bates was followed by another local pastor, Reverend Gray of the Community Church, who "gave a very convincing talk on the favorable influence yielded by the daily use of the Bible in the home and in the school," offering his own endorsement of the Klan's Protestant agenda. The audience then took in a few more songs by the choir; "several vocal trios" from local residents Mrs. B. A. Cover, A. A. Holthouse, and B. A. Cober; and then Shaw's lecture. "Following the meeting," the *Logue* concluded, "refreshments were served."

Interestingly, by the time of these community events in 1927, the national Klan and Oregon Klan's influence had waned; the US Supreme Court ruled the Compulsory School Bill unconstitutional in 1924, for example. The continued enthusiasm for the Klan in Mill City reveals not just the persistence of white supremacy in the area, but also that the Klan operated both in and of the North Santiam Canyon, organized and driven by the local white Protestant community.

A poem featured on the front page of the *Mill City Logue* (published at the IOOF hall) in March 1927 further reveals how this broader trend of white supremacy developed within the specific conditions of life and work in the canyon. While the Klan had lost direct political clout by the mid-1920s, its legacy of anti-immigrant nativism continued, especially in the effects of the National Origins Act passed by Congress in 1924. That act severely curtailed immigration from southern and eastern Europe and eliminated any immigration from Asia.[91] Those were precisely the populations attacked by the poem published in the *Logue*.

Written by an anonymous "contributor," the ten-verse poem, "Third Record Cut," seeks to explain to readers a recent record-setting success of the Hammond mill: "Hurrah, Hurrah, they have did it again / But there is no use to shout, / So sit you down until I begin / And I'll tell you what it's all about." The poem starts with praise for a vaguely defined "noble saw mill crew" of "large and husky lads" who are defined primarily by their opposite: "never a man was late . . . they were never known to shirk." The poem gets to its ugly point in the fifth verse: "The third record cut that they have made / in the last few months, methinks, / These are men of American grade, / It can't be done with Japs or Chinks." The author goes on to attack "rag heads" (referring to the Sikh population) and Greeks. Drawing on nativist tropes then and now in fashion, the poem accused Asian and non–Western European immigrants of undermining the local economy when they "sent their money back to their native land," in addition to having been "late" to or "shirking" work. The poem's author also raises the threat of rape and violation of middle-class white domesticity: "Our mothers and wives can [now] go / And get themselves a seat / In our moving picture show / Without sitting next to a Greek."

Such were the problems of the "olden days of yore," before the Oregon Klan, the restrictive 1924 National Origins Act, and the widespread anti-immigrant sentiment and behavior of the 1920s. In fact, the non–Western European immigrant population in the area declined in this period. The 1930 census counted just eighteen people of Japanese descent living in Mill City, compared to forty-nine in 1920. In other words, the white supremacist objectives of the Klan and the National Origins Act had been achieved in the canyon. And so the poem concludes with praise while also echoing the specter cast by the previous month's lecture on the "unclean" by Klan speaker Bearcat Allison: "The plant has prospered, without a doubt / As can plainly be seen. / And if we can keep the foreigner out, / We can keep our village clean." The "men of American grade" and their families should take pride in the prosperity they created through Hammond's timber operations—a prosperity, many believed, meant only for suitable types of white Americans.

All of these forms of racism, from delighting in the "real thrill" of a flood destroying Japanese homes to the explicit hatred expressed by the Mill City Klan and the "Third Record Cut" poem, represented angry ambivalence about and resistance to Hammond's influence. When residents attended Klan meetings or nodded their heads in agreement to the stanzas of "Third Record Cut," they were expressing anger and frustration with demographic transformations; specifically, the presence of "Japs," "Chinks," "ragheads," and other "unclean" nonwhites. These changes were not some unintended and unnecessary effect of the expansion of Hammond's timber and milling operations. They were essential to that growth. The Hammond Lumber Company recruited and hired foreign workers for its operations.[92] But white supremacists like the poem's author wanted the benefits of a booming timber industry—good-paying jobs and access to middle-class consumer goods and services—while also rejecting the changes wrought by such a boom.

The IOOF hall represented these paradoxes of the canyon's relationship to A. B. Hammond. The hall itself was one of the few buildings not owned by Hammond, yet one of its tenants, the *Mill City Logue*, served as Hammond's public relations arm, proudly boasting of the mill's production records and technical investments and advances. Another tenant, Floyd Fleetwood, ran an independent restaurant and store offering confectionary delights, which locals eagerly bought up using their Hammond paychecks. Canyon residents like Leora and Wilson Stevens joined the IOOF for practical and social benefits offered independent of Hammond's careful watch, but the IOOF did not welcome other, nonwhite residents who came to work for Hammond. The IOOF hall points to the spectrum of ways—from autonomous consumerism and entrepreneurship to vicious and exclusionary white supremacy—that canyon residents sought to shape their worlds within Hammond's inescapable shadow.

That shadow loomed large. The Hammond Lumber Company and the outside economic forces it represented shaped life and work in the

canyon despite the various efforts—creative, malevolent, and otherwise—of local residents to exercise agency in their lives. The resources
and connections at the company's disposal gave it the advantage from
the beginning. Hammond bought the railroad and the mills during the
depression of 1893, when few other capitalists in Oregon, and certainly
no one locally, had sufficient assets to make such an investment. And
it was Hammond who primarily profited from these investments. By
1907, the company recorded profits of $750,000, thanks to the logging
and milling operations in Mill City joined by Hammond's larger empire,
which included a railroad and timber operation Astoria, another railroad
and massive redwood holdings in Northern California, a shipping fleet,
and sixty-five lumberyards in California.[93] When A. B. Hammond died in
1934 at the age of eighty-four, he was worth $60,000,000.[94]

The North Santiam Canyon, however, had no millionaires. While
Hammond's Mill City properties appraised at $1.5 million in 1929, the
median home value in Mill City in 1930—before the Great Depression
decimated wealth—was $900, according to the US Census. Such calcula-
tions do not tell the whole story of these families and their lives. The
census does not include the photographs residents so carefully staged
and treasured as part of their middle-class identity. Hammond paycheck
stubs do not record the variety of consumer goods people bought to fill
their homes, nor do they show the myriad ways that they entertained and
enjoyed themselves with their families and as a community outside of
Hammond's control. But even as residents found ways to work with and
even challenge the company, they continued to rely on the connections to
external markets by which local options diminished and outsider influence increased. This would become painfully obvious during the 1930s,
when the Great Depression revealed just how connected—and dependent—the North Santiam Canyon had become.

4

The Great Depression in the Canyon

The Great Depression hit the North Santiam Canyon as it did the rest of the country, with widespread unemployment and a reduced standard of living. Much of this material suffering resulted from the loss of the Hammond Lumbering Company, whose logging, milling, and other operations had connected the local economy to the world and made it dependent on that outside world. Other connections, some tangible and some intangible, also disappeared or shrank during the Great Depression: regular train service to the Willamette Valley, the local newspaper, and post offices that closed as the population decreased. These contractions produced hardships for residents, as recollections and records from the period attest.

Yet these recollections also reveal that while connections to the outside world decreased, so did some of external influence, requiring increased independence and self-sufficiency for some people in the canyon. As in the situation of Coos Bay, Oregon, explored by William Robbins in the classic community history *Hard Times in Paradise*, the Great Depression brought out both creative resourcefulness as well as the demands for government assistance so common in the history of the American West.[1] Even as local residents continued to look for opportunities and support from outside—especially New Deal programs like the Civilian Conservation Corps—they also looked to themselves and each other to survive and thrive. The Great Depression lasted a short time compared to the preceding Hammond era and the following decades of dramatic economic growth and change. But that brief period produced a revealing situation in which the communities of the North Santiam Canyon simultaneously lost economic prosperity but gained, however briefly, some autonomy.

THE DEATH OF HAMMOND

In the first months of the Depression, canyon residents expressed a confidence that their community and the rest of the country was not doomed. On December 12, 1929, two months after the market crash that signaled the onset of the Depression, the *Mill City Logue* ran an

77

editorial that reflected this faith. "The stock market collapse, temporary business depressions, or financial crises are momentary phenomenon," said the *Logue*, dismissing concerns about a long-term crisis. Drawing on patriotic reserve and notions of American exceptionalism (and implying the inferiority of other countries), the *Logue* confidently asserted that "American business is the soundest in the world, the most progressive, the wealthiest." Readers had nothing to worry about, because America's "tremendous reserve in capital and credit are steadily building up new enterprises, improving the employment problem and increasing the national payroll." Cautioning those who might be tempted by the bold promises of Soviet communism, the *Logue* reassured readers that "This is no mythical prosperity of ours, but an actual prosperity whose benefits accrue mainly to the great mass of American citizens and wage-earners."[2] Look around, the *Logue* seemed to be saying, and see the loggers and the millworkers and the smoke and steam from industry. The Hammond Lumber Company and connections to the market had made it all possible, and the company and the market were just fine.

Local economic signs and conditions gave people every reason to be confident. By the time of the stock market crash, the Hammond Lumber Company had been established in the North Santiam Canyon for almost thirty years. In addition to investment in technology and capacity, the company further expanded its operations in an effort to defeat the Depression through growth. On October 31, just two days after Black Tuesday on Wall Street, the *Mill City Logue* announced the Hammond Lumber Company's purchase of eight hundred acres of timberland, "One of the largest land transfers recorded in Linn County."[3] This purchase added more stock to the Hammond Lumber Company's timber base with the hope that increased production would bring increased profits, a policy that would continue during the first few years of the Depression. The company bought out the Little River Redwood company of California in February 1931, consolidating over one hundred thousand acres of redwood timberland in the Hammond Lumber Company's hands.[4] The *Mill City Logue* expressed confidence that "The combined holdings will be sufficient to furnish logs for the company's mills for the next 50 or 60 years." The Hammond Lumber Company, it seemed, would continue to provide work for many years to come.

Hammond was fighting a shrinking lumber market and an accelerating global economic catastrophe. When expansion did not stave off the Depression, the company began looking for ways to save more, rather than earn more. Problems in the lumber market had reached the canyon as early as May 1928, when the *Mill City Logue* reported that "the Hammond Lumber Company mill will this week . . . start working on a five day a week basis until conditions are improved, the mill to be shut down each Saturday."[5] The *Logue* explained that Hammond made this decision "on account of the depressed condition of the lumber market, and in an effort to stimulate the prices" and that the action was taken "in conjunction with the majority of other large mills around the country," an explanation that both sought to reassure residents of the health of the timber industry and pointed to the nationwide decay in that industry. Closures increased as the Depression deepened. Some logging camps, such as Camp 24 and Camp 17 (current-day Detroit), closed owing to "surplus logs"; other camps that closed during the winter or fire season did not reopen when conditions improved. The Hammond Lumber Company mill made repeated reductions in its operating hours, culminating in August 1931, when the mill cut back to two days a week, each with only a single six-hour shift.[6] The newspaper expressed hope that it was a "temporary shut down" owing to "shortage of water to float the logs." But it was becoming increasingly clear that Hammond and his company were not invincible.

The final blow to the Hammond Lumber Company and its operations in Mill City came in 1934, when A. B. Hammond died at the age of eighty-four. Hammond's son Leonard promised to keep the mill open—a promise he could not keep. In July 1934, the Hammond Lumber Company's board of directors ordered a complete review of the company's business. The report found that the Mill City operations had lost over $500,000 since 1925—a shocking contrast to the public confidence exuded by the *Mill City Logue*. The study concluded that "It appears impossible to revise the operation in any manner, or at any reasonable cost, to change the operating figures sufficiently to make a profit." The conclusion was inescapable: "It was therefore recommended that logging operations be discontinued [and] that the plant be shut down."[7]

Hammond's Mill City interests languished for another year. On July 1, 1935, the *Four L Lumber News* ran an obituary for the company's operations in the canyon: "The big sawmill at Mill City, Oregon cut its last logs March 23rd. Manager Fred Olin, of the Hammond Lumber Co., announced recently that all of its lumber operations are being closed permanently." Hammond intended to not just shut down its operations, but also to pull its assets out and recoup some of its expenses, as the *Lumber News* reported: "The logging railroad is being taken up and logging equipment is being sold. The planing and shipping departments will be run until stocks of lumber are disposed of."[8] Hammond hired a Eugene-based company to tear down the mill and remove all the machinery, to be sold off to pay for other company debts.[9] Although the Hammond Lumber Company would hold land in the area for decades to come, it had ceased to exist as an industrial concern in the North Santiam Canyon.

The decline and fall of Hammond Lumber Company were felt most immediately in paychecks. During its last few years, the company repeatedly reduced wages, chopping pay checks ten percent at a time until, after seven cuts, the minimum wage at the mill had dropped to one dollar per day or twenty cents per hour. The *Mill City Logue*, desperate to prop up spirits and maintain the illusion of a strong local economy, tried to put the best spin on the situation: "Naturally, a wage cut is not received with satisfaction, and although it apparently will be difficult for many families to subsist on the announced minimum wage, it is not thought that there will be any trouble in securing the necessary amount of workmen under the present unemployment conditions."[10] The *Logue* did not acknowledge an additional hardship: these lower wages were paid in scrip that was only good at the company store. This increased dependency on Hammond brought with it further vulnerability, as one longtime resident remembered: "You rented your house, you bought your water and lights, you bought your groceries and your clothing and everything from Hammond or you didn't work for him. And when you ran out of scrip during the Depression, you didn't get anything."[11]

The standard of living only got worse when the company finally went under and the entire economic structure of the canyon fell apart. In addition to the hundreds of millworkers who lost their jobs, the logging camps shut down, hotels shuttered their windows, and stores closed. The *Mill City Logue* bore witness. The paper dutifully reported business closures, such as the closing of the Mill City Theater in December 1932—forced out, as the paper explained with ambiguity, by "the press of other business."[12] The *Logue*'s declining advertising base belied the paper's efforts to dismiss or explain away the canyon's economic troubles. In 1929, the *Logue* averaged around fifty advertisers per issue. By 1933, the local paper could only find five advertisers. Residents had come to depend on the Hammond Lumber Company, and when it vanished, so did the area's economic prosperity.

CONTRACTION IN THE CANYON

The Great Depression and the dissolution of the Hammond Lumber Company led to the loss of other connections to the outside world that had become integrated into the community. Most noticeably, railroad

This undated (ca. 1930) postcard of the "Old Detroit Road" shows one of the road's particularly dangerous sections, which the postcard's sender describes as "3 sharp curves with 3 points sticking up skyward on rocks on each curve and straight down the other side." From "Old Detroit Road," photo book, page 1, Canyon Life Museum.

service steadily dwindled throughout the Great Depression. Freight trains ran less often and with considerably less cargo; gone were the days when the Albany-bound train, loaded down with twenty-five to thirty cars of logs, would have to back up to Gates in order to make it over the hill outside of Mill City. In 1930, the Southern Pacific ran two trains daily into the canyon, with stops in Lyons, Fox Valley, Mill City, Gates, Niagara, Breitenbush, and Detroit. By 1933, there was only one freight train with three stops, the farthest being Mill City, and no more passenger trains ran on Southern Pacific's tracks.[13]

As rail transportation contracted, the only way in and out of the area was by means of a narrow county road that had been built in 1924 (more about this road in chap. 5). Originally eight feet wide, the North Santiam Highway, as it would eventually be known, was doubled in width all the way to Detroit in 1926, ostensibly providing for two-way traffic. In practice, the road was slow, uncomfortable, and dangerous. The road "was naturally 'surfaced' during the thirties; that is, boulders, a measure of crushed rock and a plethora of potholes," remembers one longtime resident of Detroit. "In places, the width hardly accommodated one car . . . It would not be unfair to describe the drive from Niagara to Detroit as cause for fear and near-terminal distress."[14] The hazards and inconvenience of this rough road made transportation of products, goods, and services much more difficult; the county highway could not replace the economic connections provided by the Southern Pacific. The loss of Hammond and the railroad effectively cut the North Santiam Canyon off from the external economy it had come to depend on.

The area also lost the local newspaper. The *Mill City Logue* had been in operation since August 26, 1926, when its editor stated plainly the newspaper's intent: "we hope, with your assistance to keep a Log (record) of the activities of the North Santiam valley."[15] In columns like "Lyons Pickings," "Gates Gatherings," "Mehama Locals," and "Detroit Squibs," the *Logue* kept readers abreast of everything that happened in the area, from news of local industry to community dance announcements. The *Logue* also connected the area to the outside world, both through its reports on national and world affairs as well as by delivering local news to subscribers throughout Oregon and Washington. As the Depression wore on, that news was increasingly grim, with solemn reports of wage cuts and the closure of local businesses eclipsing optimistic forecasts of the economy's imminent rebound.

By 1933 the *Logue* had faded, much like the Hammond Lumber Company and the rest of the local economy. After passing through the ownership of three different editors, in 1930 the *Logue* ended up in the hands of Albert and Arlene Van Dahl; they both worked as linotypers at the Salem *Capital Journal*, and Albert had previously co-published the Baker *Herald* in eastern Oregon. Albert was also a passionate philatelist, and he devoted more and more of his time to a small hobby weekly called *The Western Stamp Collector*. Van Dahl continued to run the papers separately until February 9, 1933, when he combined the new papers and announced that "the name of *Mill City Logue* has been discontinued while the local publication adopts the name [*Western Stamp Collector*] which conforms with the future field of its endeavors. The local subscribers will receive a special local edition until such time as subscriptions have expired after which the local page will be discontinued entirely."[16]

The local page continued for another four months and then finally closed on May 25, 1933, with a bitter announcement by Van Dahl, who

derided the community for a lack of advertising revenue and a paying subscriber base of just "FIVE true-blue readers."[17] The Van Dahls
packed up their equipment and moved the *Western Stamp Collector* to
Albany, where they ran their stamp paper until the 1970s. Back in Mill
City, the offices of the *Logue* inside the Independent Order of Odd Fellows (IOOF) building went dark. The second issue of the *Logue* had
promised that it would be "a champion of the community's rights, and
a direct avenue of the advancement of its civic conditions."[18] With the
newspaper's closure, the community lost that champion as well as an
important communication channel with the outside world.

Canyon residents experienced other kinds of loss during the Great
Depression. The post office at Niagara closed in 1934, with all service
transferred to Gates, four long miles away down the rough county road.
That left the rest of the upper canyon with just a single post office at
Detroit (and a smaller station at Breitenbush, which opened in 1928).
That same year, the Mill City Hospital burned to the ground, leaving
area residents without reliable medical service until 1938, when Dr.
David Reid opened a community clinic in Mill City. The Depression also
visited the area in the form of hungry transients from elsewhere. Tom
La Duke, who lived in Mill City at the beginning of the Great Depression, remembers one such "gentleman of the road" begging for a few
eggs and onions.[19] Henry Bock, who grew up in Gates, recalls his family
being visited by a "vagabond Frenchman" named Cole Chapelle who
lived on "flapjacks and Hoover sandwiches," the latter being "a slice of
bread between two slices of turnip."[20] These experiences of depravation
and loss contributed to a sense of vulnerability and disconnection in the
North Santiam Canyon.

CREATIVITY AND COMMUNITY DURING THE DEPRESSION
Although links to the outside world contracted during the Great Depression, they did not completely disappear. The county road was rough, but
it provided access to markets and government agencies in the Willamette
Valley and beyond, and local residents used these connections as best
they could to survive the hard times. Some people cultivated a few niche
markets to secure precious cash. Al Fisher of Detroit split wood for use
in cookstoves, loaded it on a flatbed truck, and drove it down to Salem,
where, as Fisher's son remembers, "Prospective customers, although
mostly poor, could afford to be selective in their purchases and would
not buy wood with a knot or too much pitch."[21] There was also a small
market for the bark of the Cascara tree—chittum bark, as it was called,

an ingredient used in laxatives. Longtime canyon resident Henry Bock collected enough of the bark to sell for eight dollars, which he used to purchase a Sears bolt-action .22 rifle.[22] Stanley Chance of Mill City also remembered scavenging "anything for a dollar: chittum bark, scrap iron, moss" that he could sell in Salem.[23]

The firewood and chittum bark trade hardly provided enough income to put food on the table. And so, like many Americans during the Great Depression, canyon residents looked to the federal government for assistance. New Deal relief work and projects made a lasting impression on the landscape and the community through the Civilian Conservation Corps (CCC).[24] In 1933, the CCC built Mary's Creek Camp just up the river from Detroit.[25] The camp housed and employed two hundred young men, including some from Mill City, Gates, Detroit, and other communities, as well as Willamette Valley towns such as Woodburn, Albany, and Mt. Angel.[26] Though the Army ran the camp, the US Forest Service took charge of the recruits, putting them to work on projects throughout the area. In addition to blazing trails, building roads, and fighting forest fires, Mary's Creek CCC recruits took on a number of sizable projects, including a Forest Service guard station along Breitenbush Creek, a triplex apartment building at the old Detroit ranger station (now submerged under Detroit reservoir) and, at the very end of the CCC program in 1939-40, the two-and-a-half-story Santiam Pass Ski Lodge, big enough for sixty skiers and all their equipment.[27] Walter Seamster, who grew up on a farm outside of Gates and worked at Mary's Creek between 1933 and 1934, recalls his time there as "a learning experience. I learned some good work ethics, how to live in close quarters with other men, how to accept the good with the bad."[28] Like other CCC recruits, Seamster considered himself "fortunate" for those lessons, the experience, and the government paycheck.

Seamster was indeed fortunate. Although the CCC offered paying work for some local residents, there were fewer positions than applicants, and getting into the CCC did not ensure placement at the local Mary's Creek facility; there were dozens of CCC camps all over Oregon. Nor could Mary's Creek CCC recruits depend on permanent placement in the canyon. In June 1935, the Forest Service sent the Mary's Creek crew three hundred miles away to Bear Wallow in Union County. The young bachelor Walter Seamster found the experience interesting, but it presented more challenges to married men like Al Fisher, who joined the CCC and was then shipped off to Union County, far from his wife and son back in Detroit.[29]

The difficulty in finding government work led to expressions of frustration that revealed the persistence of anti-immigrant and anti-outsider sentiment and biases. As Marion County slowly continued construction on the highway, locals were distraught to see "foreign labor" doing much of the work. In July 1931, J. F. Bewley led a delegation of Detroit citizens to the Marion County court and filed a complaint against the road contractors who "have employed between 40 and 50 Austrians on the work and that residents of the vicinity who are out of employment are given no favorable consideration when putting in applications for jobs. . . . They told the court that there are from 10 to 15 families in Detroit, heads of which have no work and are badly in need of it."[30] They had some success, with the government promising to require that contractors "[employ] a certain number of men taken from the county relief list and agree to pay a minimum wage."[31] It was difficult and hardly lucrative work—for example, Scott Young of Marion Forks made sixty cents per hour clearing rockslides, removing uprooted trees, and driving a makeshift snowplow.[32] But local residents were desperate for—and jealous of—any kind of paying work during the Great Depression.

As the economic crisis continued and connections to the outside world contracted and offered insufficient means, many residents looked to subsistence activities to get by. People who lived in the canyon during the Depression remember that, as Clyde Rogers recalls, "many families were dependent on venison for supplementing their meals during these difficult times."[33] Don Jenkins remembers his uncle, an out-of-work saw filer, supplementing his diet with venison; Al Fisher once shot a bear at the local Detroit dump and brought it back to his family's garage for skinning, salting, and drying.[34] Fisher also employed his skills at fly-fishing to produce meals of "fish [served] with fish," as his son recalls. Subsistence farming and berry collecting contributed to dietary needs, some eaten fresh and the rest canned for later in the year. The wild game, berries, and small farming opportunities even drew some new people to the area, participating in a dispersed back-to-the-land movement seen elsewhere in the United States in the early twentieth century.[35] Glen Shelton and his family moved from Illinois and then to California before heading up to the North Santiam country, which to Glen "sounded like a good place to be. There I could raise most of our food, fish and hunt to supply our meat."[36]

Canyon residents utilized a variety of other methods to get by during the Depression, and memories from the period focus on creative resourcefulness. Shelton learned to "make do" in a number of new fields. He repaired leaky water pipes by cutting rubber inner tubes into strips and then wrapping the rubber around the pipes with hay wire. "I had a good many 'blow-outs,'" recalled Shelton, "but after a while the water was running up the hill to the house." The Fisher family of Detroit also made good use of all they had at hand. "I have a vivid recollection of pouring canned milk over my cereal," remembers Tom Fisher. "It was never poured from a can at the table, but from a blue Shirley Temple pitcher that once had come as a premium in a cereal box. After all, we did have some social graces, if not a touch of class!"[37] Fisher would often go exploring through Detroit's town dump, where "young people were treated to a productive archeological hunting ground." Young people like Tom often did all they could to help out their families. Lowell Fleetwood would add to the family coffers by cutting and stacking wood or washing cars for fifty cents each.[38] The Leisey family picked blackberries and sold them to Lowell's dad, Floyd Fleetwood, for three cents a pound.[39]

Some residents turned to illicit activity during the Depression. The forests offered deer, elk, and wild game that not a few residents poached out of season. Clyde Rogers's brother-in-law committed just such a crime in 1933, bringing home in the middle of the night a deer for the family to butcher, eat, and fret over, for poaching brought a rumored fifty- to seventy-five-dollar fine. Clyde's father constructed an ingenious hideaway for the meat behind false cabinet doors in the family kitchen. Other canyon residents with a more entrepreneurial and daring streak took up moonshine and bootlegging. Willis Grafe of Gates writes, "Some of the local high school boys were accessory to this enterprise, providing a little much needed cash."[40] The authorities sometimes got wind of these operations, as they did in June 1932, when they arrested Delbert Devine in the forests around Gates. Devine had been running a ninety-gallon still and was caught with fifty gallons of mash and ten gallons of liquor. "The still," wrote the local newspaper, "was equipped with a gasoline burner and the most modern attachments. Devine, it is understood, was given a fine of $50 and 30 days in jail."[41] Illegal it may have been, but moonshining was nevertheless one way that canyon residents looked to themselves to find a way to survive during the Depression.

The entrepreneurial spirit evinced by Delbert Devine manifested itself in other, more legal ways during the Great Depression. Louis Rada, the Czech immigrant who had started the Hill Top Store in 1927, sold that operation in 1936 and bought the Mill City Hotel, next to which he built a row of cabins.[42] Floyd Fleetwood pursued a number of economic interests. Fleetwood would drive to the Oregon coast, buy fish, and then return to sell the fish the next day. He and his wife also ran the small Hamman Stage Line depot in Mill City, transporting by car the few residents or visitors who came and went.[43] Roy Newport of Detroit was one of the most ambitious entrepreneurs, owning Baxter's Grocery Store, a tavern, and a mink and fox fur farm, as well as "nearly all the commercial real estate" in Detroit.[44] His real estate holdings and grocery store made him the "central figure during the thirties," extending store credit that he meticulously tracked on small white tablets behind the counter. Newport's high prices and rather flamboyant lifestyle—he had gold teeth, drove a Buick coupe, and traveled to eastern Oregon for sport hunting—irritated some people in Detroit, evincing simmering class tensions. But local memories of the time subsume such resentment in a general sense of shared struggle and scrappiness to get through tough times.

Such scrappiness and entrepreneurship, when paired with an opportunistic eye to connections with the outside world and some luck, created some local enterprises that far outlasted the Great Depression and would shape the area's economy for decades to come. A good example is Marion Forks Lodge and the associated businesses of the Young family of Marion Forks. Located sixteen miles southeast of Detroit, Marion Forks lies at the far end of the upper North Santiam Canyon, along the path of the highway that was slowly making its way into the mountains. In the 1930s, the remote area provided opportunities for both work and investment. In 1932, while working as a supervisor for burning rights-of-way for the highway, Scott Young purchased property at the confluence of the North Santiam River and Marion Creek. Two years later, Young moved there with his wife Nan and their children, Bob and Dottie. While Scott did occasional road maintenance work, the family built a cabin for themselves and then built a lodge to serve road workers. "With the help of friends," wrote Bob Young later, "we ran a cook house boarding 14 engineers and 40 construction men working on the building of the road towards Sisters."[45] With the completion of the highway (see chap. 5), the lodge focused on serving tourists passing through and recreationalists that came to camp and fish at Marion Lake and other nearby streams. Marion Forks Lodge became an important local institution, so much so that when the original building burned in 1946, "neighbors and the community helped [rebuild], and it was up and ready to serve people in six weeks," as Scott's daughter Dottie

Originally catering to road construction crews, Marion Forks Lodge became a stopover for long-haul truckers, loggers, and tourists alike—a symbol of the North Santiam Canyon's hybrid economy and identity. From "Old Breitenbush," photo book, page 1, image 2, Canyon Life Museum.

recalled. After all, the restaurant had "a 'beer to go' license that they did not want to lose."[46] The lodge and restaurant would continue to serve locals and tourists alike for decades to come.

Meanwhile, Scott Young continued to explore other investment opportunities. He partnered with Jewels Myers of Detroit to form Myers and Young Logging, a small outfit equipped with a large Caterpillar tractor to drag logs off the steep hillsides of the upper canyon. The highway was critical to this business. Initially, Myers and Young Logging used trucks to get their logs to the railhead in Idanha, from whence the logs would travel to the Silver Falls Lumber Company mill in Silverton. Scott Young and Boots Myers eventually parted ways, but the Youngs stayed in the logging business. Scott's son Bob partnered with neighbor Vern Morgan to form Young & Morgan, Inc., which would become one of the largest and most influential logging companies in the North Santiam Canyon, with extensive timber property holdings, numerous mills, and a fleet of logging trucks running through the 1980s.

Other canyon residents looked with hope to the area's Douglas fir forests and external lumber markets. Although the collapse of the Hammond Lumber Company produced economic ruin, the company's departure, and its eagerness to sell off its assets, created opportunities for some ambitious entrepreneurs. Carl Kelly had worked as a dry kiln and planing mill foreman for Hammond Lumber Company from 1919 to 1925. The

Kelly family left the canyon in 1925 to chase logging opportunities elsewhere in Washington and Oregon. When the Hammond operations in the canyon shut down, the Kellys returned to Mill City "to see all that had happened with the demise of Hammond," and they found that "there were a lot of small family mills in the area that had no means of planing or shipping lumber."[47] In 1935, Kelly joined with four friends, all of them former Hammond employees, and bought the Hammond mill site on the Marion County side of the river and some remaining infrastructure, including kilns, dry sheds, storage buildings, the planer shed, and railroad siding and loading docks. Kelly and his partners called their company the Mill City Planing and Processing Company, which hired other former Hammond employees.

The next year, another group of former Hammond employees, including Otto Witt, Frank Potter, Bill Quinn, J. T. Smith, and Frank Rada, formed the Mill City Manufacturing Company (MCMC), a worker-owned and -operated logging and milling cooperative. MCMC bought eighty acres of the former Hammond mill site on the Linn County side of the river and the shuttered Darlin-Singer mill in Clatskanie, up on the Columbia River west of Portland.[48] MCMC worker-owners disassembled the Clatskanie mill, loaded it onto trucks, drove 140 miles to Mill City, and then reassembled the mill on part of the old Hammond mill site. In June 1936, just a few months after starting the company, MCMC shipped out $35,000 worth of Douglas fir harvested from another tract of Hammond land close to Mill City. The next year, MCMC started another logging camp drawing timber from both Hammond land and federal government timber sales. By 1945, MCMC employed more than one hundred men, many of them former Hammond employees. Like Mill City Planing and Processing, the Mill City Manufacturing Company would survive through the Depression and into the postwar era, a testament, in the eyes of local residents, of the resiliency of the people of the North Santiam Canyon.

A number of other mills and lumber operations started up during the Great Depression, and these operations would come to represent and dominate the local timber industry and shape the community's relationship to the outside world. Among the Mill City Planing and Processing Company's earliest customers were the Freres and Frank lumber companies, both built during the Depression. Thomas G. Freres and his brother had been running a small mill outside of Stayton for a dozen years when in 1934 Thomas bought another small mill on the Little North Fork and moved his family to the area. Freres invested heavily in canyon timber during the Great Depression; in 1936, for example, Freres spent $7,500 on three timber sales, amounting to 3.4 million board feet of Douglas fir timber.[49] The Freres Lumber Company would become one of the largest and longest-lasting locally owned timber companies in the area. Among the Freres Company's later acquisitions was the Mt. Jefferson Lumber Company, formed in Lyons in 1937.[50] That same year, Amandus Frank moved a small lumber mill to the Lyons area; "Mandy" Frank would eventually own three local mills, and he later partnered with Freres Lumber before going out on his own again.[51] At the same time up in Marion Forks, Scott Young was beginning to develop the family business that would become Young & Morgan. Each of these operations expressed confidence that the lumber market would rebound and bring economic prosperity. Their origins in this period of difficulty would figure into the image of rugged, locally based self-sufficiency that became so central to the canyon's postwar identity.

Such confidence may have seem misplaced during the early years of the Great Depression. But the local economic degradation that resulted from national and global economic catastrophe in many ways brought the communities of the North Santiam Canyon together to survive and thrive. The McRae family of Fox Valley lost their house to a fire in 1933, and without insurance—which had lapsed because the family could not sell enough farm produce to pay the premium—it looked as though the McRaes would be homeless. John McRae recalls how the family was saved: "The community came together and helped us build a small unpainted house in our large apple orchard. I felt warm and secure in that little house. Those wonderful neighbors brought us their spare clothing and utensils."[52] People in the canyon relied on each other not only for help in times of emergency, but also for their social needs. The school that John McRae attended was also where the people of Fox Valley came together for "pie auctions, spelling bees, and school and community theater." In Mill City, Walt Leisy and a few others formed the "Corn Cob Pipe Club" and played music at the old Hammond Hall on Saturday nights, "charging a dime admission—if you had it!"[53] Religion continued to play an important role, too. Mehama ran its first vacation Bible school for students on summer break during 1935, and in Gates, an evening youth group formed and was quite active in the community. "No homes were closed to it," writes Gates's historian, "and even many families without young people were pleased to host the meetings. This group was a great asset to the community, affording the young people...an opportunity for service and fellowship in a Christian environment."[54] As they looked to one another for fellowship and support during the Great Depression, canyon residents built community and developed a narrative of local resiliency in the face of abstract external pressures and forces.

Some of these impressions of community, compassion, and happiness during the Great Depression are clearly the product of nostalgia—a simpler time seen through rose-colored glasses that blur memories of hunger and hardship. Yet such memories and the real experience of the Great Depression reveal something important about the tension in small communities between local autonomy and connections to outside forces. The Depression had such a dramatic effect because the people along the North Santiam River had become intimately connected to and dependent on external forces such as the railroad, external markets, and especially the Hammond Lumber Company. When these forces shrank or evaporated, the North Santiam Canyon experienced severe economic difficulty and material hardship, as jobs were lost and people reverted to a subsistence lifestyle. Canyon residents, like other Americans, looked to the federal government for support in the form of programs like the CCC. At the same time, however, the Depression encouraged some autonomy from outside forces, as residents looked to themselves and their fellow community members for some well-being and happiness.

The Great Depression, then, presented something of a paradox, whereby people of the North Santiam Canyon gained some independence while losing economic stability. Could they not have both? For residents of the canyon—and especially the entrepreneurs creating new timber companies—a developing narrative and identity provided a clear answer to that question: not only could local control coexist with economic prosperity, but also such prosperity directly depended on their own determination, creativity, and self-sufficiency. As the Depression faded and the economy boomed during and after World War II, residents jumped at the chance to reestablish connections to the outside world, particularly in the form of state and federal government projects. Residents hoped to improve their quality of life while also exercising local control, but the connections they encouraged would erode the little autonomy they had developed during the Great Depression.

5

The Highway and the Dam

Between the Great Depression and the onset of the Cold War, the North Santiam Canyon underwent a series of dramatic transformations. Immense physical changes began during the 1930s, when the rough county road that dead-ended in Idanha became a smooth state highway passing over the Cascades. Meanwhile, engineers and boosters from the Willamette Valley and beyond began planning a massive flood-control project for the North Santiam River: Detroit Dam, an Army Corps of Engineers project completed in 1953 that, among other changes, resulted in the drowning of what would become known as "old Detroit." The highway and the dam strengthened the area's connections to the Willamette Valley to the west, central Oregon to the east, and far beyond. Those connections were as much economic, political, and social as they were physical, and they fundamentally changed the area. In less than two decades, the North Santiam Canyon had transformed from what the local paper called a "minor gulch" to an important component of Oregon and the nation's transportation, flood control, and hydropower infrastructure. That process transformed the area's economy, identity, and relationships—real and perceived—to the outside world.

Enthusiasm for these transformations was widespread, both in and out of the canyon. The national road-building boom that began in the 1920s barely slowed during the Great Depression and World War II, urged on by automobile enthusiasts seeking smoother and safer roads, engineers and administrators pursuing more efficient routes of travel, and boosters boasting the economic benefits of faster and more decentralized transportation.[1] Willamette Valley tourists, planners, and business interests made similar arguments in favor of an improved highway through the North Santiam Canyon, and they found enthusiastic local supporters, particularly in the *Mill City Logue* newspaper and its successor, the *Mill City Enterprise*. Likewise, the local newspaper and other businesses followed the lead of Willamette Valley farmers and chambers of commerce that wanted to control the North Santiam River, particularly as justification for dam projects shifted from flood control to "multipurpose" projects that promised hydropower, pollution abatement, irrigation, recreation, and, more generally and vaguely, "economic development."[2] Such arguments were widespread during the postwar boom years of river development in the American West as economic, political, and bureaucratic interests aligned to dam and otherwise dramatically transform river systems, including especially the Columbia River, into which the North Santiam River's waters eventually flow.[3] For many people inside and outside of the North Santiam Canyon, rationalized roads and rivers promised a path to a better, more prosperous future.

But some residents expressed concern about the highway, dam, and the transformations they would bring. This included arguments that the highway and dam would not only change their environment, but also destroy their rural and relatively isolated way of life. More often, though, "resistance" meant demanding that external forces, from Marion County assessors to engineers from the Army Corps of Engineers, make small concessions and compromises to mitigate the social and cultural impacts of the highway and dam. These muted voices of resistance did not seek to stop the physical transformations, nor did they oppose the general enthusiasm for economic development driving the projects. But resistance to the highway and dam, whether moderate or vehement, revealed anxiety about how these new connections might destroy—figuratively and literally—the homes and ways of life in the canyon. Moreover, this resistance and anxiety marked a transition to an increased sense of victimization and a narrative of powerlessness in the area, with local residents defining themselves as "us" versus "them" on the outside. The highway and the dam bound the North Santiam Canyon to the world outside, and those ties led to both enthusiasm and resentment.

THE HIGHWAY: A NEW AVENUE OF POWER

By the turn of the century, there was still no practical way to travel through the North Santiam Canyon from the Willamette Valley to central Oregon. All good roads terminated twenty-five miles east of Salem, with pavement ending in Mehama and graded gravel reaching Niagara. A rough, ungraded gravel road continued past Idanha, but the route was used mostly by loggers and a few isolated residents. Travelers still heading east after Idanha often had to go by foot if they wished to continue on to Sisters, Bend, and other places on the east side of the mountains. In reality, though, few used this route on their way across the Cascades. Instead, the upper canyon was a dead-end, represented by the railroad turntable in Detroit, a device at the end of the tracks on which railroad engines were literally turned around 180 degrees, pointing them west for their return trip to the Willamette Valley below.

In the postwar enthusiasm of the 1920s, road builders once again turned their eyes toward the canyon. Motorists throughout the country clamored for better roads on which to drive their mass-produced automobiles, and, as historian Christopher Wells shows, local, state, and national authorities obliged through road-building and land-use policies that transformed the United States into "car country."[4] Motor tourism grew dramatically throughout Oregon in the 1920s, when "motoring for recreation became an important source of traffic," as the State Highway Division's official history of the North Santiam Highway summarized.[5] In 1922, Marion County conducted a survey between Niagara and Detroit, and within two years, contractors had completed the road. The road had been graded to only eight feet wide, and it quickly became apparent that it was insufficient for the logging trucks and other traffic traveling up to Detroit. The "Old Detroit Road" was extremely dangerous, only to be attempted by the reckless and fearless, as longtime residents recall. Stanley Chance remembers making the trip between Detroit and Mill City: "Just throw that little Chevrolet wide open and ride the horn . . . that was a one-way road; if you made enough noise, they'd hear you coming and they'd pull over."[6] Visitors rattled by a journey up the road "would consistently stop in Detroit to inquire about an alternate route home," says Tom Fisher.[7] Learning there was none, they would enlist the services of local teenagers, who "used to make pretty good spending money in the summer driving flatlanders over that road," according to Lowell Fleetwood.[8] The county made further efforts to improve the road through the 1920s, widening it to sixteen feet in 1926 and conducting more surveys in 1928, 1929, and 1930.

The Depression years slowed plans for expanding and improving the road into a proper highway. As the Oregon State Highway Division's history of the road records, "Maintenance took precedence over new construction." There were fits and starts to road expansion during the 1930s, as county, state, and federal agencies and the Southern Pacific Railroad Company bickered over right-of-way, cost allocation, and the exact route for the highway. Although the highway would cross from Marion into Linn County, the latter argued that "almost the entire benefit derived [from the highway] would inure to Marion County and the citizens and taxpayers thereof," and therefore demanded that Marion County pay for the road's extension; Marion County agreed in 1931, thereby clearing a major bureaucratic hurdle. The Southern Pacific complicated plans in 1935, when the company officially denied the State Highway's Commission's demand to give up the railroad line above Mill City, forcing the Highway Commission to alter the highway's route. At the same time, the Highway Commission learned about tentative plans of the US Army Corps of Engineers to build a dam on the North Santiam River near Detroit, which, if the plans went through, would flood parts of the existing roadway. When those plans came to a stop—temporarily, as it turned out—the State Highway Department continued road construction as planned, and by 1939, the highway had been paved all the way to the Santiam Junction, where the new road intersected with an existing highway along the South Santiam River. It had been eighty years since John Minto—or was it Eph Henness?—"discovered" the pass, but the Willamette Valley finally had its direct connection to central Oregon running through the North Santiam Canyon.[9]

The North Santiam Highway underwent more transformations after World War II during the construction of Detroit Dam on the North Santiam River from 1949 to 1953. The planned reservoir would inundate the highway, which still snaked around the North Santiam River, requiring relocation of the road above the new high water line. The State Highway Department seized the opportunity, demanding that the federal government pay not only to move the road, but also to build a straighter and wider road than the Army Corps of Engineers proposed. Eventually, eager to complete the road and focus on dam construction, the corps agreed to the Highway Department's plans for a modern twenty-foot roadway with four-foot shoulders and relatively gentle ten-degree curves. Engineers took the opportunity to straighten both the highway and the North Santiam River itself, moving the river's channel to reduce the number of twists and turns. This straighter, rationalized river allowed for a faster and more efficient highway that effectively replaced the railroad, long a real and symbolic connection between the North Santiam Canyon and the Willamette Valley.

From its earliest phases, the North Santiam Highway was driven by the dreams and desires of people living outside the area. John Minto and others in the nineteenth century fantasized over the possibilities for Euro American emigration through the canyon. As towns and cities like Bend and Salem grew on both sides of the Cascades, it became even more attractive to build a road that would connect these communities, their finished products, and especially their natural resources. That was the promise of Hogg's failed Oregon Pacific Railroad, and it was a dream that

Willamette Valley boosters were eager to realize throughout the twentieth century. Both major Salem newspapers, the *Capital Journal* and *Oregon Statesman*, were enthusiastic about a direct route to central Oregon to replace the existing route proceeding first south and then east, which was often closed during winter. The North Santiam Highway, as the editors of the *Capital Journal* happily noted, will "provide a short cut from Salem." Editors of the *Oregon Statesman* enthused about the highway's efficiencies: "The road is very practical from an engineering standpoint, and will provide nearly an all-year connection between the valley and eastern Oregon, and the low grade and low pass make the route very desirable from every angle." The highway promised much more than faster transportation between the Willamette Valley and central Oregon. By "linking the two great sections of Oregon," the highway opened "another epoch in the progress and development of Salem and Marion county," as the *Capital Journal* explained. The North Santiam Highway was not just another road: it was a route to growth and prosperity for Salem and the Willamette Valley.[10]

While the Salem press raved about the economic opportunities made possible by passing *through* the canyon, tourists from the Willamette Valley and elsewhere anticipated traveling *to* the area. The North Santiam Canyon's identity had long been connected to recreational tourism opportunities for Willamette Valley residents, from John Minto's family seeking health and relaxation in the pure mountain air, to librarian Lucy Lewis and her group of Corvallis mountaineers summiting Mt. Jefferson. Minto had walked and Lewis had taken the train, but the automobile and roads promised additional opportunities. For those willing to brave the dangerous pre-highway road and rustic conditions, the area offered stunning mountain vistas, bountiful hunting, and fishing on the North Santiam River.

The new and improved highway would improve access to all these recreational opportunities, particularly in the heretofore nearly inaccessible upper canyon. The 1936 *North Santiam Recreation Guide* distributed by the US Forest Service invited tourists to different recreational opportunities along the highway, including the trail to Pamelia Lake (former homestead of John Heidecke of the Oregon land fraud trials) at mile 13; Forest Service camps, summer homes, and trails into the Mt. Jefferson Primitive Area—a "fisherman's paradise"—starting from Marion Forks at mile 17; and at mile 38, direct access to the Skyline Trail (later part of the Pacific Crest Trail) running along the spine of the Cascades.[11] Travelers who continued east another few miles reached the Santiam Pass

Ski Lodge built by Mary's Creek CCC workers in 1939-40. Before the war, the Santiam Pass Recreation Area offered skiers just two rope tows; immediately after the war, another rope tow was installed. The widening, straightening, and paving of the North Santiam Highway made the area more accessible to skiers from both sides of the Cascades, and so in 1948 the recreation area now known as Hoodoo Ski Bowl built a four-thousand-foot-long chair lift and a new three-story lodge accommodating as many as one hundred skiers and their gear.[12] The highway had opened up the entire North Santiam Canyon for tourists from the Willamette Valley and beyond.

For year-round recreation and relaxation of a different kind, tourists looked to Breitenbush Hot Springs Resort, twelve miles north of Detroit.[13] Breitenbush's thirty-plus springs, pouring forth mineral-rich waters at nearly two hundred degrees Fahrenheit, had attracted the interest of tourists since the turn of the century, and its history was intimately bound up with the history of trails, paths, and roads into and through the canyon. John Minto coined the name "Breitenbush" after John Breightenbush (a "one-armed hunter and nothing else," as Minto recorded), who had settled at the confluence of the Breitenbush and North Santiam Rivers, and whom Minto met during his 1873 effort to locate a pass over the Cascades.[14] Another early road enthusiast from the Willamette Valley, John Waldo, began visiting the hot springs in the mid-1880s, recording in 1887 that "the water is helping me and could not well do otherwise if there is any virtue in it, for I sit for two hours of a morning snuffing it through a tube." An increasing number of valley visitors came to relax at the springs and fish on the river, especially after the Oregon Pacific Railroad reached Detroit in 1889. One needed to take the train and walk two hours to reach the springs, where, by 1893, a few enterprising souls had built a primitive log bath and steam house. During a visit that year, Waldo complained about the "disfigurement" caused by "the hand of progress and development" but nevertheless enjoyed the bath house, which made a "very agreeable chamber to bath [sic] in."[15]

The growing popularity of Breitenbush attracted the interests of speculators and investors who dreamed of a resort and tourist attraction. The first effort was a professional and personal mess. Claude Mansfield arrived in the late nineteenth century and staked a claim at Breitenbush, which was only finalized in 1904 after years of legal wrangling with the superintendent of the Cascade Forest Reserve, Captain Salmon B. Ormsby (who was at the time party to the Stephen Puter and John Heidecke land scam). Mansfield and his wife, Hattie Ross, developed a private "resort" at Breitenbush, offering free tent sites, a store for camp supplies, and "very reasonable" rates at a small hotel.[16] But just a year after the Mansfield homestead claim was finalized, Claude and Hattie separated in what the Salem *Daily Journal* called a "well-known divorce suit," with Hattie getting custody of their two children plus a one-third interest in "the famous Breitenbush hot springs." Less than a year later, Claude Mansfield died, leaving his uncle and his ex-wife to share in the management of the homestead and resort. The confusing state of Breitenbush's ownership complicated efforts to improve the property. A 1912 US Geological Survey report called Breitenbush "a crude 'health resort'" that nevertheless attracted "many patients [who] take the waters each year." But the biggest obstacle to Breitenbush's development was the lack of a good road. "If the place were more readily accessible," concluded the 1912 report, Breitenbush "would undoubtedly enjoy a large patronage."[17]

Ongoing improvements to the highway attracted new speculators to Breitenbush. In 1924, a Portland-based investment group calling itself the "Breitenbush Hot Springs Company" secured a fifty-year lease to Mansfield's former homestead and resort, seeking to build a more substantial health resort. The company had ambitious plans, including four "modern and complete" bath houses served by attendants and resident physicians, "private mineral water and mineral mud baths," and a natatorium to be built on a small island on the river. As the company's prospectus advised, guests from the Willamette Valley and beyond would find "remarkable cures of Rheumatism in all its forms, Neuritis, Diabetes, Pyorrhea, Gout, Goitre, Constipation, Dyspepsia, Female Pelvic Disorders, Nicotine habit, Skin and Blood diseases, and many other chronic ailments."[18] The prospectus included a map that emphasized the proximity of Breitenbush to the Willamette Valley and especially Portland, with a dotted line tracing the fifty-six-mile distance. This presentation was disingenuous, as travel to Breitenbush still required taking the train to Detroit and hiking twelve miles up a US Forest Service trail. "Inaccessibility of the place," the prospectus admitted, "has been an added difficulty." The Breitenbush Hot Springs Company reassured potential investors that this difficulty would soon be overcome, as the company planned to build a railroad spur to Idanha and an automobile highway to Detroit; furthermore, the company would assist the State Highway Department in completing the North Santiam Highway "in time for this summer's patronage." The summer of 1924 came and went without the highway, and the Breitenbush Hot Springs Company dissolved.

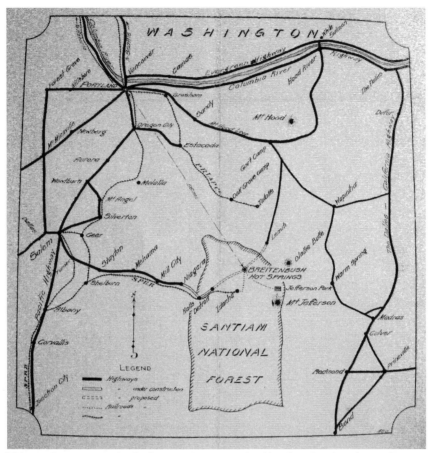

This map from a 1924 Breitenbush Hot Springs promotional brochure imagines the North Santiam Canyon as the center of a vast network of Pacific Northwest highways and railroads—some real, some not yet complete, and some "proposed." Courtesy of Canyon Life Museum.

Breitenbush's development awaited the North Santiam Highway, which finally reached Detroit in 1925. That same year, Merle Bruckman—a friend of former Breitenbush owner Hattie Ross, whom he would marry in 1941—secured the lease on the Mansfield property and began building Bruckman's Breitenbush Springs resort. By 1929, the Bruckmans had completed a hotel with a dance floor, fifty cabins and tent sites, and electricity provided by a local hydroelectric plant.[19] Although part of the road from Detroit to Breitenbush remained unpaved and "rutty in places," the *Mill City Logue* insisted "the trip is an easy one." Despite the rutty road and global economic catastrophe, Bruckman's Breitenbush Springs survived the Depression and World War II and was ready to thrive with postwar transportation development. A 1952 brochure advertised numerous improvements at Breitenbush: a forty-by-one hundred-foot swimming pool, sixty-two cabins with running water, electric lights, and "Beauty-rest" mattresses ($3 to $6 per day, depending on options), a thirty-two-room hotel ($3.50 to $5 per day for "European plan" accommodations), a store equipped with refrigeration and fresh food, and massages at a rate of $1 to $3 each. Most importantly, guests would now enjoy a "beautiful scenic drive up the North Santiam Gorge, with its fine new highway" and continue onto Breitenbush via "another new highway [that] leads you to our resort." With Bruckman's resort and the smooth, straight, and fast highway, the North Santiam Canyon had become both a destination and throughway for tourists from the Willamette Valley and beyond.

LOCAL RESPONSES TO THE NEW ROAD

Enthusiasm for the highway and what it brought was not limited to outsiders. Many residents eagerly supported development of this powerful connection to the outside world, anticipating the economic growth it would spur. This enthusiasm had its loudest and most consistent voice in the *Mill City Logue* newspaper, which from the beginning supported the project. The *Logue* ran a weekly column titled "Road Building" that featured stories on the latest in construction technology, the benefits of roads, and projects in other parts of the country. When Marion County and the federal government first approved highway extension in 1930, the *Mill City Logue* ran a banner headline: "North Santiam Highway Okeh'd."[20] The paper enthusiastically reported that "the highway will be completed through to central Oregon and will open one of the largest periods of progress and development of Marion county," echoing the praise of the *Capital Journal* and *Oregon Statesman*.

The *Logue*'s successor, the *Mill City Enterprise*, continued to push for highway improvements. Founded in 1944, the *Enterprise* came into being while the State Highway Department and the US Army Corps of Engineers argued about where to relocate the highway to make way for Detroit Dam. The *Enterprise* sided with the Highway Department and its demands for a broader, smoother, and gentler road than the Corps of Engineers originally proposed. Through such a modern transformation, wrote the editor in 1948, "The new North Santiam highway offers a new future to the region." Echoing Hogg's grandiose claims about the Oregon Pacific Railroad seventy years before, the paper promised that the modern highway "will, when finished . . . place the Canyon on major transcontinental highways, to south and east. The permanent and lasting benefits of the road are hard even now to realize."[21] The *Enterprise* effused joy when the State Highway Commission allocated the remaining funds for completing the road's realignment and improvement in 1950: "HIGHWAY APPROVED!" ran the headline.[22]

Chambers of commerce in Mill City, Gates, and elsewhere added their voices of approval, and various citizen action groups formed to encourage county, state, and federal agencies to finish the project. Signaling their support, communities repeatedly voted for new taxes to help with road development, such as a levy in 1926 that increased the county's fund for oiling the gravel road between Mill City and Mehama.[23] Local residents advocated with some success for employment opportunities on the road during the Depression. On the day the State Highway Commission approved straightening and improving the highway in 1950, a local delegation was on its way to the state capital to "protest past delays"; on hearing the news, the group congratulated the commission on its decision and returned home victorious.[24] Like road boosters in the Willamette Valley, many canyon residents saw the highway as an opportunity for economic growth.

Other people, though, were not as enthusiastic. Some even saw resistance as a path to a lucrative payday. As during construction of the railroad, it was necessary to acquire private land on which to build the highway. Like the relatively smooth experience of the Oregon Pacific Railroad, county and state officials did not encounter widespread resistance. Carmen Elaine Stafford's diary recorded a brief and straightforward transaction for the family's property in Niagara in October 1945: "State highway man here and we sold this place."[25] But earlier in the process, a few residents refused to sell their land for the highway. "NORTH SANTIAM RIGHT-OF-WAY CAUSES TROUBLE" read the worried *Mill City Logue* headline of November 27, 1930. The trouble was money. Some of the landowners along the proposed route believed that they were being swindled, and they "have already filed demand for much more damage money than the viewers board recommended."[26] The battle over land value continued until May 1932, when a county surveying crew submitted a revised compensation report that provided sufficient satisfaction for road construction to go forward.[27] These local landowners had extracted a compromise from the road builders—a small but notable achievement.

But road improvement stirred resentment that ran deeper than the desire for a bigger payoff. The *Logue* noted that the landowners demanding more money for their property "are notably hostile to encroachment of a modern highway system" and the economic, social, and cultural changes that might come with it. Although the previous road that dead-ended in Idanha was dangerous and curbed economic growth, those limitations seemed like a good thing to some residents who wanted to keep the community small and manageable. Construction and improvement of the highway, particularly in conjunction with dam construction, threatened that way of life through changes in the size and character of the community. So it seemed to some people in Detroit and Idanha during the straightening and improvement of the highway, as the local newspaper later reflected: "the upper Canyon was on the warpath." Specifically, local residents claimed that road construction had brought in outsiders, crime, and lawlessness: "Despite the influx of hundreds of workers on the North Santiam Highway projects, the County officials had done nothing whatever about the law enforcement problems of Detroit and Idanha, both unincorporated and thus unable to establish a police force."[28] Pressure from citizens eventually led to the regular posting of a deputy sheriff to the area, providing some relief from "law enforcement problems" while the highway straightening and improvement finished.

Such muted forms of resistance and complaint did not seek to stop the highway. Reluctant property owners understood that the significant political and economic power of road supporters made a "modern highway system" all but inevitable. They knew that they were outnumbered by road enthusiasts who not only made persuasive arguments about the practicalities of a more efficient highway but also tapped into deeply held and widely shared beliefs about the need for economic growth and development. A few vocal residents resisted in small ways for various reasons, including to increase the payout they would receive for access to their property or out of anxiety about the social and cultural transformations that they believed accompanied the physical changes wrought by the highway. But most accepted the highway's development and hoped to make the best of the changes it brought.

More changes were underway. In November 1948, two years after her family sold property for the highway, Carmen Stafford of Niagara wrote in her diary that "A Bonneville man was here today about right-of-way." A few months later: "Some government men were here and appraised our house and place for powerhouse." And later that summer: "putting power poles up in front of house." The federal government, in the persons of engineers, assessors, and others associated with the US Army Corps of Engineers, the Bonneville Power Administration, and their contractors, were coming to the canyon. Their work, even more than the highway, would bring fundamental physical, social, cultural, and economic transformations. These dramatic changes would challenge residents and their views of outside forces.

THE DAM: CONTROLLING WATER AND POWER

The stories of the North Santiam Highway and Detroit Dam are inextricably linked, and not just because of the need for negotiation and cooperation in regard to the relocated highway. The highway and dam were part of the same process of dramatic transformation. As the 1952 brochure for Bruckman's Breitenbush Springs noted, "the beautiful scenic drive up the North Santiam Gorge, with its fine new highway, takes you past the site of the mammoth Detroit dam (which is now under construction)." That process of construction and transformation began in the 1930s and stretched through the 1940s and 1950s, when the US Army Corps of Engineers surveyed, planned, and built Detroit Dam and its sister dam, Big Cliff Dam, on the North Santiam River. The story of the Detroit and Big Cliff Dams is usually subsumed into much broader narratives about river development in the post–World War II period. Whether told from an institutional perspective or with a more critical approach, these interpretations portray the dams as the product of external regional sources of power (downstream cities, farmers, chambers of commerce, etc.) and national or even international forces and trends, such as the long history of the Columbia River as an "organic machine" and the even deeper of "hydraulic societies."[29] It is true that the "development" of the North Santiam River had its origins in the hopes and fears of people, groups, and forces outside of the canyon. But caught up in the narrative of progress, growth, and development, such big histories reveal little about the communities most directly affected by the dams—the people who lived and worked there, their responses to dam construction, and how people experienced the destruction of homes and communities that often accompanied river development.[30] A closer look at the North Santiam Canyon and other such places shows that local residents played important roles in river development through active public support and opposition, both during the postwar dam building boom and well before.[31]

Both local and outside forces had been putting the North Santiam River and its tributaries to use for almost a century before the US Army Corps of Engineers started surveying the Detroit area. The first sawmill in the area, built near Mehama in 1857 by Ephraim Stout and his son Lewis, was located on and derived its power from Stout Creek, which was also used to power the first grist mill in Mehama, built in 1880 by D.

S. Whisler. At the Hammond Lumber Company's mills in Mill City, the river powered a number of different engines and generators, including a 250-kilowatt generator that could be used alternately for powering part of the planing mill, shooting water from a 1,500-gallon-capacity fire pump, or powering most of the town's lights—but only from seven o'clock to eleven o'clock at night.[32]

The Hammond hydropower operations were small compared to the dreams of Edward and Frank O'Neil and their partner, Charles W. Callaghan. In 1898, these three San Franciscans saw potential at Niagara, where the North Santiam River narrowed to four feet wide and doubled in depth to forty-five feet. The O'Neils and Callaghan imagined a dam that would power a paper mill employing one hundred employees and generate extra electricity for a quickly growing power market. Fifty men, including some local residents, began work on the dam in 1898, and the project was nearly finished in 1901, when spring snowmelt unleashed the fury of the North Santiam River and destroyed the dam.[33] Work continued intermittently over the next few decades, but sand and gravel rock in the surrounding river bank made the site impractical for a dam. The San Franciscans abandoned the project, leaving behind impressive stoneworks that would become a historical treat for visitors to Niagara Park.[34]

The North Santiam River was left to its own course until the 1930s and 1940s, when the Western frenzy for dam building and water management made its way into the canyon by way of the Willamette River. The Willamette Valley had long been susceptible to spring flooding caused by snowmelt and massive rains that would inundate the Willamette River and its tributaries. In 1861, the Willamette River rose nineteen feet above its banks and flooded more than three hundred thousand acres of valuable farmland. By 1936, the river had breached its banks eight more times.[35] Willamette Valley farmers, urban businessmen and industrialists, and civic leaders called on the federal government to bring the Willamette under control and protect the area's population, agriculture, and business. In 1935, the Portland-based engineering firm of Stevens & Koon prepared a report "on the proposed Navigation and Flood Control Project by Reservoirs in the Willamette River Valley" for the Corps of Engineers, focusing on the tributaries to the Willamette River, including the North Santiam River. After analyzing possible dam sites, transportation capabilities, and flood-control plans, the engineers concluded that "from the standpoint of 'dollar economy' the proposed improvements are not justified." The costs of building dams on Willamette River tributaries would outweigh the benefits of flood control and navigation.[36]

The report continued, however, "from the viewpoint of general social betterment, providing a safe residence section for a large population, and in order to furnish relief to the unemployed, the improvements herein outlined may be fully justified." The corps and politicians from the Willamette Valley seized on the idea of "social betterment," finding an argument they could use to aggressively promote river development. They shared this objective not just with the Willamette Valley's business community, as William Robbins has shown, but also with government officials, politicians, farmers, businesspeople, and a host of other dam boosters throughout the Columbia River region, as Richard White and Eve Vogel have explored.[37] In 1936, Congress passed the Flood Control Act, finding that "investigations and improvements of rivers and other waterways, including watersheds thereof, for flood-control purposes are in the interest of the general welfare."[38] A revision of the act in 1938 allocated $73,055,000 for the entire Willamette River Basin, including $13,615,000 for a dam on the North Santiam River.[39]

The corps soon began surveying the area, selecting a site on the river about ten miles downstream from Detroit. Tom Fisher remembers seeing these outsiders as a child. "Crews of engineers could be seen around town. Usually they showed up in a pair of crew vehicles." Though they attracted the occasional gawker like Fisher, the engineers went about their work methodically and quietly, and "after working on their survey and core-drilling jobs at the dam-site, they came to town for a beer at the tavern—sometimes a steak at Whitey's Cafe." These men and their equipment confused young Fisher, who "had no idea . . . how those three-legged things (the ones with a telescope on top) were used."[40] But older locals, remembered Fisher, "referred to them as 'the corps,'" and the grown-ups knew that these engineers and their survey equipment signaled major changes for the North Santiam Canyon, although the project paused during World War II.

When work resumed in 1947, the scope of the plan had increased dramatically and dam supporters had become more adamant. Flood control and navigation, while still primary, were now supplemented by what Stevens & Koon had called "social betterment" objectives: hydropower, irrigation, pollution abatement, fish and wildlife conservation, and recreation.[41] The budget for the Willamette Valley Basin project had also grown, ballooning to a whopping $3,224,265,700, with $62,433,000 estimated for Detroit Dam. That cost was worth the benefit from the perspective of chambers of commerce, farmers' unions, and other groups that initiated letter-writing campaigns and formed advocacy organizations like the Willamette Valley Flood Control Association and the Greater Willamette Valley Association.[42] They understood river control as river development—managing river systems not only to prevent dangerous and costly floods, but also to protect investments in low-lying farms and cities and, through the added benefit of hydropower, to encourage further economic growth. The corps held public meetings in Salem and Eugene in 1947, where Willamette Valley residents expressed their enthusiasm for the project. A Salem farmer stated: "We take this method of stating our belief in the necessity of the proposed Willamette valley flood control project and to urge the utmost haste in it's [sic] completion to avoid further heavy flood losses."[43] Valley residents were also interested in the hydroelectric potential of the project, as expressed by the Salem Chamber of Commerce: "Unquestionably the by-product of the electric power that the Dam will generate, will give the Willamette Valley, where industry is growing day by day, the chance to carry on this normal growth."[44] Citizens of the Willamette Valley wanted a dam in the North Santiam Canyon, and their combined voice and political power were the driving forces behind the Detroit Dam project.

Control of the planning and construction processes rested in the hands of even more distant forces. The contract for the dams went to Consolidated Builders, Inc., an interest of Henry J. Kaiser, the capitalist behind Boulder (later, Hoover) Dam, the Grand Coulee Dam, Bonneville Dam, and other projects, including the San Francisco Bay Bridge. Kaiser's company was in charge of every facet of production, from when and where the project started to who was hired and the housing in which they lived. The company even controlled access into and out of the area; the North Santiam Highway's realignment received final approval from the state only after Kaiser decided to ship supplies by rail instead of by road, thus calming highway officials who were afraid that so much truck traffic would damage the new road.[45] The company itself was subordinate to the US Army Corps of Engineers, which monitored and guided the progress of the project: selecting the site, negotiating with state and county officials for land and rights-of-way, and managing the federal funds that continued to flow to the project. Keeping a close eye on the corps, Kaiser, and the dam were the residents and politicians from the Willamette Valley whose interests were so tightly bound up to the project.

Construction began April 1, 1949, and the first bucket of concrete was poured on August 3, 1950. Three years later, on June 10, 1953, at a ceremony attended by corps officials, local residents, and national politicians, the governor of Oregon officially dedicated Detroit Dam, punctuated by a nineteen-gun salute. The local paper declared it a fitting "climax" for an "epic [that] has transformed the upper N. Santiam."[46] The project had cost nearly $50 million more than originally estimated for the dam in 1938. More than fifteen hundred workers cleared more than three thousand acres of timber, moved a highway fifteen miles, and built two dams (Detroit and its regulating dam, Big Cliff), which combined held back over 1.5 trillion gallons of water and could generate 1,800 kilowatts of power. It was indeed an epic transformation, wrought by a host of forces from beyond the canyon.

CANYON DAM BOOSTERS

Willamette Valley dam boosters found plenty of allies in the North Santiam Canyon who played a significant role in encouraging and using this new connection with the outside world. Most of the benefits of the Detroit project would accrue to bigger cities like Salem and Portland, desperate for flood control and thirsty for power and clean water. But dam advocates argued that local residents could join in shared prosperity throughout the region, specifically through the dam's recreational benefits. Lt. Col. Jack Miles, an engineer at Detroit Dam, was a self-proclaimed "one-man chamber of commerce" for recreation at the reservoir, which would attract fishermen and boaters bearing dollars for an expanded tourist economy.[47] Miles found a receptive audience among local boosters and business interests that were enthusiastic for Detroit Dam. The 1947 Corps of Engineers hearing in Salem that attracted such vociferous support from valley residents for Detroit Dam also attracted backing from local businesses, including the Mill City Furniture Company, Frank Lumber of Lyons, and Freres Lumber, also then of Lyons. Some of the most enthusiastic local support came from Charles Wolverton, editor of the *Mill City Enterprise*, who, "representing the county up there," wholeheartedly supported the dam.[48]

Wolverton and the *Mill City Enterprise* consistently and eagerly supported the Detroit Dam project, just as the editor and the paper had for the highway project. In an article titled "The Canyon in 1948—A Year of Promise," Wolverton wrote that the dam was "the Canyon's big chance to end a long and obscure history of being a minor gulch in the Willamette Valley watershed"—a chance to embrace prosperous future in service to the rest of the country by "finding a new role of becoming a major supplier of electrical current for the nation."[49] On the eve of the dam's dedication in 1953, the *Enterprise*'s editor reflected on the great opportunity and responsibility represented by the dam: "The presence of mighty Detroit Dam places in our laps a thing of great worth." Wolverton argued that his readers should understand themselves as part of a bigger world: "It is clear we must think of it in terms of use to the entire community of the Northwest. By so doing we make return to other citizens of the United States for their investment in our Canyon." That investment, Wolverton maintained, would bring not just economic development, but also a larger and more vibrant community: "In the years ahead the North Santiam hopes that it can summon to this Canyon many new citizens who will easily and happily call it home."[50] Through Detroit Dam, the area could further integrate with the region, nation, and world while also benefitting locals both new and old.

In addition to such lofty ideas about community and responsibility, residents had practical reasons to be enthusiastic: the multitude of ways to profit from this new connection between their "minor gulch" and the outside world. The project would bring good-paying jobs. For example, Robert Tompkins made $2.10 an hour as a Kaiser Consolidated Builders, Inc., construction worker assigned to Detroit Dam in 1950 at a time when Portland-area millworkers averaged $1.80 an hour and the national minimum wage was $0.75 an hour.[51] But dam jobs were temporary. Local boosters and businesses were more interested in long-term economic growth that they believed would follow dam construction and the accompanying real estate boom. In a March 1948 article, the *Mill City Enterprise* reported on "business, industrial and residential expansion totaling about three-quarters of a million dollars" underway.[52] In addition to the dam, the Kaiser interests purchased land in Mill City for a $250,000 home development project. Anticipating future growth, Freres Lumber Company of Lyons bought land for a new lumberyard in Mill City, and the city started building a new grade school. City services saw an influx of revenue from new businesses and a new permit system that the Mill City council rushed through the day before the Kaiser company bought land for its housing development. In less than a year, permits had brought almost $30,000 to the city.[53] The newspaper expanded as a result of this development, growing from two pages to twelve in less than four years.[54]

Some residents translated this real estate boom into substantial profit, earning the scorn of the *Enterprise* and other boosters who feared that such speculation would spoil their "big chance" for economic development. When in 1949 the Mill City Lions Club attempted to charge Kaiser $6,000 for land that months earlier had been worth $1,000, the newspaper reacted in outrage. "Those who are empowered to sell the homesites to Consolidated ought to get a new set of figures, go to the contractor, and tell him they're ready to deal at a reasonable price." Framing the real estate transaction as a matter of civic responsibility, the paper shamed the Lions Club and warned that "the townspeople will not easily forget if this burst of greed, just at the eve of great expectations for the city, loses us the benefits of a beautiful home development."[55] The Lions Club eventually dropped their price to $2,400, just over twice its earlier value. The *Enterprise* also shamed homeowners with rooms to rent who were trying to charge top dollar in the tight rental market. "Far be it for the paper to say that 'four rooms and path' [referring to a dilapidated, unplumbed house for rent] is not worth $80 a month," the *Enterprise* noted sarcastically. "Seriously, however, the talk one hears in the Canyon and outside of newcomers being gouged is not helping the future of the North Santiam area." The *Enterprise* urged locals to be fair to the "newcomers" or else lose a great opportunity: "Profiteering now will drive out the fine new people now locating here, and they'll quit this Canyon as soon as the work on the dams is done."[56] From real estate "gouging" to new permit systems that filled Mill City's coffers, a variety of people in the canyon found ways to benefit from the new dam on the North Santiam.

Enthusiasm for the dam was even apparent in Detroit, which would be completely submerged under the dam's reservoir. By the time the Corps of Engineers started poking around with the "three-legged things" that had so intrigued young Tom Fisher, Detroit had developed into a coherent community. Although unincorporated and unrecognized by the US Census Bureau, Detroit housed almost two hundred people in 1946.[57] For such a small town, it offered an array of services, including a hardware store, two cafes, a clothing store, and more. Residents picked up their mail from Mabel Moore at the post office (established in 1891), placed their telephone calls through Ella Johnson (who ran the switchboard from her home), and shopped at Cook's Grocery or Sophie's Market. The town also contained a small community church, although secular interests seem to have been more popular: Detroit had four taverns, two billiard houses, and a movie theater.[58] Residents found more services twenty miles west in Mill City, or they could travel thirty miles farther to Salem. Like other places in the canyon, Detroit was both a community of its own while also remaining connected to the world outside.

Detroit provided community not only to its own residents, but also to other people living in even more remote parts of the upper canyon. Isolated up at Marion Forks, Nan and Scott Young and their kids, Dottie

This 1951 postcard of Detroit shows the post office, two cafés, a tavern, a service station, and a motel, as well as pedestrians and an onlooker. Taken while Detroit Dam was under construction, the photograph suggests both the depth of the community and the impermanence brought by the dam—the rooms at the hotel were available "by day, week, or month." From "Old Detroit," photo book, page 2, image 11, Canyon Life Museum.

and Bob, depended on Detroit for services and opportunities. During the winters when the North Santiam Highway was not yet finished and still too dangerous to travel, the Youngs sent Dottie and Bob to live in Detroit and attend school. Beyond school, Detroit provided other necessities. Even after moving to Marion Forks to live full-time, Dottie Young remembers that the family would go to Detroit "for social things. The kids would buy candy bars from the candy store." Later in her high school years, Dottie traveled through Detroit on her way up to Bruckman's Breitenbush Hot Springs, where, "once the road was built . . . there were some dances on Saturday nights." With its schools, businesses, and social opportunities, Dottie remembered Detroit as "a place to go to when [she and her family] wanted a change"—a community hub for the upper canyon.

Detroit Dam would inundate that community, but, perhaps surprisingly, residents of Detroit and elsewhere supported that violent transformation. At the 1947 US Army Corps of Engineers public hearing in Salem, representatives from the Detroit Garage and Service Station, the Detroit Tavern, the Canyon Café, and the Detroit Women's Civic Club voiced their approval.[59] These business and civic organizations were eager to participate in the economic benefits of river development, just like others in the canyon and in the valley. Some Detroit residents moved to aid in the growth of other towns; the *Enterprise* happily reported that C. H.

Cass, recently of Detroit, had moved to Mill City and planned "100 feet of retail business frontage."[60]

Others stayed close to the dam, expecting a new era of prosperity. Dottie Young recalls that "the people [in Detroit and the upper canyon] in general were happy" because construction of the dam and improvement of the highway "would bring people to the area." Anticipating the flood of boaters and fishermen driving up the smooth North Santiam Highway to the new Detroit reservoir, Earl and Audrey Layman, owners of Cedar Tavern, put their business on a sled and hauled it up to higher ground in the fall of 1951.[61] Ora Leis, proud owner of a half acre in Detroit, looked forward to the reservoir washing away some of the town's less desirable elements: "Down here [in Old Detroit], too much of the property was owned by a few people who leased it out. Nobody took care of it." Leis anticipated that the dam would bring property ownership and community improvement. "Up there we will all own our own lots and I expect it will be nicely landscaped."[62] The dam would flood their town, but Detroit residents like Ora Leis were happy with the prospects of a new, better, and more permanent community brought about by the influence of forces from outside the canyon.

The US Army Corps of Engineers also seemed pleased. Despite an unseasonably cold winter and trouble with moving contractors, Detroit residents had removed most of their buildings by the deadline of June 1, 1952. To thank them, District Engineer Colonel T. H. Lipscomb sent residents a memorandum applauding the town's "foresight of planning and a definite determination to fulfill your agreements with your Government." Lipscomb concluded with optimism for the area's growth: "I sincerely hope that the Detroit Project will be the means of helping you attain your future goals."[63] It seemed that Old Detroit would pass quietly and peacefully into the past, making way for the shared vision of progress promised by Detroit Dam.

MOVING DETROIT AND TRANSFORMING THE CANYON

Underneath this tranquil surface, some people in Detroit were stirring up trouble, arguing that their dispossession violated the sanctity of private property and due process. When construction got underway in 1948, so did land speculation, as entrepreneurs sought to profit from dam building, which promised to bring more than a thousand workers to the area.[64] "Construction of residences, stores, tourist cabins, and other buildings, is progressing continuous," wrote Portland District Engineer Colonel O. E. Walsh in 1949, "they are proceeding to clean up on the boom during the construction period in every possible way."[65] Concerned with the haphazard construction boom that might interfere with the Corps of Engineers' plans, Walsh issued a stop construction order and began condemnation proceedings, pushing to pay off and move out Detroit residents. Sixteen landowners resorted to the courts to protest the corps' valuation of their property. One of them, B. G. Cochran, took the promises about tourism too seriously for the corps' liking. The corps complained that Cochran had "visions of developing his land into a recreational area," and he refused to sell his one-acre plot for the assessed value of $25. The case went to court in November 1952, when a jury awarded Cochran $500—short of his claim of $12,500 but more than the government's original offer.[66]

Others who sought to negotiate with, appeal to, or plead with the Army Corps of Engineers found themselves stymied. Frustrations began even before dam construction got underway. In May 1938, Detroit resident David B. Orr wrote to the Corps of Engineers district office in Portland. Orr had heard that the corps was exploring Detroit as a site for a dam, and he wanted the corps to know that "if our flat of several hundred acres are flooded then lots of poor people who are building homes here will be without a place to go." His own home, Orr wrote, sat on "nearly 8 acres" and "is not just land in common, but my home, and serves [the] same purpose as a million dollar Brown Stone Front." He described his place: a "large log house (good sized logs)" covering 1,600 square feet, a good well, seven apple trees, and two "large cherry trees all bearing unless you have a magic wand you can not produce them short of 15 years and they are evidently worth something."

"I am thankful for what I get," wrote Orr, but he faced challenges: "69 years old—deaf—bad eyes and worn out with hard work. . . . Nursed an invalid wife for years who recently went away to never return." And now he faced the prospect of losing his home: "If only part of flat [were to be] covered [by the dam and reservoir] and my house on an island and no store or road near, I would have to desert the place and go where I could get supplies in. Cannot afford an auto and could not drive either." Orr pleaded: "Why not the dam be put further down the valley?" he proposed; failing that, Orr asked not for a cash payment but "a home for home," something "as good as I give naturally (That's fair isn't it), near a post office and store. . . . Do not care for any great amount of land and a few trees o.k. . . . If you have a city or town place would do." Orr trusted that the corps would do the right thing: "I don't think you want to punish me or make me suffer and feel you will do best you can." The corps responded to Orr's two-page letter with a half-page note that explained that "this office has no authority to buy lands in the proposed reservoir at this time. . . . Neither has this office any means of aiding you in making a trade or sale of your place, much as it would like to be of assistance to you." It is a sad story: the corps politely turned away a deaf and half-blind widower looking for a home—the kind of interaction that would feed into the developing sense of victimization at the hands of outsiders.

Later on, other residents found that the law and the corps frustrated their honest efforts to participate in the process of dislocation. Roberta Renner, owner of a motor court in Detroit, drove one hundred miles to a US District Court hearing in Portland to ask permission to conduct business until the dam was complete. Renner thought the hearing, attended by representatives of the corps and conducted in a federal court, was the appropriate venue for such a request. The judge patiently explained otherwise: "The only purpose of this hearing is to allow the Government to take immediate possession . . . As to when they will negotiate with you, if they ever do negotiate with you . . . the Court cannot assure you about things like that."[67] Such assurances meant little to some people in Detroit. As she packed up her life in the spring of 1952, Hilma "Ma" Dickie, who had run the fourteen-room Detroit Hotel for over twenty years, told a reporter from Salem that "the government didn't give us too much for what we have." It was enough to make a person lose faith in the government, as Rayford Hiatt complained: "The way the government has conducted this, it has a little dictator tinge to it."[68] Hiatt, Dickie, Renner, Cochran, and others were caught up in the disturbing process of transformation that had been threatened by the highway and realized by the dam.

Frustrations with these transformations became especially clear in the protracted struggle for a new Detroit town site. As a rule, the US Army Corps of Engineers did not relocate towns unless specifically directed to do so by Congress. The Flood Control Act of 1938, which authorized Detroit Dam, made no such provision. "However," wrote the corps' legal team in 1948, "if the factual situation demonstrates that the acquisition of a new town site and relocation of the old town is so closely connected to the construction of the project as to constitute a necessary, natural, and proper part, though perhaps an incidental part thereof, its relocation, and the acquisition of the land required therefore, is authorized under the general authority to acquire land."[69] The corps, in short, had the power to create a new town. And there was a place to do so: the Hammond Lumber Company's old Camp 17, just above the proposed waterline of the new reservoir. In his pleading letter to the corps in 1938, David Orr had suggested exactly that spot: "Detroit could be moved up" to the site of Camp 17.[70] But it was less expensive and less complicated to pay residents for their property and wish them well in their new lives—somewhere else. It was not so easy for everyone. Ma Dickie had thought about moving east to Bend, but as she said, "that is too far from my children." At a public meeting in July 1949, Ora Leis asked, "if there is any possible site that the people could have . . . People don't want to leave here." The corps' chief of real estate responded frankly: "That's the way it is."[71]

And so began the fight for "new" Detroit, a muted struggle that adhered to legal conventions and accepted notions of civility while simultaneously revealing fault lines and frustrations. The divisions began in the community itself. In September 1949, Edison Vickers—justice of the peace, owner of Detroit's Canyon Theater, and president of the Canyon Commercial Club—filed papers in Marion County court for incorporation of a new Detroit that would merge the dry portions of Old Detroit with the village of Idanha, three miles up the canyon. Detroit and Idanha shared a long history. In 1922, Hammond Lumber Company Camp 11 at Idanha was disassembled and moved to Detroit. Decades later, when the corps started clearing out Old Detroit, some of those same buildings were again disassembled and returned to Idanha, including Vickers's Canyon Theater, which became the Village Store in Idanha.[72]

Vickers wanted to officially bring Detroit and Idanha's history together and create "the longest little city in the country." The *Enterprise* reported that Vickers had "great hopes in the future of [the new town] becoming a trading center for a large recreation area expected to develop around Detroit Dam Lake."[73] Other local residents expressed less optimism. They were more appalled than amused with the idea of a "longest little city," and they doubted that tourism would bring the economic boom the Vickers and others promised: "to incorporate such an extensive area, the larger portion of which is undeveloped, uninhabited stump land, into a city and then saddle ourselves with a tax burden in order to provide the area with public utilities is not only unsound and unreasonable but actually fantastic." This Idanha-based letter writer was not alone. By a margin of two to one, voters sent the incorporation plan down to defeat in October 1949 and again in December, when Idanha voters opted to incorporate their own town, leaving Detroit's fate uncertain.[74]

Vickers retreated, and the fight for a new town shifted to confront outside forces. In November 1949, 155 residents of Detroit signed a petition requesting that the US Army Corps of Engineers negotiate with the US Forest Service (USFS) to secure a new town site. The USFS owned much of the land above the reservoir's high waterline, and the petitioners argued that the two federal agencies had a responsibility to cooperate and relocate the town. "The petition," reported the newspaper, "was signed by residents, some of who have been in Detroit for 30 years, and others who have come here recently but have decided that the upper Canyon country would be a good place to settle permanently." The petitioners framed their struggle as one between locals and outsiders, calling them-selves "natives" and arguing that "it would not be right to 'shove them aside to make a recreation area for city people.' "[75] Responding to the petition, the corps' Colonel D. S. Burns asserted that "this office has no authority to sell any lands of the Forest Service," which was technically true, although Burns did not volunteer the relevant fact that the corps possessed the statutory authority to create new towns. Burns instead suggested that the petitioners address their complaint to the USFS. But USFS representatives had clearly rejected such an idea at a public meeting six months before, and they again declined to take land out of the public domain for a new town site.[76]

Ultimately, the residents of Detroit turned to an old acquaintance, the Hammond Lumber Company. Although Hammond had decades before sold its mills and logging operations in the canyon, the company still owned significant amounts of property in the area, including Camp 17 just above the new reservoir's waterline. In August 1950, the company subdivided the property into three hundred lots, laid down streets, and platted the town.[77] By June 1952, Hammond had sold sixty-seven lots for a sum of $42,800.[78] Residents of Old Detroit bought forty-five of those lots; the rest went to recent arrivals looking for their own lakeside retreat or hoping to cash in on the expected tourism boom. New Detroit did not include some of the institutions of Old Detroit; for example, Whitey and Hazel Goodman of Whitey's Cafe moved to Mill City, as did Ma Dickie, the owner of Dickie's Hotel who had expressed concern about the corps' behavior having a "dictator tinge to it." Others left for the Willamette Valley and beyond.[79] Finally, on June 17, 1952, as the corps burned the last remaining buildings of Old Detroit, residents of the new Detroit filed incorporation papers.[80]

As the waters of the North Santiam River backed up behind Detroit Dam in May 1952, the editor of the *Enterprise*, Charles Wolverton, paused to reflect on the meaning of the dam and its lake. Since its founding in 1944, the *Enterprise* had been a consistent and persistent advocate for the dam. With the moment of triumph at hand, Wolverton sought, again, to encourage a global perspective among his readers. "There are those who freely preach of a hell-fire depression in the offing. There are those who predict a war explosion in the Far East," wrote Wolverton, in reference to the ongoing war in Korea and the looming threat of nuclear holocaust. "Something has crept into our lives. This 'something' can be described as 'tension,' a feeling of insecurity, bewilderment, and uncertainty."[81] But the development of Detroit Dam offered refuge: "It is hoped that the presence of this lake will prove a Memorial for those souls who seek rest from the cares of that storms [sic] our senses each day." A project that started as an effort to control floods in the Willamette Valley had transformed into something much bigger. In a tumultuous world of "insecurity, bewilderment, and uncertainty," Detroit Dam offered the promise of peace, security, and prosperity.

Having overcome internal and external division, Detroit residents eagerly sought to be a part of those lofty promises and to enjoy more tangible and practical benefits. Mabel Moore, formerly the postmaster for Old Detroit and now "new" Detroit's correspondent at the *Enterprise*, reported that "the year 1952 will be recorded in Detroit history as one of great accomplishment." Detroit had much to celebrate: the opening of businesses new and old, a new dial-operated telephone system, and a new high school, paid for by the US Army Corps of Engineers.[82] The Laymans reopened Cedar Tavern, although Mrs. Moore was happier to report that "the Detroit Church of Christ is firmly established in the new town site, an example of the determination that religious-minded citizens will display in the face of serious obstacles." Mrs. Moore ended her dispatch on a triumphant note: "The year 1952 will be recorded in Detroit history as one of great accomplishment. Citizens who took part in rebuilding the city look forward to a bright future in its growth and development as a business and recreational center."[83] Even after all the turmoil and frustration, the people of Detroit had not abandoned their commitment to the prevailing vision of growth and development.

As the dam's dedication date of June 10, 1953, drew closer, excitement grew. Planning for the dedication ceremony had been underway for months, led by a committee including representatives of the Corps of Engineers and chambers of commerce from throughout the Willamette Valley, including Salem, Albany, Silverton, and Oregon City. Canyon residents participated, too. The North Santiam Chamber of Commerce sent Ken Golliet, proprietor of the IGA grocery store in Mehama, and E. C. Kennedy of Detroit, who in 1950 had taken up the lease of a smaller hot springs area just down the road from Bruckman's Breitenbush Hot Springs. Golliet and Kennedy were eager to capitalize on what Golliet anticipated would "be one of the biggest things in the State of Oregon." They proposed creating a souvenir program to distribute throughout the state, with the idea, as Golliet explained, "to publicize the dam and then on the other side bring attention to Mt. Jefferson area, Hoodoo Ski Lodge, etc." Kennedy suggested printing as many as 50,000 such brochures, noting that he himself had "put out 100,000 for my little hot springs," and promising that he would "make a substantial donation, because it will attract people there and help my business." Still, the expense would be too much for the North Santiam Chamber of Commerce to handle on its own.[84]

Golliet and Kennedy persuaded the Corps of Engineers and nine other chambers of commerce from the valley to help pay for the brochure, which was appropriate, given their shared vision for the kind of place the North Santiam Canyon should become. The front of the program featured photos of Detroit Dam and former Oregon governor and current US Secretary of the Interior Douglas McKay, who had been a strong advocate for Detroit Dam. The back of the program included a photo of "Warm Springs Indian boys who will perform at dedication ceremonies," a nod to the canyon's past. But most of the brochure looked to the future, defining the North Santiam Canyon as "A Year-Around Playground!" Photos and flowery prose described what the area offered recreationalists, from "Unsurpassed Scenery" and "Unexcelled Mountain Climbing" to opportunities for "Fishing at Its Best" and a "Winter Sports Paradise." A map at the bottom of the brochure showed the path of the North Santiam Highway, a "picturesque route [that] presents a panorama of fruit orchards, beautiful homes, evergreen forests and snow-capped mountains." The simplified map presented the vision that boosters like Golliet, Kennedy, and Wolverton had been advocating for years: the technological and engineering wonders of Detroit and Big Cliff Dams, recreational attractions like Breitenbush and Hoodoo, and the towns of the North Santiam Canyon, woven together by a smooth, wide (and deceptively straight, in the program) highway connecting the area to the outside world.[85]

But for those residents who expressed concern about the growing influence of "city people," the dam's dedication confirmed their fears about expanding external power. In addition to Secretary McKay, the guest list included the governors of Oregon, Washington, and Idaho; the vice president of construction for Kaiser's Consolidated Builders, Inc.; and Army Corps of Engineers officials from Washington, DC, and Portland. The rector of St. Paul's Episcopal Church in Salem opened the

The North Santiam Canyon is

Unsurpassed Scenery

The North Santiam River Highway is the lowest pass over the Oregon Cascades. This scenic route is open to travel all year. You will know Oregon better after traveling this picturesque route. The Santiam Highway presents a panorama of fruit orchards, beautiful homes, evergreen forests and snow-capped mountains. It gives quick access to one of the West's great recreational areas.

The largest lumber producing forest in the United States, the Willamette National Forest, makes up a large part of the recreational area. This great forest of hemlock, cedar and superb Douglas fir comprises over 1,500,000 acres.

Hundreds of miles of trail under the supervision and maintenance of the U.S. Forest Service lead in every direction. Lakes that abound in fish and are the answer to any angler's prayer, are easily reached by car, trail or pack train. There are mackinaw trout of great size in some of the lakes. The German brown and the fighting rainbow are to be found in most lakes and streams in this angler's paradise. Detroit Lake, one of the recreational assets of the North Santiam area, has been well stocked. It will soon be one of the best fishing and boating lakes in the Northwest.

Unexcelled Mountain Climbing

In no part of the West is there more diversified activity. For the nature lover or camera enthusiast, the North Santiam area offers much. In the spring, summer or fall, wild flowers and flowering shrubs make the hillsides a riot of color. Beautiful camp grounds and picnic sites located on rushing mountain streams or serene lakes provide pleasure for the tourists and campers.

For the more hardy explorer, there is the famous Skyline Trail to travel either by foot or horse. A large portion of this great wilderness area is adjacent to the North Santiam Pass. The Skyline Trail wanders leisurely some 400 miles through Oregon. Along the trail are over 200 spring-fed lakes. The scenery varies from the green alpine meadows to lofty peaks and perpetual snow fields.

Fishing at its Best

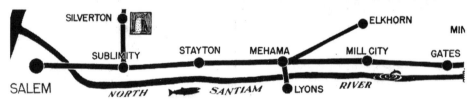

Commemorating the dedication of Detroit Dam in 1953, this brochure presents the North Santiam Canyon primarily in terms of tourist attractions, recreational opportunities, and the technological wonders of Detroit and Big Cliff Dams, made accessible to visitors from the Willamette Valley by the (deceptively straight, as portrayed here) North Santiam Highway. From "Detroit Dam," photo book, front pouch, Canyon Life Museum.

meeting with prayer, followed by remarks from Oregon's governor, who introduced McKay for the main speech. McKay's presence was meant to honor his work on the dam and create excitement, as Golliet had explained, "since this is Doug McKay's baby I think it should be quite an occasion." Instead, a quiet pall hung over the ceremony. McKay received what the usually joyous *Enterprise* termed a "mediocre greeting" from

a Year-Around Playground!

DETROIT DAM

DEDICATION CEREMONY
JUNE 10, 1953 — 1:30 P. M.

Winter Sports Paradise

Some points of great interest along the trail are the Mt. Jefferson primitive area, and the Eight Lakes Basin. Mt. Jefferson is one of the highest peaks in Oregon, and has an elevation of 10,500 feet. Its northern and eastern sides are covered with immense glaciers, and offer excellent opportunities for mountain climbing. Jefferson Park, a natural park-like setting at the northern base of the mountain, holds an array of small lakes, and a wild flower display that is unsurpassed on the North American continent. Information on how to reach this and many beautiful areas can be obtained at any U.S. Forest Ranger Station.

To you, the ski enthusiast, the area offers excellent facilities. Hoodoo Bowl affords the skier a variety of exciting terrain for winter pleasure. The cooperation of the State Highway Department and the Forest Service assure you of a snow-free winter highway with ample parking space.

Three of large group of Warm Springs Indian boys who will perform at dedication ceremonies.

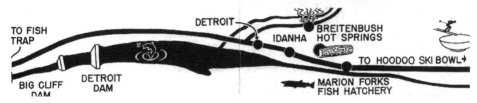

TO FISH TRAP

DETROIT

BIG CLIFF DAM

DETROIT DAM

IDANHA

BREITENBUSH HOT SPRINGS

TO HOODOO SKI BOWL→

MARION FORKS FISH HATCHERY

an audience of approximately four thousand people marked by a "conspicuous lack of cheering."[86] Perhaps the local crowd's reticence arose from the external influence evident at the ceremony, in which local residents had been reduced to the role of supporting cast. No one from the area had been invited to speak that day. All businesses closed, except restaurants and service shops. High school students from the area formed a one-hundred-piece band to provide music for the visitors. And the mayor of Mill City, the largest town in the canyon? "Albert Toman," reported the *Mill City Enterprise*, "will supervise soft drink and eating stand concessions at the dam site." The canyon's most powerful local politician became a service-sector worker—a harbinger of things to come for the people of the North Santiam Canyon.

The construction of Detroit Dam and the North Santiam Highway represented a transformative moment in the history of the canyon. Many residents embraced these dam and highway as they had earlier connections to the outside world, and some especially enthusiastic boosters eagerly encouraged the rapid changes that would come to the local economy, population, and identity. But a growing awareness of the increasing influence of outside forces and the corresponding loss of options tempered the enthusiasm of other residents. The dam and road would not be stopped— this much was clear. And so people made important choices from their limited options. Landowners in the way of the highway sued for greater compensation. The people of Detroit got a town. Mill City landowners "gouged" Kaiser's Consolidated Builders, Inc., and businessmen capitalized on the opportunity to sell their community to the outside world. In this sense, residents took control of their lives and forced compromise from outside forces. But they had also integrated the highway and the dam into their communities, developing a dependency on the outside world against which more and more residents bristled and defined themselves and their place: "us" in the canyon victimized by "them" elsewhere.

6

Becoming a Timber Community

With the completion of Detroit Dam and the North Santiam Highway, the canyon incorporated powerful connections to the outside world that led to new opportunities, old vulnerabilities, and a transformed identity based in the local timber industry. The highway improved access to local forests and outside markets and facilitated increased logging and milling. Residents embraced the economic opportunities that favored local timber companies and workers as well as those that came at the hands of outside forces. Complex relationships developed between the owners and managers of timber companies and their employees, with organized labor briefly providing a means by which to negotiate—and highlight—differences among people within the industry. Over time, the local timber industry and its supporters shifted attention away from divisions within the canyon and toward perceived threats from the outside. In an effort to lower federal timber sale prices and ward off external competition, local timber companies developed relationships that they considered innocently cooperative but that federal prosecutors and judges determined illegally collusive. Timber company executives and their allies portrayed these trials as unfair not just to the local timber industry, but to everyone in the area. This affair contributed to a narrative of victimization in the North Santiam Canyon, whereby people came to think of themselves as part of a "timber community"—an identity defined both by an industry and by a shared sense of powerlessness in the face of outside forces.[1]

GROWING THE CANYON'S TIMBER INDUSTRY

The transportation connections running into and through the canyon grew after World War II, facilitating the expansion of logging. According to local mythology, the first log truck, a converted flatbed, was put into use in Mill City in 1933, before the Hammond mill had shut down and while trains still ran through the area. The details of the story seem apocryphal—an expression of the kind of rugged, independent creativity

Heavy-duty trucks and trailers, coupled with a rapidly expanding network of logging roads, facilitated the expansion of the timber industry in the North Santiam Canyon after World War II. Note the size of the enormous stump (left), the remains of an ancient tree cut down and processed as part of the industrial logging process. From "Logging," photo book 110, page 2, photo 3, Canyon Life Museum.

that local residents pride themselves on—but it is true that throughout the Pacific Northwest after World War II, logging companies relied on trucks, as well other technologies, to open up new forests and new extractive possibilities for the industry.[2] The process accelerated in the North Santiam Canyon after August 1949, when the Southern Pacific abandoned its railroad line above Gates, as required by the filling of Detroit Reservoir.[3] The end of rail service to the upper canyon was an occasion meriting brief historical reflection in the diary of Niagara resident Carmen Elaine Stafford, who wrote on August 12, 1949, "The last train load of logs went down here tonight. Started in 1880's." Trains continued to run between Mill City and Gates until 1959, when the Southern Pacific shuttered the line above Mill City, too. Local timber companies encouraged state and federal agencies to develop a vast and intricate network of roads to move logs quickly to mills and off to market. When the Oregon State Highway Department moved the highway to make way for the new Detroit Reservoir, it made sure to plan a road that was "wide enough and curves gentle enough to accommodate the increasing number of heavy log trucks," a process that continued through the 1950s.[4]

The US Forest Service played an important and active role in building out the area's logging road network. The *Mill City Enterprise* reported that in 1952 the Detroit Ranger District contained 139 miles of timber access roads, with 13 more miles constructed the following year. Furthermore, "Two hundred miles of main line roads are needed to make national forest timber in the North Santiam drainage fully accessible, according to S.T. Moore [Detroit district ranger]." The Forest Service would supervise the construction of these roads, and the agency would organize the timber sales leading to even more roads opening up even more timberland, as Moore explained: "Large timber sales in remote sections of the forest will make it possible for future operators to continue the road development on the district."[5] The 200-mile estimate was far too low. Over the next few decades, many hundreds of miles of roads would be built, and by 2004, there were more than 1,000 miles of roads crisscrossing the Detroit Ranger District, opening up thousands of acres of timber to logging.[6] The road building boom, facilitated by the Forest Service, exemplifies the agency's accelerating efforts to accommodate and encourage the expansion of the timber industry throughout the postwar era.[7]

These transportation developments coupled with a market for lumber that increased dramatically during the postwar years. The housing market boomed after World War II and into the 1970s, and timber production increased in response to market demand. In the Willamette National Forest (which includes the North Santiam Canyon), loggers cut an average of around 450 million board feet a year in the 1950s; in the 1960s and 1970s, the average had increased to 700 million board feet a year, with peaks as high as 940 million board feet.[8] In the North Santiam Canyon's Detroit Ranger District, the area harvested increased from less than six thousand acres in the 1950s to more than thirteen thousand acres in both the 1960s and 1970s.[9]

The timber economy revitalized by expanded transportation and market connections generated enthusiasm in the North Santiam Canyon. The *Mill City Enterprise* devoted most of its attention to the boom in logging and milling. Whenever the Forest Service put a new tract of timber up for sale, it was front-page news. "Forest Timber Sale Yields $623,447," ran the January 22, 1953, headline. Three weeks later: "Large Timber Sale Planned: Detroit—Sixty-seven million feet will be sold on the Detroit district in an estimated 28 tracts." And again two weeks after that: "Timber Sale Brings High Prices at Eugene Monday . . . contract with Pamelia Lumber Company of Idanha for removal of three million feet of timber in the Marion Forks area."[10]

When the *Mill City Enterprise* was not keeping the community notified of timber sales, it was reporting on the dozens of new mills and logging firms that sprouted up in the postwar years, encouraged by the growing network of public Forest Service roads. As one resident of Mill City reminisced in 2001, "About 15 years ago, there were 15-20 logging companies in the Canyon"; another resident has listed more than forty mills running at one time or another.[11] In September 1953, the *Mill City Enterprise* ran a story on the Termite Lumber Company, a new business going in on the site where another shingle mill had burned to the ground just three months earlier.[12] The Termite Mill was just one of many new mills and logging operations that seemed to start every month. Most of these outfits were small operations, like the Santiam Shake Mill, a four-man business founded in Mill City in 1961. These modest businesses picked up small contracts from the Forest Service or cut and processed timber from private holdings in the area, and they usually closed up shop within a few years—Termite Lumber Company, for instance, lasted less than ten years.

While most logging and milling businesses remained relatively small and short-lived, three local timber firms expanded significantly and became influential in the canyon's economy and identity. Young & Morgan of Marion Forks, Freres Lumber Company of Lyons, and Frank Lumber Company of Mill City were three of the largest and more important local timber businesses of the postwar period. These three family-owned and -operated companies were the successful bidders on many Forest Service timber sales in the last half of the twentieth century. A review of the *Mill City Enterprise* in the 1950s, 1960s, and 1970s reveals these companies' dominance in local timber sales, with regular stories such as "Young & Morgan Top Bidder on Mansfield Sale" and "Freres Veneer Company purchases 5 million board feet."[13] That dominance continued well into the 1980s. In the first quarter of fiscal year 1984-85, the Forest Service sold over 79,000,000 board feet of timber from the Detroit Ranger District. It was the largest sale quantity in district history, and most of those sales went to Freres, Frank, and Young & Morgan.[14] Transportation and market connections had yielded significant economic opportunities, and local timber companies, some small and a few big, profited from those connections.

LOVING AND HATING OUTSIDE TIMBER COMPANIES

The roads utilized by local timber companies also made the area accessible to outside firms, who increasingly challenged canyon logging and milling operations. For a brief time during the years of the Great Depression and World War II, small firms dominated the local timber industry; hence the need for Mill City Planing and Processing Company and the Mill City Manufacturing Company (MCMC), which provided planing, shipping, and other services the small logging companies and mills could not. But before too long, external capitalists were swooping in. In 1937, Portland lumberman Coleman H. Wheeler Jr. bought eighty percent of MCMC's stock. The transaction returned a locally owned mill, started from the wreckage of the Hammond Lumber Company, to the hands of outsiders.

Local companies simply could not compete with better resourced, larger outside firms that could afford expensive logging and milling technology and whose economies of scale drove them to extensive and expensive purchases of land and timber sales, as W. Scott Prudhom has explained.[15] This became clear during the construction of Detroit Dam, which was supposed to offer opportunities for small, independent loggers called gyppos. The US Army Corps of Engineers needed to get the reservoir area clear of all trees, and as District Engineer Col. Walsh explained to the Salem Chamber of Commerce, "It is planned to cut up the job of clearing land in small contracts so that residents of the upper Santiam country can bid on the work." That was welcome news, as the *Mill City Enterprise* reported in May 1949, for these "gyppo logging companies have had it tough," but they "are currently being given a good break by the Forest Service," which was responsible for overseeing timber sales.[16] Unfortunately for these local companies, outside firms too often got the contracts. For example, in February 1949, five small local logging firms came together to bid for the right to clear some of the trees for Detroit Reservoir, but the group lost half its members, and the remaining partnership made a bid that was "far out of line," as the *Mill City Enterprise* reported, compared to the winning bid from an outside firm.[17] Companies from Roseburg, Tillamook, and Albany secured later reservoir clearing contracts, amounting to more than one million board feet of timber cut by logging companies from outside the canyon.[18]

By the 1950s, "small mills were disappearing from the scene," as Mill City Planing and Processing Company's Carl Kelly Jr. recalled, and many were being bought up by external capitalists. One of the most consequential acquisitions occurred in 1953, when Portland firm M & M Wood Working purchased a veneer plant in Idanha and a plywood plant in Lyons. At the time, M & M was the third-largest plywood manufacturer in the United States, and the company's operations included plywood mills in Albany, Portland, and Eureka, California, as well as billions of board feet of timber in Oregon and California. Many people in the canyon, especially the boosters at the *Mill City Enterprise*, embraced the outside timber companies that had operations along the North Santiam River. The *Mill City Enterprise* reported every development of M & M Wood Working and was particularly enthusiastic about the M & M plywood plant, which grew from an eighty-man operation in 1953 to a four-hundred-employee firm one year later. In September 1955, in honor of an M & M "open house celebration," the *Mill City Enterprise* triumphantly wrote, "the Lyons Plywood Division of the M & M Wood Working Company, at Lyons, Oregon, is one of the nation's most modern and complete mills. The latest electronic equipment and 400 skilled employees enable this plant to produce 75 million feet of plywood annually."[19] The power of outside capital was bringing technological innovation and jobs to the canyon, and the *Mill City Enterprise* could not have been more pleased.

This was not simply a case of overzealous *Enterprise* boosterism; that same issue included numerous full-page advertisements of support taken out by local businesses and groups. In one such advertisement, a group of taverns, grocery stores, a women's club, and other organizations and businesses claiming to represent "The Communities of Detroit and Idanha" declared that they were "glad to join other communities the North Santiam Canyon in congratulating M and M on their plywood plant located at Lyons." These civic groups and businesses anticipated that external investment in the timber industry downstream would lead to a growth in tourism upstream: "We of the upper Canyon Area invite you and your men to vacation in our scenic wonderland. We are sure you will have fun fishing and hunting up here." The *Mill City Enterprise* reported that thousands visited the open house celebration of the M & M plywood plant, indicating enthusiasm for the economic opportunities presented by the plant. Some residents, then, welcomed the investments of outside forces, just as they had advocated for the establishment of the highway and road system that facilitated such investment.

Enthusiasm for outside corporations was hardly universal, however. In the decades after the war, some residents became increasingly wary of outside control in the timber industry, and for good reason. History and memory suggested that outside corporations held too much power and could not be trusted. Some locals had been around long enough to remember Colonel Hogg and his broken railroad promises. Even more had direct experience with the Hammond Lumber Company abandoning the community. In March 1951, an angry canyon resident penned an editorial to the *Mill City Enterprise*, reminding readers and neighbors of what outside lumbermen could do: "Hammond Lumber Company

Built from the ruins of the Hammond Lumber Company, the Mill City Manufacturing Company's grand opening in 1936 represented to local residents the resiliency of the North Santiam Canyon, but its closure in 1949 highlighted the area's vulnerability to external markets and investors. Undated photograph from "Mill City Views," photo book 127, page 24, photo 102.

slaughtered much of our virgin timber and then pulled stakes. This little deal left Mill City a wreck and shambles."[20]

That letter came in the aftermath of what seemed like yet another betrayal: the decision of the Mill City Manufacturing Company's Portland investors to shutter the business in the spring of 1949. For months, business had been tough for MCMC and its employees, who were no longer worker-owners, since Portland lumberman Coleman Wheeler's investment in the company. On Thanksgiving Day 1948, the company announced that the mill would close indefinitely, "affecting the employment," as the *Mill City Enterprise* explained, "of about 60 or more in the mill and indirectly affect[ing] the jobs of others in transportation connected with its operations." The company blamed the closure on "market uncertainties and the decline in prices of some grades of lumber," a reference to a slight drop in prices over the previous two months.[21] The mill reopened in March, a source of relief for MCMC's employees, and also, as the *Mill City Enterprise* explained, "a welcome event for local businesses" that depended on the "resumption of the mill payroll."[22]

But dark clouds were on the horizon. Soon after the mill resumed operations, Frank Rada retired. Rada, the son of Austrian immigrant Louis Rada, had been MCMC's millwright, and he was one of the former Hammond employees who had formed Mill City Manufacturing as a locally owned and operated cooperative. Rada had decided that "real estate interests" were more promising than the mill. And he was right. The lumber market decline continued into the spring, and the mill shut down again at the end of April. Wheeler's office in Portland denied rumors that the mill had been sold, but by June, the Mill City Manufacturing Company was dead.

The closure and sale of MCMC brought the normally pro-business *Mill City Enterprise* to a state of apoplexy. In a vitriolic article titled "An Industry Dies: An Obituary," the paper eloquently vented local anger at this latest betrayal by outsiders.[23] "With a casual stroke of a pen," Wheeler and his fellow Portland investors had "struck off in a moment this week what had taken years of labor and sacrifice to build. The words the pen wrote were: Junk it!" The products of local "labor and sacrifice" would now be sold off to the lowest bidder: "The men who deal in junk are here. They're figuring on the machinery—that used to be the sinews of a fine local industry and the tools of livelihood for 150 families—at so much per pound." The *Mill City Enterprise* hoped that not all was lost; perhaps "here and there a machine will go to another mill—to produce lumber and payrolls for others," but the paper also expressed cynicism about the community's economic base, asserting that "unquestionably the industry itself is all being junked." The paper highlighted the tragic irony of MCMC's death: "The mill was built by the donated labor of many men here—left stranded by the junking of another enterprise, the Hammond mill here." Betrayed twice by outsiders, "most of the workers who gave their labor to that effort are either too old to start out again, or too disillusioned to try—remembering how connivers grabbed, then tossed aside, their own mill."

The article concluded with damning poetic reflection. "Obituaries are written for human beings," wrote the *Mill City Enterprise*, and "perhaps one ought to be penned for wrecked mills, ruined land or mismanaged endeavors they live by." The paper proposed an obituary that praised what had been made and lost locally, and condemned the outsiders who had profited from and abandoned the community: "Mill City M., born in travail, lived in prosperity, enriching its owner, died through neglect; survived by well-rewarded ingrates, plus a host of honest workmen, cast off as casually as the corpse was interred."

The dirt over Mill City Manufacturing Company's grave had barely settled when, in 1956, Seattle-based Simpson Logging Company bought M & M Wood Working for $50 million.[24] M & M was hardly a small local company; the four hundred people who worked at the plywood plant in Lyons and the veneer plant in Idanha represented a sixth of the company's twenty-six hundred employees in its operations in Oregon and California in 1956.[25] But Simpson was even more distant and its corporate goals even more opaque than M & M. The same year it bought M & M, the company's first foray into the Oregon timber industry, Simpson also acquired two other lumber companies in California, leveraging an unknown reserve of capital to dramatically expand its operations in dimensional lumber, plywood, and veneer in both Douglas fir and redwood trees.[26] Despite the danger that had accompanied such distant capital and control in the recent and distant past, the *Mill City Enterprise* expressed optimism about Simpson's takeover of M & M. The paper pointed out to its readers that "the company has long been a leader in perpetual-yield management of its forest lands," suggesting that the Simpson company would have a long and sustainable presence in the canyon.[27] The *Mill City Enterprise* also printed an interview with the company's public relations director under the headline "History of Steady Growth of Simpson Co.," with the subtitle "Employees Have Many Benefits."

But memories of past betrayals haunted local residents, who could not help but notice that outside corporations were making decisions that directly, and often negatively, affected the local timber industry and, consequently, their lives. Workers at the Simpson plants at Lyons and Idanha felt acutely decisions made at company headquarters in Seattle. In February 1957, just three months after taking over at M & M Wood Working, Simpson cut production to four days a week at all its plywood production plants on the West Coast, including its facilities in the canyon. The company cited a "lack of orders," pointing to a ten percent drop in plywood prices over the past year.[28] Blaming the market was nothing new—MCMC had done the same thing in the years leading up to its closure, and Hammond had often curtailed production in line with market demand. But those two examples did not bode well for residents dependent on Simpson's mills.

The company's finger-pointing at abstract markets left local workers and their families understandably confused when Simpson made decisions that seemed contradictory to the supposedly inexorable laws of supply and demand. In June 1960, the company added more equipment to its Lyons plant to increase production, suggesting that it saw the opportunity for growth. But plywood prices were down, as the *Mill City Enterprise* pointed out, and the paper asked whether workers should expect contraction, not expansion. The company reassured workers and the *Mill City Enterprise*'s readers that Simpson "did not plan any layoffs at the present time, and certainly hoped the market for plywood would strengthen soon."[29] Three months later, the company again cut back to a four-day workweek. The company's vice president explained that "with plywood prices below the cost of production, there is no alternative but to continue production curtailment."[30] The justification provided cold comfort to the three hundred employees of the Lyons mill whose paychecks had just been cut by twenty percent. Simpson decisions continued to buffet the canyon until 1967, when the company permanently shuttered both its Lyons plywood mill and its Idanha veneer mill, putting four hundred people out of work. "The reason for the closure," reported the *Mill City Enterprise*, "was given as a weak plywood market," although the price for plywood was actually up.[31] Simpson sold thirty thousand acres of timberland and its Lyons and Idanha mills to U.S. Plywood, which kept the plywood mill idle. After all, the market was down.

COOPERATION AND CONFLICT: UNIONS

The combined influence of outside corporations and local, family-owned firms in the growth of the timber industry in the postwar era produced complicated relationships between owners, managers, and workers. Thousands of people either worked in or depended on the timber industry. Logging was the central source of income throughout the postwar period, with nearly three-quarters of the workforce employed in the woods and mills in 1980.[32] Industrial relations in the area had always been complex, eschewing standard categories and expectations about class conflict or cooperation. During the Hammond era, the labor conflicts that affected timber production areas elsewhere in the Pacific Northwest in the early twentieth century did not come to the canyon, much to the delight of the Hammond Lumber Company.[33] While Hammond engaged in anti-labor and union-busting efforts at his facilities in California, the Mill City workforce challenged him mostly through independent economic activities, especially frequent job changes.

In the early twentieth century, the radical Industrial Workers of the World haunted the nightmares of Hammond and his managers, but the Wobblies had little presence in the canyon.[34] John Jackson, who grew up at Hammond's Camp 17 in the Detroit area, recalled that "my father and some of the men in the bunk houses were I.W.W. members but they never burned the sand shed or dynamited the company commissary."[35] Many Hammond employees were instead members of the 4L—the Loyal Legion of Loggers and Lumbermen—an industry-wide, timber company–friendly union created by the federal government, working in close cooperation with timber companies, that prohibited strikes, demanded loyalty pledges, and instituted eight-hour days and better conditions. Members of 4L wore membership buttons, started a vocational school for workers (taught by the mill's superintendent and chief engineer), and sent delegates to the 4L semiannual meeting in Portland. For the 1921 meeting, the union sent mill manager Frederick Olin, a revealing sign of the company-friendly nature of the 4L union and, more broadly, the canyon during the Hammond era.

During and after the Great Depression and World War II, when the federal government under Franklin Roosevelt's New Deal became much more supportive of unions as a "countervailing" force against the power of capitalists, the labor movement in the canyon became more independent while remaining generally cooperative.[36] National unions, both those of the American Federation of Labor and the Congress of Industrial Organizations (which merged in 1955 to become the AFL-CIO), established local chapters in conjunction with the construction of Detroit Dam and the rebounding local timber industry. In 1942, for example, the father of Carmen Elaine Stafford of Niagara went to work for Mt. Jefferson Lumber, where he became a member of the International Woodworkers of America (IWA, a CIO union) and attended union meetings, as Stafford recorded in her diary.[37] The unions became important advocates for the interests of workers, whether they were employed by local companies or outside firms. For example, although local timber firms failed to secure contracts for clearing Detroit reservoir, the local chapter of the IWA negotiated contracts with the outside companies to employ its canyon members.[38] In an interview with the *Mill City Enterprise*, the IWA's local representative highlighted not only the practical benefits of the contract, such as new "vacation pay plan based on hours worked," but also the value of union workers: "The IWA has the most experienced group of workers to draw from for work in the woods."

The unions kept the peace with employers and kept employees happy through deliberate and thoughtful procedural steps, including carefully negotiated and elaborately detailed contracts.[39] Some contracts were specific to the industry and work at hand; for instance, a 1949 contract between Detroit Dam subcontractor Morris-Knudson (M-K) and the Building and Construction Trades Department of the American Federation of Labor stated, "when required, rubber boots shall be furnished by the Employer on concrete, tunnel, sewer, and water-main work. When required, slickers shall be furnished on tunnel work."[40] More generally, contracts established a steady and dependable relationship between the companies and union employees. That 1949 contract between M-K and the AFL, for example, guaranteed the stability of the union by requiring all workers to be union members. The contract also guaranteed the company a reliable workforce by banning strikes and lockouts. For those seeking economic harmony and growth, contractually negotiated peaceful relations between employers and employees offered an amicable solution.

But the contracts also revealed a fundamental tension between employees on the one hand and employers—local or outside—on the other. When canyon unions and employers negotiated terms, they did so as part of larger, regional organizations. At Freres Lumber, workers participated in and were represented by the Western States Regional Council of the International Woodworkers of America, while their boss Bob Freres participated in and was represented by the Timber Operators Council, Inc. The agreements covered myriad "bread and butter" worker issues, from guaranteeing holidays and a standard forty-hour work week to regularizing wages at standard and overtime rates. At the Freres plants in Lyons, union members saw regular pay increases come through contract negotiations: 7.5-cent increases in 1958 and again in 1959, followed by a 3.5 percent increase in 1960 and another 1 percent increase the next year.[41] In 1960, pay rates started at $2.20 per hour on the green chain (where unskilled laborers pulled lumber through the mill) and up to $3.53 per hour for the more skilled work of saw filers; in 1963, those rates were at $2.34 and $3.69, respectively, and that year's contract stipulated a 5-cent raise the next year and 6-cent raises for the next two years after that. Those wages matched other timber workers in the Pacific Northwest's Douglas fir region: an average $2.45 for green chain and $3.61 for saw filers in 1964.[42]

Unions secured other benefits meant to improve the quality of life for timber workers, such as employer-sponsored insurance benefits, covering health, life, and accidental death and dismemberment. In 1961, the IWA scored a major victory for its members at Freres: a new pension plan into which Freres would pay ten cents per hour for every hourly employee. Moreover, these agreements sought at some level to equalize the playing field between employees and owners. Timber workers gained some power through contract provisions that prevented employers from requiring overtime, the establishment of employee "Plant Committees" responsible for bringing grievances to employers, and the empowerment of employee safety committees to "go into any part of the plant or operation at any time for safety inspection when called upon to do so by any employee of the operation," as the 1959 agreement between the IWA and

Freres explained. Such provisions recognized the reality that different and sometimes competing interests pitted canyon timber workers against timber companies, whether locally owned or not.

Sometimes those competing interests could not be reconciled, and simmering tensions between employees and their employers boiled over into outright conflict. Canyon timber workers were not afraid to confront and challenge their employers, even when those employers were neighbors. In May and June 1945, workers at Mt. Jefferson Lumber in Lyons went on strike. The walkout affected the home life of families like the Staffords in Niagara, as Carmen Stafford recorded: "May 31, 1945: Jeff on strike, Dad didn't work. . . . June 3, 1945: They are still on strike at Jeff."[43] The strike also pitted neighbors against each other; although Mt. Jefferson Lumber was based in Portland, its Lyons plant was managed by local resident Walt Miller. For a few decades after the war, timber workers continued to assert themselves through their unions. In the spring of 1950, the local chapter of the IWA authorized a strike in response to employer recalcitrance during contract negotiations.[44] In July 1955, AFL workers at the M & M plywood plant in Lyons joined other M & M workers in Oregon and California in a strike when M & M refused to renew an existing contract; the strike lasted for a month before M & M backed down.[45] Another strike came in 1963, when workers at the Simpson (formerly M & M) plywood mill demanded, and eventually secured, wage increases.

The period of union power in the North Santiam Canyon lasted briefly. Reflecting broader national trends in the labor movement, and especially among timber workers, the International Woodworkers of America became increasingly irrelevant.[46] A variety of factors contributed to the IWA's fall, including union infighting, persistent challenges by employers, and, perhaps most importantly, the diminishing presence in the area of the larger outside timber corporations with whom the IWA had previously engaged and negotiated. By the 1980s, there was just one union mill in the canyon: Champion Lumber's plywood mill in Idanha, which closed in 1985. The *Mill City Enterprise*, for one, was grateful, editorializing in 1988 that "Non union labor facilitates frank and open communication between owners and their employees," suggesting that local workers and local timber companies got along better without external influence.[47] But the decades of union influence had revealed fractures in the canyon, showing that there were tensions not only between locals and outsiders, but also between neighbors: workers, managers, and owners.

CORPORATE COOPERATION: "GABFESTS" OR COLLUSION?

Among timber companies in the area, a sense of unity and purpose in the face of external opposition dominated. When U.S. Plywood bought out Simpson in 1967, an unnamed local "businessman" told the *Mill City Enterprise*, "this will do us no good, but this area has received rougher blows and has survived and continued to grow."[48] This positive attitude coupled with a spirit of cooperation among local timber company owners and managers to help the area "survive and grow." That cooperative approach had previously manifested itself in the creation of locally owned businesses like Mill City Planing and Processing and Mill City Manufacturing Company. As smaller companies and mills sold out or shut down, the local timber industry consolidated into three companies: Young & Morgan, Freres Lumber Company, and Frank Lumber Company. These three businesses had their origins in the crucible of the Great Depression, and the companies had grown together during and after World War II. Together, they developed a series of understandings and strategies to retain local control in the face of outside forces.

The companies' owners and managers knew each other well, and they would occasionally meet to share information and discuss business. As the biographer of the Freres family business explains, these conversations established and reinforced general agreements and assumptions about efficient business practices in the local timber industry.[49] Acknowledging the relative strengths and specialties of each other's operations, the companies would trade or sell each other logs. For example, Frank Lumber Company's mills ran on hemlock, while Freres' operations used Douglas fir, so if Freres bought a timber sale that contained hemlock, Freres would sell those hemlock logs to Frank. The companies also acknowledged each other's operating areas and jurisdiction, with Young & Morgan in the upper canyon and Freres and Frank in the lower canyon. Because, as Freres would later explain, "Logs were heavy and no one wanted to haul them any further than they had to," it made more economic sense for Young & Morgan to take timber from the upper canyon and Freres and Frank to take timber from the lower canyon. This information and these assumptions informed conversations about upcoming federal timber sales: how many board feet, the type and quality of the timber, and whose mills and processing facilities would best be suited for each different kind of sale. From the perspective of the companies, these discussions were "like informal gabfests," as a timber cruiser for Freres Lumber explained.[50]

One of the practical effects of these "gabfests" and the arrangements they produced was to reduce competition between Freres, Frank, and

Young & Morgan. Specifically, the agreements helped tamp down on the vicious bidding wars for federal timber sales that plagued the canyon. These live auctions often resulted in timber tracts selling for three times or more of their appraised value.[51] The bidding wars became such a problem that in 1965 Detroit District Ranger Wendell Jones gave a presentation titled "Timber Price Structure" to the North Santiam Chamber of Commerce. After explaining the US Forest Service's method for appraising timber sales, Wendell was forced to admit that "he did not have any answer for the overbidding on timber sales." When someone suggested moving to written, sealed bids instead of live auctions, Wendell said "he felt that local bidders would not like this situation as it would leave too large a chance for outside bidders to come in and take the timber from mill operating operators here."[52] That was exactly what local timber companies were trying to avoid.

With the Forest Service not offering any solutions to the problem of overbidding, canyon timber company gabfests took on increasing importance in deciding who got what timber sale for what price. By acknowledging each other's strengths and jurisdiction and discussing which sales they were interested in, the companies could cooperate, stepping out of the way when a timber sale better suited another operation. In practice, that meant fewer bids at live auctions, lower prices for many timber sales, and less revenue from public lands. This arrangement became increasingly effective in the late 1960s, with timber sale prices dropping to less than five percent above the appraised value of the lumber in some cases. For example, in January 1967, Freres secured 10,700,000 board feet of timber for $628,865.00 after a bidding war that more reached more than double the appraised value of $283,074.00. But at a sale in May 1968, Young & Morgan bought 2,100,000 board feet for $49,529.90, just seven percent more than the appraised value of $46,095.80. The *Mill City Enterprise* observed, "Although there was [sic] four qualified bidders only one bid was cast," but the paper did not venture an explanation for that curious fact.[53] The *Mill City Enterprise* also reported without commentary other timber sales at low prices, such as a September 1968 sale of 138,000 board feet to Frank for $24 per thousand, appraised at $23.60 per thousand, and a September 1969 sale of 3.6 million board feet to Young & Morgan for $77.30 per thousand, appraised at $69.75 per thousand.[54] It seemed that local timber companies had arranged a truce on timber bidding wars.

For the federal government, the conversations that led to this truce and lower prices were not just casual gabfests. They represented conspiracy, collusion, and theft from the American people. In September 1974, the

US District Attorney brought federal antitrust charges against Bob Freres of Freres Lumber, Amandus Frank of Frank Lumber, Vernon Morgan of Young & Morgan and Bugaboo Timber (a Young & Morgan subsidiary), and L. James Bagley of Champion International. Bagley was the logging and timber manager for the Oregon Division of Champion International, a New York–based company that merged with U.S. Plywood in 1967 and ran a veneer plant in Idanha (which Freres would buy and shut down in 1985). The indictment accused the companies of collusion, focusing on the period from 1968 to 1971. The companies faced charges of running a sophisticated two-pronged conspiracy intended to protect their business interests. For local timber sales that only interested Freres, Frank, Young & Morgan, and Champion, the companies would limit bids and keep the sale price low; for timber sales that attracted outside timber companies, the conspirators would bid high so as to keep the timber in their mills and hopefully drive off the outside competition. The Forest Service could point to public evidence of this in the *Mill City Enterprise*. At a timber sale in September 1969, Young & Morgan bought 23.6 million board feet for $77.30 per thousand, ten percent above the appraised value of $69.75 per thousand.[55] A month later, Frank Lumber paid more than twice the appraised value for 2.164 million board feet in an auction that also attracted a bid from San Francisco–based timber giant Crown Zellerbach.[56] The conclusion was hard to escape: local timber companies had conspired to control timber sale prices and reduce competition, a clear violation of federal antitrust laws.

The trial came down to a fundamental difference of perspective from inside and outside the canyon on the intent and purpose of cooperation among the timber companies. Whereas the *Mill City Enterprise* saw little to comment on regarding timber sales like that of May 1968, in which the sole bidder Young & Morgan got the sale for just a little over the appraised value, the federal government saw a smoking gun—clear evidence that the companies had plotted together to keep timber sale prices down, and in so doing robbed the American public of a just price for logs from national forests. The companies admitted that yes, they had met, and yes, they had discussed upcoming timber sales and who was interested in them, although the companies denied having discussed prices. Federal prosecutors, meanwhile, argued that even if prices were not discussed, the meetings still resulted in agreement about who would purchase which timber sale, thereby effectively and illegally eliminating competition. What to the federal government amounted to a conspiracy to defraud the American public of millions of dollars in federal timber sales was to local timber companies a genuine, innocent practice among friends and fellow community members to prevent ruinous competition and protect the most important industry in the North Santiam Canyon.

In July 1975, federal judge Robert C. Belloni issued his verdict. Belloni had already acquitted Frank and Bagley in June, concluding that the federal government had insufficient evidence to try the two men. He found the Freres and Young & Morgan companies guilty of "an implied agreement: to eliminate competition for these timber sales; to reduce the price being paid for these timber sales; and, to allocate these timber sales among themselves." Belloni concluded that, beginning sometime in late 1967, the companies had started to meet to discuss their interest in timber sales, resulting in "implied agreements to act on this information" and to reduce competition on federal timber sales between March 1968 and into the fall of 1971. "A line must be drawn," wrote the judge, between legal "exchanges of information" and illegal conspiracies to defraud the government and the American people, and "the defendants crossed that line."[57] The judge fined all companies involved in the case: $50,000 for Champion and $30,000 each for Freres Lumber and Young & Morgan. As for the individual defendants Vernon Morgan and Robert Freres, Belloni concluded that they "are not bad people. They're good people" who were nevertheless guilty of "technical business violations."[58] Belloni fined the men $5,000 each and sentenced them to five years' probation and sixty days of community service.[59] Attorneys for the defendants appealed the decision, but the Ninth Circuit Court of Appeals upheld the ruling, and the Supreme Court declined to hear the case. Belloni added another $400,000 in fines during a civil trial three years later. Meanwhile, timber sale prices went up dramatically; the *Mill City Enterprise* reported a year after the verdict that live auctions were bringing in "about double the appraised price."[60]

Although the expensive timber, fines, probation, and community service penalties stung, the real pain started in October 1977, when the US Forest Service announced that, based on the guilty verdict, it would prohibit Freres and Young & Morgan from participating in federal timber sales in the canyon for two years. The companies were livid and portrayed the penalty as an attack on the entire community. While they continued to maintain their innocence, they also argued that the prohibition—debarment, in Forest Service parlance—would result in economic catastrophe. In September 1977, while defense attorneys appealed to the courts and various Oregon politicians pressured the Forest Service to back down, the timber companies warned local residents of the consequences of debarment. "A capacity crowd filled the Frontier Inn at the North Santiam Chamber of Commerce dinner meeting," reported the *Mill City Enterprise*, "to hear Robert T. Freres of Freres Lumber, Lyons; Vernon R. Morgan and Robert Young, of Young & Morgan, Mill City." The timber men explained "what would happen in the Canyon area if the Forest Service is successful in preventing the mill owners from bidding on national forest timber sales for two years as the agency proposes to do." Freres, Young, and Morgan warned of dire consequences: "The proposed debarment against three of the area's largest lumber mills will directly affect the employment of about 700 employees."[61] And that would be just the beginning; the effects of hundreds of unemployed millworkers would extend to every other sector of the North Santiam Canyon economy, from the loggers that fed the mills timber to the restaurants that fed the millworkers.

Over the next few weeks, conversation in the area focused on how the North Santiam Canyon communities needed to come together to prevent what the paper and the companies framed as economic disaster brought by the outside forces of the federal government. The Detroit City Council weighed in, sending a letter "giving non-support for debarment of local mills. Council felt prosecution, if warranted, should be on an individual basis only."[62] The Forest Service acknowledged that the debarment would create economic difficulties. But it also argued that it had a responsibility to represent the public interest; after all, the collusion brought down prices on timber from national forests, thereby robbing taxpayers of millions of dollars in revenue. Ultimately, the Forest Service decided to reduce the debarment period to one year. Judge Belloni thought the decision "too severe," and he released Vernon Morgan and Bob Freres from their court-ordered sixty days of community service. The companies paid their fines and served their times, including a year away from timber sales. Debarment from federal timber sales in the Detroit Ranger District led to some economic disruption; Freres Lumber, for example, blamed the debarment for its decision to lay off one shift at the mill for a brief period. But the companies continued to purchase lumber from other ranger districts as well as state lands—the industry "survived and continued to grow."[63]

From the perspective of many locals, the collusion conviction reinforced an increasingly popular and powerful narrative: outsiders did not understand and could not be trusted. The canyon had to unite as a "timber community" and confront outside forces by whatever means possible, even if those means might appear illegal. In July 1992, a federal jury convicted Paul Knapp, a sixty-four-year-old retired log scaler from Detroit, of defrauding the federal government. The jury found that between 1985 and 1988, Knapp had falsely appraised good, usable logs as cull (that is, worthless), thereby allowing logging companies to take the logs without paying for them. The federal prosecutor in the case alleged that Knapp had acted on behalf of a number of local logging companies. For his services, Knapp allegedly received cash payments, a discounted Ford Bronco truck from Young & Morgan's car dealership, and whiskey. The jury acquitted Knapp of conspiracy, and the federal prosecutor did not bring the alleged co-conspirators to trial for lack of evidence, but the prosecutor was convinced that Knapp had not acted on his own.[64] The federal prosecutor continued to pursue the case, and in 1993, Young & Morgan paid $1.7 million in civil fines for its role in the log theft scheme.[65] The fraud conviction echoed similar themes from the collusion trial fifteen years before, with local timber companies explaining their actions as innocent efforts to retain local control in the face of abusive and excessive federal power and intervention.

This narrative of canyon versus outsiders competed with the reality that not everyone had the same perspective and in fact held competing interests. In June 1988, a dozen employees of North Santiam Plywood, a Young & Morgan company, penned a letter to the *Mill City Enterprise* complaining about poor pay and required employee contributions to the company's health insurance and retirement plans.[66] The plant's management explained that employees still had the opportunity to work overtime and that the company had also instituted a production bonus system; workers responded that "people are getting hurt trying to correct problems" that came from working too fast for the bonuses.[67] Tensions simmered for the next few months, until February 15, 1989, when the 150 workers at North Santiam Plywood held a vote to decide whether to form a union. Two months before, the company had warned its employees that it might cut three-quarters of the jobs at North Santiam Plywood—if the plant could remain open at all. The December announcement explained that "The plywood plant no longer has the ability to show a reasonable profit" and that the cutbacks or closure were slated as soon as February 15—the day scheduled for the union vote. The vote failed. The next day, workers found a new notice posted at North Santiam Plywood. "Due to an unexpected stronger plywood market, we will continue to operate on the present basis for the short range." The notice did not mention the union vote of the day before, but the timing suggested a clear message: workers and owners of the canyon timber community should stick together rather than following class divisions to economic catastrophe.

Both the log-scaling trial and the North Santiam Plywood union vote unfolded under the shadow of what the local timber industry portrayed as a new outside threat: environmentalism. In the December 1988 note warning of impending layoffs, North Santiam Plywood explained that there were "factors no longer under the company's control." One of those factors was "competing substitute products" (referring to OSB, a cheaper alternative to plywood), but another was "higher prices for raw material brought about by an increasingly smaller supply of public timber." Everyone who read the memo knew exactly what that meant: the US Forest Service was no longer selling as much timber as it did during the boom decades of the 1950s, 1960s, and 1970s. The cause of these problems, said many canyon residents and especially timber company officials, was outside environmentalists who had taken up the cause of an endangered species, the spotted owl, which lived in old-growth forests, including those in the North Santiam Canyon. To timber companies, timber workers, and the "timber community" of the North Santiam Canyon, urban environmentalists presented a new external, and even existential, threat.

7

Environmentalism and Tourism in the Canyon

In the last quarter of the twentieth century, the belief that the canyon was under siege by powerful external forces became an essential part of local identity. The local timber industry and supporters cast the community as the victim of well-organized, politically connected, and legally savvy environmental preservation groups (and their growing base of support) that sought to protect wild and beautiful places throughout the United States, and especially in the American West.[1] The North Santiam Canyon became one of the most visible and vitriolic sites of confrontation over differing ideas about nature. Those confrontations first centered on the area's old-growth forests, the habitat of the endangered spotted owl and the main source of raw material for the local timber industry. Those fights transformed the logging and milling business and encouraged a shift toward a tourism-based economy. Then, a new struggle arose over the waters of the North Santiam and how the river would be shared among its various stakeholders: downstream urban residents using it for drinking water and pollution abatement, struggling fish populations needing streamflow for survival, and the local tourism businesses depending on the river's allure. In both the old-growth and river-use struggles, environmentalism and environmental concerns, represented through preservationist as well as recreational tourists, became an increasingly abstract and powerful force against which some people reacted with anger and vitriol. That ire became a central part of local identity—us versus them—environmentalists, the federal governments, and urbanites.

CONSERVATION AND PRESERVATION IN THE CANYON

In the North Santiam Canyon as elsewhere in the American West, discussions about the myriad different values of the nonhuman world stretched much further into the past than the angry debates of the 1980s and 1990s would suggest. The Kalapuyans, Molallans, and other native peoples regarded different specific places in the area, such as Mt. Jefferson, as

This commemorative plate produced in 1974 highlights different elements of the North Santiam Canyon's identity: the timber industry (seven of the fifteen encircling images are of milling facilities), tourism and recreation (including Marion Forks Lodge and Hoodoo Ski Bowl), and wilderness (Mt. Jefferson) and technology (Detroit Dam). From the author's personal collection.

sacred.[2] Mid-nineteenth-century gold prospectors commented on the scenic value of the canyon, calling it "most grand and sublime." Ephraim Henness drew on turn-of-the-century Progressive Era ideas about conservationism when he complained in 1907 about A. B. Hammond's "wasteful" logging practices, preferring that the forests be entrusted in "the hands of the people and not in the hands of the large timber monopolies." The *Mill City Logue* in 1929 praised local wilderness, marveling at the "virgin forest of stately firs, unmarred by the work of humans," on the road up to Breitenbush.[3] From the spiritual and sublime values of nature to conservationism and preservationism, the full spectrum of environmentalist philosophy had been on display for as long as humans had occupied the area.[4]

In the decades after World War II, environmental conservation efforts directed at the North Santiam Canyon elicited mixed responses based on the effects those efforts would have on the local economy. Residents sometimes acted as concerned conservationists when they perceived a threat to the potential for tourism revenue. In January 1960, the North Santiam Sportsman's Club "went on record as being against the construction of a third dam on the North Santiam above Niagara."[5] The club worried that this new dam, a $25 million private project, would "ruin 10 miles of the best spawning grounds on the North Santiam River." The project never got past the hypothetical stage; instead, Marion County and the State of Oregon created a park at Niagara in 1961.[6] Local concerns about the environment and tourism extended outside the area, as well. In 1953, the North Santiam Chamber of Commerce signaled its disapproval for the proposed Beaver Marsh hydroelectric project on the McKenzie River, another tributary to the Willamette River located about seventy-five miles south of the North Santiam River.[7] The chamber gave $25 to a McKenzie River preservationist group and asserted that "anything that would damage this scenic area would be harmful to tourist business, as well as ruining one of the favorite fishing spots of local sportsmen."[8] Such sentiments demonstrated an appreciation of the scenic, recreational, and economic value of nature left to a "wild" state.

But when environmental conservation and preservation efforts seemed to pose a threat to economic development, the scenic and recreational values of nature were quickly discarded. For example, the North Santiam Chamber of Commerce, which opposed development of the McKenzie River in 1953, fully supported the failed hydroelectric project at Niagara seven years later, stating that the hydroelectric and corresponding economic development "benefits outweighed the losses."[9] This particular cost-benefit analysis—framing environmental protection as opposed to economic development—became especially clear and acrimonious when the local timber industry's unfettered access to public forest land was challenged by environmental protection efforts, starting with debates over wilderness in the 1960s. Nationally, these debates centered on the drafting and passage of the 1964 Wilderness Act, although as Paul Sutter, Mark Harvey, and other historians have shown, fights over wilderness areas began much earlier.[10] In the Pacific Northwest, such debates centered on the creation and expansion of wilderness areas in national forests, and as Kevin Marsh has shown, the boundaries of these areas were "a joint product of competing interest groups"—environmentalists and timber industry advocates. One such boundary was drawn in the North Santiam Canyon in 1968, when Congress approved a US Forest Service recommendation to expand the Mt. Jefferson Primitive Area from 85,000 to 95,540 acres.[11] Although the resulting Mt. Jefferson Wilderness included popular recreation areas around Marion and Pamelia Lakes, it deliberately did not include much valuable timberland—certainly not as much as environmental protection groups had asked for in their own 125,000-acre proposal for the wilderness area. Because of the relatively limited nature of the Forest Service's proposal, as Marsh writes, "there was a relative lack of concerted, public opposition on the part of the timber industry in the Oregon."[12]

But any expansion of the Mt. Jefferson Primitive Area elicited fierce opposition among timber industry advocates in the North Santiam Canyon. The editor of the *Mill City Enterprise* raised an initially muted alarm that pointed the finger at environmental preservation groups: "The Sierra Club and other outdoor clubs no doubt do a lot of good, but I do feel that they are getting over ambitious in tying up timber land." In this framing of the debate, any increase in environmental protection represented a threat to the local economy and local residents: "Soon, unless it is brought to a halt, the conservationists will have all the land tied up, and there will be nothing left to be utilized by the general public."[13] Although the expanded Mt. Jefferson Wilderness Area left out thirty thousand acres of valuable timberland when Congress approved the area in 1968, the *Mill City Enterprise* nevertheless lamented what it portrayed as the loss of local power in the face of outside forces: "Local residents who were battling to keep Marion Lake out of the Wilderness area lost their fight. Many telegrams were sent to Washington, but to no avail. Evidently the Sierra Club and the Western Outdoor Clubs had enough lobby power to get their way."[14] From this perspective, even though the timber industry maintained access to timber that might have been "tied up" in a wilderness area, the North Santiam Canyon had fallen victim to the "lobby power" of far-off, abstract environmental protection organizations.

That sense of victimization continued and intensified—and occasionally transformed into fear and hate—during the old-growth forest controversies of the 1980s and 1990s. As the struggle over the expansion of the Mt. Jefferson Wilderness demonstrates and the work of historians has shown, this fight over logging on public lands—variously referred to as the ancient forest, old-growth, and spotted owl debates, controversies, and crises—had been decades in the making.[15] After World War II, timber companies began cutting ever more trees on more public land in more obviously destructive ways, while conservation and preservation groups increasingly demanded more environmental protection for recreational, aesthetic, and other reasons, and resource management agencies—especially the Forest Service—tried to accommodate such demands while still prioritizing timber extraction in what the historian Paul Hirt has called a "conspiracy of optimism."[16] The pressure finally broke in 1988, when a number of environmental groups, initially led by an organization based in Boston, Massachusetts, successfully petitioned the federal government to consider the northern spotted owl (*Strix occidentalis caurina*) as a protected species under the Endangered Species Act (ESA). The ESA raised concerned eyebrows in the canyon at the time of its passage in

1973; Dennis Frank, president of Frank Lumber, remembers being told by then-Senator Mark Hatfield not to worry about what Hatfield considered a harmless salve to environmentalists.[17] Hatfield could not have been more wrong. The push to list the spotted owl under the ESA would require the federal government to protect the owl's old-growth forest habitat, which was precisely the point. Preservationists sought to protect complex ancient forest ecosystems, and the northern spotted owl served as an indicator species for the health of those forests.

The effort to protect the owl had an immediate chilling effect on timber sales on public land in the Pacific Northwest. In the Willamette National Forest's Detroit District, where North Santiam Canyon timber companies got most of their logs, sales of federal timber dropped from 29,000,000 board feet in the first quarter of fiscal year 1988-89 to less than 400,000 board feet in the second quarter.[18] In June 1990, the US Fish and Wildlife Service listed the owl as an endangered species, and in May 1991, a federal judge issued an injunction barring timber sales in spotted owl habitat, bringing logging in the North Santiam Canyon to an effective standstill. When Dennis Frank called Senator Hatfield and asked what he should do now that the power of the ESA had become so obvious, Hatfield could only offer one suggestion: "pray."[19]

At the same time that timber companies were losing access to public federal forests, they also feared that state efforts might shut them out of public forest lands at the headwaters of the Little North Fork of the North Santiam River. Near a small stream called Opal Creek, Douglas fir trees towered over the wreckage and detritus of mining operations, creating what preservation groups called one of the last remaining low-altitude old-growth forests in the United States. Earlier efforts to protect Opal Creek had failed, but by 1989, heightened public interest in preservation and the improved legislative and legal savvy of environmental groups led to an effort to create the Opal Creek Ancient Forest State Park.[20] That state legislation failed, but efforts to protect Opal Creek continued, drawing national media attention and discussions in the US Senate. Taken together, the efforts to preserve Opal Creek and spotted owl habitat—all part of a broader push to protect old growth forests—posed an existential threat to the timber industry and timber communities.

That crisis was real, but the causes were much more complex than owls, parks, and environmentalism. As studies by W. Scott Prudham, Paul Hirt, and others have shown, those factors included intensified factory-style extraction and production in the timber industry, federal forest policy that overpromised the capacity of a limited resource (large old-growth trees), increasing productivity in logging and milling, and the boom/bust nature of lumber market.[21] These forces coalesced to undermine the long-term sustainability of the timber industry and the stability of income and employment in the woods well before environmentalists started talking about the spotted owl and Opal Creek. And some of those factors came from the way the local timber industry had evolved in the decades before the ancient forest debates. Freres, Frank, and Young & Morgan had all come to depend heavily on timber sales from public lands—Frank Lumber, for example, got around ninety percent of its logs from public land. Moreover, the local timber industry had decided to invest heavily in mill equipment specifically and exclusively designed for the enormous old-growth trees that came out of the national forests. As the use of those public lands shifted from timber production to habitat and ecosystem preservation, the timber industry—and the communities that had come to depend on that industry—claimed that environmentalism threatened their existence, simplifying the existential threat faced by places like the North Santiam Canyon.

RESPONDING TO ENVIRONMENTALISM

In their initial response to this crisis, loggers, millworkers, and their families in the North Santiam Canyon joined with similar Oregon communities in a series of protests called Yellow Ribbon Rallies.[22] The first of these occurred in August 1988, when around ten thousand people, bedecked in yellow clothes and riding in buses, vans, and log trucks decorated with yellow ribbons and flags, descended on the Josephine County Fairground in Grants Pass, Oregon, for the "Silver Fire Round-Up." The previous summer, the Silver Complex Fire had burned nearly a hundred thousand acres in the Siskyou National Forest in southwestern Oregon, and environmental protection groups had successfully prevented timber industry efforts to cut the area. Protestors came, as the *Mill City Enterprise* explained, to support "salvaging as much of the burned timber as quickly as possible to mitigate the effects of decay and return the area to a thriving forest."[23] Robert Freres—son of Bob Freres, and the company's government liaison officer since 1979—told the *Mill City Enterprise* that the roundup had been "the biggest show of solidarity in the state's history," seizing on and cultivating a particular sense of unity as "timber communities" that would hopefully sustain—and certainly come to define—the North Santiam Canyon.

These convoys and rallies, and the yellow ribbons that featured so prominently in the protests, became the symbol of efforts to continue

At Yellow Ribbon Rallies, individuals and families from the North Santiam Canyon participated in the ancient forest controversies of the 1980s and 1990s in a variety of ways, from frustrated protest to the more whimsical approach shown in this undated (probably 1989) photograph. Courtesy of Myles and Sue McMillan.

logging apace in the North Santiam Canyon and throughout the West. Yellow Ribbon Rallies were held at numerous locations throughout the state, including the high school gymnasium in the small town of Sweet Home, the Oregon State Capitol in Salem, and Pioneer Courthouse Square in downtown Portland. Although these rallies were most frequently associated with the spotted owl controversy, rallies were also held to protest efforts to protect the Opal Creek area. The canyon made a strong showing at all of these rallies. Hundreds of area timber workers and their families traveled to Salem in February 1989 to protest the creation of Opal Creek State Park. For the Pioneer Courthouse Square event in 1990, schools, mills, and most businesses closed for the day, and entire families traveled to Portland, dressed in yellow t-shirts and hats.[24] The affairs were designed to encourage and display a united front as a timber community; the Freres Lumber Company of Lyons even paid its employees to attend a rally in Salem.[25] Myles McMillan worked with Young & Morgan at the time and attended the Portland rally with his family, and he remembers the energy as something that "nobody had ever seen or expected."[26] But he also recalls a sense of frustration and futility, with everyone returning home after the rallies, wondering whether their actions had done any good.

In 1989, a group of North Santiam Canyon residents formed an advocacy group called Communities for a Great Oregon (CGO) to present a more organized and hopefully more efficacious and fulfilling response. The CGO wanted to "support a stable timber supply for Oregon's economy," as the *Mill City Enterprise* explained, and sought especially "education of the public as an objective." The group brought together timber companies large and small: its founding president was Tom Hirons, owner and operator of Mad Creek Logging, an independent "gyppo" outfit, its vice president was Robert Freres, and the board also included Jim Morgan of Young & Morgan and Dennis Frank of Frank Lumber. The CGO quickly developed into a sophisticated political organization that pursued a variety of strategies to defend the timber industry. The group hired a full-time administrative assistant and published a newsletter distributed to its growing membership base as well as to local and state legislators and the media. CGO representatives actively lobbied legislators to support bills that would protect the timber industry and demanded that they reject environmental protection legislation. The CGO organized letter-writing campaigns to politicians and the media, and it published voters' guides comparing politician scores from the Oregon League of Conservation Voters (the lower the score the better) and the Oregon Farm Bureau (the higher the better). Beyond politics, the CGO encouraged its members to boycott businesses that supported environmental causes, including REI, Levi's, Patagonia, Target, and Amway; organized "Earth Day Forestry Tours" of local mills and forests to "educate the public about the wise use of our public lands, specifically timber"; and informed its members about aid programs like Oregon's Dislocated Worker Program, which provided unemployment and job-training benefits.[27]

The CGO also cultivated relationships and developed partnerships outside of the North Santiam Canyon. The Mill City CGO encouraged the formation of CGO chapters in other Oregon timber communities such as Sweet Home; it joined with other natural resource-dependent Oregon businesses to form the umbrella group Oregon Lands Coalition (OLC); and the CGO also helped form the Alliance for America, a national group that, as Hirons explained to the *Statesman Journal*, "would seek to defend private property rights and to challenge additional limits on grazing, logging and mining on public lands."[28] The CGO leveraged these regional and national connections in various ways: publishing reports from "OLC Network News" in the CGO newsletter, bringing in OLC staff to facilitate strategic planning sessions and presenting a united front to politicians, as the group did in September 1992, when CGO members joined OLC and Alliance for America representatives on a trip to Washington, DC, meant to "educate government decision-makers and the media about the need for sensible environmental decisions and protection of private property rights," as the CGO newsletter summarized.[29]

Communities for a Great Oregon (CGO) supported the timber industry and cultivated a "timber community" identity in many ways, such as by holding a softball tournament at the 1992 Timber Fest. One of the softball teams called itself "Bye Bye Babe," referring to the effort to recall Oregon Democratic governor Barbara Roberts, portrayed by the CGO and other timber industry groups as antagonistic to timber communities. From the Liz VanLeeuewen Spotted Owl Collection, Series III, Box 4, folder "CGO – Mill City – 1991-1992," Special Collections and Archives Research Center, Oregon State University Libraries.

In many ways, the CGO was an outward facing organization. In a newsletter article titled "The Loggers Image," for example, the CGO encouraged its members to become more public relations and media savvy, and to "put a human face on logging."[30] But the CGO sought above all to cultivate a sense of shared fate and consciousness among people in the canyon. Upon her election to the CGO's presidency in 1992, Karen Clark explained the different identities that came together to make her a timber community activist: "I am a wife of a logger, mother of a 19 year old son, and a payroll clerk in a logging office."[31] From this perspective, no matter where one fit in the hierarchy of power in the local timber industry, everyone was in this together. The group organized social events to help develop this shared identity. The CGO created a float for the Fourth of July parade in Mill City—the biggest community festival of the year—and put on a summer Timber Fest, complete with dunk tanks, raffles, and a softball tournament.[32]

The CGO, local timber industry, and their supporters sought to include everyone in this identity. In the same newsletter calling for a boycott of pro-environment groups, CGO member George Nelson penned "A Community Plea," drawing attention to out-of-work residents and calling on "local mills and businesses [to] pledge to employ Canyon subcontractors and employees first for whatever work is available," Local consumers had an equally important role, for "every dollar spent locally generates a ripple effect that can support entire communities. Those dollars spent outside our area to achieve a savings of a few cents can be the death knell of us all." Nelson ended his plea with both despair and hope, calling on his neighbors to "Refuse to help in the construction of a coffin for our timber communities, instead pledge to contribute to the effort to provide a future for everyone."[33] In this dire framing of the old-growth controversy, "locals"—timber company executives, millworkers, gyppo loggers, retail business owners, families, and everyone in the canyon—needed to join together to confront the threat posed by the "outside."

For observers in the media, the controversy represented an irresistible story. The situation offered too many easy dichotomies: old-growth forests versus small communities, urban sophisticates in the courtroom versus rural Americans in taverns, and, most infamously, owls versus jobs. The North Santiam Canyon emerged as one of the most dramatic and well-known battlegrounds in this "timber war," and journalists descended on the area. In 1990, Oregon Public Broadcasting partnered with the BBC and West Virginia Public Broadcasting to produce a documentary film called *Mill City*, focusing on the community where the "struggle is raging between environmentalists who want to save the remaining ancient forests and loggers who are dependant [sic] upon cutting the forests for their survival." Turner Broadcasting System and WETA-TV from Washington, DC, created a film about Opal Creek called *Ancient Forests: Rage over Trees*, narrated by Paul Newman, who two decades earlier directed and produced a film version of Ken Kesey's pro–gyppo logger novel *Sometimes a Great Notion*. The journalist David Seidemann came to the canyon to gather material for *Showdown at Opal Creek: The Battle for America's Last Wilderness*, a best-selling book about Opal Creek that featured compelling characters and caricatures from the area, including its protagonists Tom Hirons, the independent logger fighting to save his way of life, and his former friend George Atiyeh, a governor's nephew and miner-turned-environmentalist at Opal Creek. Although the books, films, news reports, and newspaper articles sometimes sought to portray nuances of power, each one reinforced a story of conflict between the people of the North Santiam Canyon and the outside world.

Residents helped create that narrative, too. The pages of the *Mill City Enterprise* filled with reports, editorials, and letters blasting environmentalists, politicians, and outsiders more generally. In a 1989 letter to the editor, Mill City resident and twenty-four-year employee of North Santiam Plywood John Wheisenhut took up the "jobs versus owl" and "us versus them" narrative, taking aim at "a group of people who want to put all of us out of work because of a little bird called the spotted owl. These people call themselves preservationists. If they get their way, then we the people of the logging and timber industry will be the ones that are threatened and endangered." These preservationists, Wheisenhut continued, not only came from outside but also exploited hard-working taxpayers: "A vast majority of these people work for the state or federal government with large incomes and with little or no concern for the mill workers and loggers that will lose their jobs."[34] Another North Santiam Plywood employee wrote that it "upsets me to think that a small, well-funded, minority of preservationists can put the axe to a large majority of mill workers and loggers."[35]

Communities for a Great Oregon cultivated a multifaceted explanation of and attack against outsiders. Its newsletter warned parents that the movie *FernGully* was an "attack by a preservationist movement aimed at children," that the cartoon TV show *Teenage Mutant Ninja Turtles* advanced a "mis-informed" pro-environment and anti-logger message, and blasted *The Simpsons* for an episode showing a logger bribing politicians in Washington, DC.[36] The CGO associated preservationism with communism—a newsletter article noted that "Soviet Scientists Petition President Bush to Save Opal Creek"—and took shots at its opponents, from Andy Kerr, a prominent spokesperson for the environmentalist group Oregon Natural Resources Council, to Jack Ward Thomas, a US Forest Service biologist who led agency efforts to plan for spotted owl protection and served as chief of the agency under President Bill Clinton. CGO and its Oregon Lands Coalition allies circulated surveys that highlighted the affluence of Sierra Club members and contrasted the tenets of "Preservationist Philosophy" (including "If it's public, lock it up" and "If it gives someone a job, take the job away") to "Our Philosophy" (starting with "Keep our families together" and "Keep our communities strong").[37] In these and other ways, North Santiam Canyon residents helped reinforce the narrative of the old-growth controversy as a story of the powerful

"them" (preservationists, Hollywood, urbanites, etc.) versus the perse-
cuted "us"—loggers, mill owners, and everyone else in the canyon.

That story reached a conclusion of sorts in the mid-1990s with decisions about federal forests leading to negative economic effects in the
North Santiam Canyon. In April 1993, President Clinton held a "Timber
Summit" in Portland, which brought together environmentalists, timber
industry officials, timber workers, scientists and other interested parties to air their grievances and discuss their ideas for Northwest forests.
Following the summit, the Clinton administration assembled a group
of scientists into a Forest Ecosystem Management Assessment Team
(FEMAT) that produced a one-thousand-page report that became the
basis of the Northwest Forest Plan.[38] That plan, adopted by the federal
government in 1994, protected eighty percent of existing mature and old-
growth federal forests. The remaining twenty percent would be available
for timber sales, which the plan anticipated would reduce timber harvests to twenty percent of their historical levels. That did not bode well
for timber companies that had come to depend on federal forests. Rob
Freres of Freres Lumber told the *Statesman Journal*, "It's our wish to
stay the same size, but it's doubtful we'd be able to."[39] The Northwest
Forest Plan included Opal Creek in its preservation plans, but Congress
went a step further in 1996, creating the thirty-four-thousand-acre Opal
Creek Wilderness and Scenic Recreation Areas, permanently setting
aside that area from timber sales.

The loss of federal timber quickly undermined the local timber
industry, represented most dramatically by the fate of Young & Morgan,
which had heavily invested in large, old-growth log-milling equipment.
Although Young & Morgan was still advertising to hire green chain
pullers, choke setters, and truck drivers in August 1996, one year later
the company filed for bankruptcy. In October 1997, the company shuttered its Green Veneer mill in Idanha; in November, its North Santiam
Plywood plant in Mill City closed; and in July 1998, the company sold
its remaining assets to a Seattle company. That company closed the last
of Young & Morgan's canyon timber operations in 2001, but by then
the local timber industry seemed to be in free fall, with the 2000 Mill
City census counting only nineteen timber workers compared to fifty-
five in 1980. The passing of Young & Morgan, a nearly sixty-year-old
company, represented the dramatic decline of logging and milling in the
canyon.

Other local timber companies fared better. Between 1988 and 1990,
while Freres Lumber Company officials helped organize Yellow Ribbon

Rallies, form Communities for a Great Oregon, and fight environmentalists and the federal government in court, the company also aggressively
expanded its operations, buying three sawmills and two veneer plants.[40]
Freres shuttered one of those veneer plants and a mill in 1993 and 1995,
respectively, but in 1997, Freres bought Young & Morgan's bankrupted
North Santiam Plywood Company, and within five years, that mill
nearly doubled Freres Lumber Company's annual revenue.[41] Meanwhile,
the company shifted from sixty percent of its logs from public land and
forty percent from private land to the reverse, with most logs coming
from its own land or from the open market.[42] Between 1999 and 2003,
Freres invested $14 million in its operations, too, including retooling its
mills to process smaller logs from second-growth timber, and adding
and upgrading technology to increase the efficiency and capacity of its
mills. As Jim Petersen, the company's biographer, writes, "2004 was the
best year in the Freres Lumber Company's 82-year history," with the
company adding $2 million to its own investment portfolio and paying
out $840,000 in bonuses to its four hundred employees. Frank Lumber
survived and thrived, too; by 2006, the company was operating three
sawmills employing around two hundred people. With retooled mills,
new sources for logs, and new business practices that did not rely so
heavily on public timber sales, the canyon's timber industry had transformed, not died.

Meanwhile, the area's demographics changed in both size and connection to place. While the number of residents in the North Santiam
Canyon remained relatively stable (8,803 in 2000 compared to 8,656 in
1990), the places those people live did not. Detroit and Idanha, in the
upper canyon (the home of Young & Morgan), both saw decreases in
their populations between 1990 and 2000, dropping from a combined
620 residents in 1990 to 494 in 2000. Mill City, the approximate midway
point of the canyon and the site of Frank Lumber, remained relatively
stable, and in the lower canyon near the Freres plants, Lyons grew by
70 residents and Mehama expanded so much that the US Census Bureau
included it as a separate place for the first time in 2000, with 283 residents.
Other changes followed this population shift. The high school in Detroit
closed in 1995 owing to lack of enrollment and decreasing revenue from
federal timber sales, and the elementary and middle school shut its doors
in 1998. Students instead bussed to the high school in Mill City, which
itself shrank and changed. As a longtime resident of Mill City put it in
2002, "Ten years ago, there used to be four beauty shops, now there's one.
There used to be a bunch of grocery stores, now there is one. There used

to be a True Value [hardware store] but it's gone. Six restaurants, now there are three."[43] George Long, who as editor of the *Mill City Enterprise* had railed against environmentalism and rallied canyon communities since buying the paper in 1972, sold the paper in January 1994. Four years later, the newspaper's new owner, Tree Fredrickson, changed the *Mill City Enterprise*'s name to the *Mill City Independent Press*, a declaration of what many residents sought in the aftermath of the old-growth conflict: independence from what seemed like powerful, uncontrollable, and abstract outside forces.

TURNING TO TOURISM

As the timber industry contracted and transformed, tourism became an increasingly important part of the local economy and culture. During the logging controversies, some residents had mocked the idea that the area could or should become a tourist destination. In a cheeky 1989 letter to the editor, one unnamed author satirized the future of tourism in the area.[44] "Imagine if you will, a well-paved path filled with tourists in their sleek Spandex shorts peddling their way through a mass of joggers in Reeboks, all elbowing their way from one city limit sign to the other," evoking images of well-heeled, out-of-touch urbanites. To the critique that tourism jobs would hire fewer people at lower wages than the timber industry, the letter writer offered this sarcastic hope: "I can see where a few entrepreneurs could really clean up. . . . Along this trail, you'd have several hot dog and pop stands, a bike fix-it shop, a sportswear boutique, a bed and breakfast, a tenny runner retread shop, and a podiatrist at trail's end." And in contrast to those who said that Willamette Valley tourists would rather continue on to established tourism destinations in Sisters, Bend, and elsewhere in central Oregon, the letter writer pointed to Mill City's own vistas and recreational opportunities: "As they are loping and gliding up and down the famous path, our visitors might be able to enjoy the scenic view through the blackberry brush and the trees. Among our real eye catchers is the back side of Kimmel Park with its boat ramp ten feet above the water, and the 7th Street Park that you can't drive into unless your vehicle is a Sherman tank." The thin veil of humor hardly hid the author's disdain at the idea and desirability of the North Santiam Canyon becoming a tourism destination.

But, in fact, tourism had long been an integral part of the North Santiam Canyon's identity. Recreationalists from the Willamette Valley had been visiting the area for more than a century, from the two hunters who in 1873 suggested to John Minto where he might find a pass, to the pack trains carrying fishermen into Pamelia Lake at the turn of the century, to the "flatlanders" winding their way up the old Detroit road to Breitenbush Hot Springs in the early twentieth century. The combination of the modern North Santiam Highway and Detroit Dam made the canyon an even more attractive place for tourists. The Detroit reservoir—called Detroit Lake by most residents and visitors, suggesting that the artificial reservoir was a natural, permanent feature—became an important Oregon recreation destination, offering fishing, swimming, waterskiing, boating, and other water activities. Detroit Lake State Park, built simultaneously with the dam and enlarged throughout the following decades, drew tens of thousands of visitors every summer. By 1990, Detroit Lake State Park had served over two million visitors, with an average of more than seventy thousand visitors each summer.[45]

Other opportunities, particularly camping and hiking, drew recreationalists to the area. The Forest Service established campsites and trailheads next to the lake as well as on the surrounding mountainsides, providing a significant source of revenue to federal coffers (more than $200,000 in 1998).[46] Tourists used the North Santiam Highway not only to access the natural wonders of the area, but also to pass through—hopefully stopping for gas or food—on their way to the growing tourism destinations in central Oregon, particularly the Mt. Bachelor ski resort and the private vacation villages of Black Butte and Sunriver. Detroit Dam and the new state highway had made the North Santiam Canyon both a destination and a road through for tourists and recreationalists.

Many people in the North Santiam Canyon embraced the new economic opportunities brought by tourism and happily encouraged connections with the outside world. The *Mill City Enterprise* heralded the new dam and highway as a promising sign of a bright future, venturing to predict in 1954, "With improved roads, parks, and fishing conditions, recreation may play a large part in the 'booming' North Santiam Canyon."[47] It did play a large part in the area's economic development, encouraged by local residents. In 1956, the North Santiam Chamber of Commerce successfully petitioned to have the North Santiam Highway included on maps printed by the American Automobile Association (AAA) in an effort to draw more tourists.[48] Four years later, the chamber asked the state highway division for a new exit sign off of the Interstate 5 freeway, the state's main artery. The sign at that time simply read "N. Santiam," but the chamber wanted to call tourists' attention to the attractions in the canyon by adding "Detroit Dam," "Mill City," and other locales to the sign. Although the state highway division declined to install such an elaborate sign, it did eventually honor the chamber's request with a new marker reading "Stayton / Detroit Lake." The chamber also printed and distributed a six-page brochure showing "the recreational advantages of this area," according to the *Mill City Enterprise*.[49]

Local entrepreneurs took advantage of the new connections to the outside world, establishing various businesses to cater to tourists. In Mill City, the highway attracted tourist shops and restaurants, such as Giovanni Mountain Pizza and Poppa Al's Burgers, which eventually became local institutions. Boat facilities grew along the banks of Detroit Lake, including Kane's Marina and Detroit Lake Marina. Marion Forks Restaurant, which originally served mostly road builders, dam crews, loggers, and truckers, became a stopping point for skiers on their way to or from nearby Hoodoo Ski Area in the winter, and hikers, campers, and motor tourists in the summer. In the 1990s, more than twenty-five businesses aimed toward tourists and visitors were established in the canyon, including a half dozen drive-through coffee stands along the highway.[50] These businesses came to represent a shift in the local economy, now centered on serving tourists zipping through rather than local residents living and working there.

Beyond simply seeking to attract and serve tourists, communities in the North Santiam Canyon even went so far as to model themselves as tourist destinations. In doing so, they transformed the local economy as well as the local image and identity, a complex process fraught with potential peril, as Bonnie Christensen and Hal Rothman have shown in their studies of tourism in the American West.[51] This process of changing the canyon to appeal to outsiders took multiple forms, including festivals and celebrations. Prior to construction of the dam, the most important community festivals were the Thanksgiving Day, Christmas Day, and Fourth of July celebrations, where residents came together for food, music, and fellowship. In May 1963, Mill City hosted its first Whitewater Challenge, a festival intended to attract visitors, in contrast to the canyon's prior communal activities. The first Whitewater Challenge was "one of the biggest events held in these parts for the past 10 years," wrote the *Mill City Enterprise*. "Thousands of spectators lined the banks of the rushing North Santiam River to view some 60 water craft of all descriptions make the precarious trip down over the many frothy rapids."[52] Most of these spectators and competitors came from the Willamette Valley, which of course was the intention of the festival.

This shift to tourism accelerated during the 1980s and 1990s. With fewer mills and timber companies, many people who chose to stay sought to embrace the possibilities of tourism. In 1994, as fears about the effects of the Northwest Forest Plan grew, Mill City's mayor, Grant Merrill, told the local paper, "I believe it is possible to combine tourism, the timber industry, and other future industry to build a good future for the Santiam Canyon and Mill City."[53] In an effort to help encourage that new economy, the North Santiam Chamber of Commerce in 1996 formed the North Santiam Economic Development Corporation (NSEDC) to provide technical support for the growing tourism economy. The NSEDC created tourism marketing plans, organized the North Santiam Canyon Tourism Coalition to bring together tourism business owners, and published a yearly *Information Guide and Business Services Directory* to highlight the scenic and recreational opportunities of the canyon. The 2002 directory boasted that "the Canyon has something for everyone," including even those preservationists who had contributed to the timber industry's fall: "With trails for hiking, wetlands for observing and rivers for fishing, the Canyon offers a world of wonder for the outdoor enthusiast."

The city of Detroit in particular sought to develop an identity as a tourism destination. In 1985, Detroit's city council even explored changing the town's name to "Detroit Lake," because, as councilmember Bob Smith observed, "Everyone seems to know where Detroit Lake is but not where 'Detroit' is located."[54] The name-change motion failed, but Detroit's focus on tourism did not. The city developed a number of celebrations and festivals to attract tourists. In the 1960s, the town began holding a Water Pageant (later changed to the Water Festival), a summer event that featured boating and fishing competitions and drew thousands of tourists each August. By the turn of the century, Detroit was hosting five festivals a year, including the 50s Cruz-In at the Lake for old-car enthusiasts and a bluegrass festival called Music on the Mountain. In Detroit and throughout the canyon, business and community boosters utilized the road, the dam, and other connections to the outside world to change its image from a timber producer to "Gateway to the Heart of Nature's Empire," as the *Mill City Enterprise*'s masthead read, thus attracting tourists and their money.

THE DROUGHT AND DISASTER OF 2001

As people in the North Santiam Canyon utilized the connections with the outside world to develop and profit from tourism, they also became dependent on and vulnerable to outside forces that used those same connections to access and influence the area. Specifically, the local tourism industry, so focused on Detroit Lake and other water-based recreational

tourism, was vulnerable to one force beyond its control—the weather—
and another force that seemed increasingly remote and untouchable: the
US Army Corps of Engineers. These vulnerabilities started to come into
view in 1977 during the worst drought up to that point in the recorded
history of Oregon. For the 1976-77 rain year (October 1 to September
30), only 53.48 inches of precipitation fell at Detroit Dam, more than 36
inches below the average for the previous twenty years.[55] Beginning in
March 1977, the *Oregon Statesman* in Salem ran a "Drought Watch" column on the front page, tracking the discouraging lack of rain throughout
the spring. The effects of the drought were felt throughout the West; also
in March, *Time* magazine ran an article on "The Great Western Drought
of 1977," reporting that "the drought's full impact is not expected until
summertime," when the Northwest could expect forest fires, farm loses,
and electricity shortages.[56]

In the North Santiam Canyon, however, the drought seemed not to
give cause for alarm. The local newspaper, the *Mill City Enterprise*, ran
occasional articles on the status of the dry weather, but when Detroit
Lake filled in mid-May—right on schedule—the mundane event only
merited a one-column story on the fifth page. The paper reported that at
Detroit Lake State Park "the reservation line started forming at 3:20pm
. . . a six-hour wait. By late afternoon a block-long line had formed. In
the nine years since Mrs. [Thelma] Story [from Oregon State Parks and
Recreation] has been a clerk at the park, this is the earliest that the reservation line has started to form, she said."[57] The lake was full of water and
campsites were full of tourists with dollars to spend, and the potentially
disastrous drought of 1977 left only a few memories and, unfortunately,
even fewer lessons.

The same could not be said of the 2001 drought, which burned
the North Santiam Canyon. With 60 inches of precipitation, the 2000-
2001 rain year was second driest only to 1976-77, yet the effects of and
reactions to the drought were starkly different.[58] It was the summer
of brownouts and blackouts during the "California energy crisis," confrontations over irrigation headgates in the Klamath Basin, and dried-up
streambeds throughout the Pacific Northwest. *The Oregonian* warned
readers in March that "Summer Fun Could Evaporate," reporting that
"[Army] Corps [of Engineers] officials don't expect to have enough
water in their reservoirs for summer recreation."[59] In the North Santiam
Canyon, no news was bigger than the drought. The *Mill City Independent Press* ran alarmed all-caps headlines throughout the winter and
spring: "RECORD LOW WATER LEVELS AT DETROIT LAKE

During the drought of 2001, the reservoir for Detroit Dam did not fill, leaving boat docks high and dry, uncovering stumps on a cracked and caked lakebed, and revealing the importance and vulnerabilities of the North Santiam Canyon's tourism economy. Photograph courtesy of Cara Kelly, Detroit Ranger Station, US Department of Agriculture Forest Service.

HAS LOCALS WORRIED," "PUBLIC MEETINGS ON LOW LAKE LEVELS SCHEDULED," and "CORPS OF ENGINEERS' REGULATIONS UNBENDING IN CONTROLLING DETROIT RESERVOIR LEVELS."[60] Local business owners formed the Detroit Lake Recreation Business Association to publicize the opportunities — and needs — of the tourism industry in Detroit, and by March, dozens of area residents were making the hour-long drive to the state capitol in Salem to voice their concerns.

They had good reason to be worried: the reservoir behind Detroit Dam was not filling. Rather than a glass-topped pool, dry earth and dead stumps covered the reservoir bed, and beached boat docks sat uselessly distant from the trickle of water flowing down the North Santiam River. One local resident said in February that the reservoir was "Lower than I've ever seen it in all the years I've been here, and that's since childhood."[61] This was perhaps an overstatement; through the middle of April, the reservoir pool was actually higher than it had been in 1977. But by the end of May 2001, Detroit Lake was sixty feet below its average height, whereas in 1977, the lake had by that time filled to normal. It would be a long, dry, and desperate summer for the North Santiam Canyon, as tourists — and their precious dollars — stayed away. The number of visitors to Detroit Lake State Park dropped from eighty-four thousand in 2000 to just over forty-seven thousand in 2001, and Forest Service revenue from its parks in the area dropped by thirty percent, a sample of lost tourism income.[62] Don & Penny Hiebert of Detroit Marina lost $500,000 and had to take out an extra mortgage to keep their business alive; other tourist-dependent businesses like the Burger Stop and Detroit Motel closed permanently.[63] The canyon could not escape the effects of the 2001 drought as it had in 1977, because the Army Corps of Engineers did not allow Detroit Lake to fill. And throughout the spring and summer, residents angrily demanded to know why.

The low pool did not come as a surprise. Beginning in February 2001, the US Army Corps of Engineers had warned, often and publicly, that it would not be able to fill the reservoir. The weather during 2001 was simply too dry: it was an "extreme low water year," "a water-tight year," with "extremely dry conditions," as the corps repeated throughout the summer.[64] The corps dispatched public relations agents to explain the situation to the press, its Reservoir Control Center sought the input of myriad state and federal agencies, and corps officials held six public meetings in Stayton, Eugene, Springfield, and Sweet Home. As winter turned to spring, the corps finalized its summer operating plan for the Willamette Basin, and by the last public meeting held on April 26 in Stayton, the agency had decided Detroit's fate. The *Mill City Independent Press* bore the bad news: "The Corps, joined this time by the Bonneville Power Administration, National Marine Fisheries Service, Oregon Water Resources Department, Oregon Department of Fish and Wildlife, Oregon Department of Environmental Quality" — such a long list of external power! — "told the audience that the top priority position of Detroit Lake had been abruptly reversed to the bottom of the list," an accusation of betrayal (with little substantiation, the corps would claim) that resonated with the *Mill City Independent Press*'s readers, who had come to see themselves as victims of powerful, abstract, distant forces. The paper continued with a combination of resignation and resentment: "Since it was evident to these professionals that the weather was not going to cooperate and, since it was obvious to them that the lake would not fill anyway, they decided to pull the plug."[65]

The corps "pulled the plug" for three reasons, as Col. Randall Butler, commander of the US Army Corps of Engineers Northwest Project, explained in a May 2001 memo: the need for pollution mitigation, hydropower demands, and protection of endangered fish species.[66] Downstream, the city of Salem had grown significantly since 1977, up fifty percent to 136,000 residents in 2001, and this growing population needed the North Santiam's cool, clean water for pollution mitigation.[67] The practice of diluting urban waste with water from the Willamette River and its tributaries—hardly unique to Salem among cities along the Willamette River—had a long history.[68] When the Army Corps of Engineers mapped its plan for the Willamette River Basin in 1948, it incorporated pollution mitigation as one of the justifications for manipulating the North Santiam and other Willamette River tributaries. The corps even went so far as to argue that "recreational opportunities along the main stream and principal tributaries would be enhanced by pollution abatement," a justification that would seem bitterly ironic to the residents of the North Santiam Canyon in 2001.[69] Willamette Valley population increases and environmental legislation since the 1950s had only heightened the downstream need for the North Santiam's water. As Col. Butler explained, "water stored in the reservoirs is historically used to meet summer and fall flow augmentation targets in the Willamette River . . . Flow augmentation is absolutely essential for enabling the state to meet water quality standards mandated by the Clean Water Act."[70] The Willamette Valley's filth required clean water, and the North San-tiam River would provide it.

The demand for the North Santiam's water extended well beyond Salem and the Willamette River, though: the West wanted electricity, and Detroit Dam's turbines—the most productive in the Willamette River basin—could help. The Bonneville Power Administration (BPA) declared a hydropower emergency in March 2001, "in recognition," as Col. Butler summarized, "that there is insufficient water throughout the entire Columbia River basin for all regional power needs." Butler went on to explain that while "the hydropower plants [of] the Willamette Basin Project are a very small portion of the total hydropower production potential marketed by BPA . . . Nevertheless, these projects are needed for maintaining stability of the Willamette Basin portion of the regional power grid." The BPA needed hydropower from all the dams in the Willamette River Basin, no matter how small, and the corps agreed to maintain "hydropower generation through the remainder of the dry season while still meeting other authorized uses."

Of those "other authorized uses," protection of Chinook salmon featured most prominently in Col. Butler's memo and in corps public statements throughout that summer. In March 1999, the National Marine

Fisheries Service (NMFS) of the National Oceanic and Atmospheric Administration (NOAA) determined that spring-run Chinook salmon in the Upper Willamette River Basin, which includes the North Santiam River, "are at risk of becoming endangered in the foreseeable future and will be listed as threatened species under the ESA [Endangered Species Act]."[71] This decision, the result of years of study of fish populations on the West Coast, opened the floodgates (literally) of salmon protection measures, particularly the release of reservoir water to augment the flow of the Willamette River. On the North Santiam River, the Corps of Engineers had increased the average daily outflow from Detroit Lake during the spring and early summer of 1999 and 2000 by more than twenty-five percent over the preceding five years.[72] In those two years, there had been enough water in the basin to provide for this increased flow while still maintaining a full pool in Detroit Lake; the 1998-99 rain year was the fourth wettest in Detroit since 1954, and precipitation in 1999-2000 had been above average at ninety-two inches.

But the drought of 2001, argued the corps, made fish protection nearly impossible. Although "the Willamette Projects were operated to meet the spring flow targets [for fish] in 1999 and 2000," Col. Butler regretted to report that "because of exceptionally low flow conditions this year, we have not been able to fully meet all of the biologically based targets." Nevertheless, Col. Butler promised to "manage releases of water from reservoir storage to provide as high flows as possible in the mainstem Willamette during the spring and early summer to ensure that the needs of endangered salmonids are served."[73] Although the spring/early summer average outflow from Detroit Lake decreased to 1,742 cubic feet per second (cfs) in 2001 from the 2,086 cfs average in 2000, outflow in 2001 was still greater than the five-year average (1,593 cfs) and helped provide enough water to satisfy flow requirements on the Willamette River.

Addressing these three demands for fish, power, and waste treatment, argued the corps, necessitated the drawdown of Detroit Lake, a regrettable but unavoidable decision. "We are very much aware of the adverse impacts to lakeside recreation and to the economic welfare of nearby communities and businesses," lamented Col. Butler in the May 2001 memo. "However, given the severity of the water shortage, there was nothing that could be done to avoid recreation being severely impacted. The only real choice was and is how to manage our reservoirs so as to avoid equally serious impacts to the other critical user communities and interests listed above." And so, beginning on May 21, 2001—just one week before the Memorial Day weekend, when tourists usually began flooding the North

Santiam Canyon—the corps uncorked Detroit Dam. In its view of events, the Corps of Engineers had taken an objective and rational approach to a difficult situation.

RESPONDING TO DROUGHT AND DISASTER

From the perspective of people in the North Santiam Canyon, though, the corps bore responsibility for its actions. Residents argued that the corps did not have to leave the reservoir empty and that the agency could have made different decisions and thereby avoided economic catastrophe. And they had a point. A comparison to the drought of 1977 muddies the clear water of the corps' straightforward claims to rationality and objectivity. The agency's defenses in 2001—that it was an exceptionally dry rain year, and that demand for pollution mitigation, power production, and fish production had increased—fall short of explaining the dramatic difference between 2001 and 1977. Weather conditions in the two years were similar; since 1977 was even drier than 2001, the lack of precipitation itself is not the only reason for the corps' decision to empty Detroit Lake. Water quality in the Willamette River was certainly a concern in 2001, but it was also a concern in 1977, when Congress passed the Clean Water Act to strengthen pollution control. The West's electrical grid was under enormous pressure in the summer of 2001, but demand and tensions were also high in 1977 during that decade's energy crisis. The Pacific Northwest's power outlook in 1977 was "ominous," reported BPA's administrator Sterling Munro that year, who warned that "downward revisions in regional load forecasts are more than matched by continuing delays in the licensing and construction of planned thermal generation," referring to the failed nuclear projects of the Washington Public Power Supply System (WPPSS).[74] In terms of drought, water-quality concerns, and power conditions, 1977 and 2001 seemed to have much in common.

The corps' most vehement defense in 2001 was that Congress had saddled the agency with the responsibility of protecting winter steelhead, chub, and the recently ESA-listed Chinook salmon. This represented an increased demand on the corps' management juggling act, but preserving fish was not an entirely new demand. The corps had taken fish into consideration in its development plans for the Columbia and its tributaries during the 1940s and 1950s, relying on technical solutions such as fish ladders, hatcheries, and egg collection stations on the North Santiam River. The Oregon Department of Fish and Wildlife's fish hatchery at Marion Forks, built by the US Army Corps of Engineers in 1950 to mitigate fish loss from Detroit Dam, was hailed by the corps and canyon boosters alike as a technological triumph that would conserve the North Santiam's valuable fish stocks.[75]

But these efforts did not sufficiently mitigate the damage caused to fish runs by dams and altered habitat, and by 1977, the corps was aware of the dire situation. That spring, the Army Corps of Engineers spent almost $800,000 on Operation Fish Run II, an effort to save spring salmon fingerlings by transporting them downriver on barges, trucks, and even airplanes.[76] The *Mill City Enterprise* noted such fish population rescue efforts, reporting on the corps' work to upgrade fish hatchery facilities and a recent release of thirteen hundred steelhead into the North Santiam River.[77] In short, while the demand for fish protection, power production, and pollution mitigation had increased since 1977, those demands were not unprecedented nor unexpected. More importantly, the variation in these demands was not commensurate with the difference in lake levels in 1977 and 2001. The corps made a different decision in 2001 than in 1977 — why, wondered canyon residents, this choice at this time?

In explaining the dry reservoir bed, the US Army Corps of Engineers, like many state and federal agencies, portrayed itself as a disinterested servant of the public will, following the rules it had been given. It is true that a variety of mechanisms constrain the corps' activities in the North Santiam Canyon. The Flood Control Act of 1936 provided the initial enabling legislation for manipulation of the Columbia River and its tributaries; Congress further elaborated Detroit Dam's authorized purposes and management in 1938 and 1948. This last congressional document was a seven-volume "comprehensive plan for development of the Columbia River and its tributaries [including the North Santiam River] for flood control, navigation, power development, irrigation, and other purposes, including fish and wildlife conservation and recreation."[78]

The corps addressed these directions in the *Reservoir Regulation Manual for Detroit and Big Cliff Reservoirs* of 1953, literally the rulebook for the management of Detroit Dam and its sister dam. The manual provides instructions for flood control, management of hydroelectric production and irrigation, and, most interestingly in the case of 1977 and 2001, the dam's mandated outflow and "Rule Curve." The Rule Curve stipulates exactly how much water should be maintained in Detroit Lake at different times throughout the year, based on flood concerns during the spring and power and irrigation needs throughout the summer and fall. The corps made these calculations in 1948 as part of the comprehensive study behind House Document 531; this study was based on a requirement of House Document 544 in 1938 that set five hundred cubic feet per second as the minimum outflow from the dam, "to satisfy fish requirements."[79] The corps incorporated these limits into the regulation manual in 1953, which remained in use ever since.

But the rules were bent—if not completely broken—in both 1977 and 2001. Whereas in 2001 Detroit Lake remained well below the Rule Curve, in 1977, the pool filled to normal, although not until later than scheduled, as the corps sought to satisfy downstream users in the spring before quickly filling the pool by the beginning of summer. Even more striking is a comparison of outflow during the two years; during the drought of 1977, outflow sometimes dropped below the minimum flow of five hundred cubic feet per second; in 2001, the corps kept the outflow at no less than double the authorized minimum. People living in the canyon noticed all that water spilling out of Detroit and Big Cliff Dams, and they could not help but wonder, and become frustrated, at the corps' decision to leave Detroit Reservoir empty. History and experience seemed to demonstrate that the agency had a choice, and that it had chosen to leave the lake dry and let businesses die.

Residents did not shy away from challenging and blaming the corps. "Residents don't buy" the corps' insistence that there was nothing it could do, as a correspondent for the Salem *Statesman Journal* summarized. "[Residents] say that even in past dry years, such as the last major drought in the 1970s, there's always been enough water to float the docks."[80] At a public meeting in March, a canyon resident "questioned why the COE [Corps of Engineers] could not draw down the reservoir later in the season; or not draw it down quite so far—letting it out later if there were exceptional rainfall," as the local paper reported. The corps responded that "it would quite literally take an act of Congress to make any changes in the reservoir regulation curves; and also the prioritization of reasons for controls."[81] That answer remained unsatisfactory to those who believed the agency had more discretion than it would admit. At another public forum in June, Corps of Engineers representative Matt Rea sat at the front of the crowd, "holding the 'hot seat' for the evening," reported the paper, as attendees continued to challenge the corps' assertion that it had no choice.

Canyon residents also directed their frustration at more diffuse outside forces, especially the City of Salem and its residents. As the corps had frequently and vigorously explained, Salem depended on the North Santiam River for drinking water, pollution abatement, and sewage treatment. From the upstream perspective, Salem's behavior was negligent and exploitive, as the *Mill City Independent Press* explained: "The years of abundant rain have allowed Salem to avoid the consequences of their deteriorating sewer system and the inadequate water treatment plant. . . . Salem is hogging all the available water to squander on their watershed system."[82] Some even suspected a conspiracy of outside power, with the City of Salem plotting with the Army Corps of Engineers to keep Detroit dry.

Mike Swaim, Salem's mayor, insisted that Salem should not be blamed. In June 2001, Swaim wrote Detroit mayor Pam Hill to "express my sincere concerns about the low levels of Detroit Reservoir and the economic hardships this is creating for your beautiful city." Swaim wanted to "assure you the rumors that have been circulated about the City of Salem requesting lowering the reservoir is totally untrue. We have never discussed this with the Corps of Engineers and we have never considered this in any way."[83] Swaim even compared Detroit's economic pain to the inconvenience that Salem-based recreationalists would suffer: "The citizens of Salem enjoy Detroit Reservoir as a favorite recreation site and believe the conditions this summer will be a major loss to many families." Swaim's defense and expression of empathy did little to reassure those who blamed Salem for the dry lake bed, and it certainly did nothing to fill that reservoir.

Canyon residents did not simply complain about outsiders and sit idly by while the lake bed dried out. In May 2001, with the spring rains not coming and the corps posting notice that Detroit reservoir would be dry, businesses owners, civic organizations, and other interested individuals formed the Save Our Lake (SOL) committee. SOL lobbied to get federal disaster aid to compensate area businesses for their losses; that effort failed in part because, as the local paper explained, "any injury to the community has to be agriculture related, which Detroit isn't." SOL turned to a broader and longer-term goal: to "put Detroit at the top of the Corps' priority list," according to one of the organizers.[84]

To bring attention to its cause, SOL organized an event familiar to veterans of the Yellow Ribbon Coalition: a caravan of protestors would drive to Salem for a rally on June 9. In the call for the rally, SOL organizers explained what was at stake and who was to blame: "They are stealing our beautiful, clear, pure water where we swim, boat, camp, fish and rejuvenate. To what purpose are we losing this precious gem? We are losing Detroit Lake so that Salem can flush the filth out of their river." But the people of the canyon were not powerless, the rally organizers insisted: "With your help, we can stop the city of Salem from making

Detroit Lake its own watershed to be used up and shut down at the whim of whoever is looking out for the interests of Salem." Such a show of unity and force would "make the people in other agencies be responsible to the public at large and stop selling us down the river. We can save the beautiful lake that we all need."[85]

The rally succeeded at getting public attention. A seven-mile-long caravan of cars, motorcycles, trucks, and boats traveled down the North Santiam Highway between Salem and Detroit. KGW television news from Portland had a camera crew and reporter on-site, as did the Salem *Statesman Journal* and the Portland *Oregonian*. Speakers included Salem's mayor—eager to de-villainize the city—and two representatives from the state legislature; Oregon's two US senators sent messages of support and promised action. A letter from Tootie Smith, Republican state legislator and former director of the pro–timber industry Oregon Lands Coalition, explicitly blamed environmentalism for Detroit's problems: "Although I can't be there in person today, I am with you 100 percent in sprit . . . I think it's time we pass an endangered species act for rural Oregon families!"[86] Later that summer, SOL received a visit from Senator Gordon Smith, who signed a petition to put recreation at Detroit Lake at the top of the corps' list of priorities. Smith apologized that he could not do anything to save the 2001 recreational season, but "he [would] be working fervently toward this not happening again," according to the local paper.[87]

In the following years, the SOL committee and other organizations such as the Detroit Lake Recreation Area Business Association continued to push for a reprioritization of recreation at Detroit. This change was apparent in the winter of 2005, when a lack of snow and rainfall seemed to be leading toward a summer like 2001. Fortunately, a wet spring brought the reservoir much needed water; furthermore, the corps publicly declared that it was "now giving higher priority to recreation, especially Detroit, as [the corps must] balance competing needs for water, including the needs of fish runs, hydropower, and water quality."[88] Canyon groups petitioned to include Detroit Lake as one of thirty-two "Reservoirs of Opportunity" by the Federal Lakes Recreation Leadership Council (FLRLC), a collaboration of federal agencies (US Army Corps of Engineers, US Fish and Wildlife, and others) working to "determine how recreation can be enhanced at the nation's more than 1,780 federally constructed lakes."[89] SOL used all of the canyon's connections to the outside—information channels, access to federal agencies, political allies, and even the road itself for a rally—to exercise local power.

The summer of 2001 was a harsh reality check. For some people, the dry lake bed represented yet another breach of trust by the government. Chuck Brennan, the proprietor of the doomed Detroit Motel, told the Salem *Statesman Journal* at the end of the summer that "I just don't understand how the state and the federal government could do this to people who pay their taxes."[90] Others saw a broader array of outside and abstract forces aligned against the canyon: "fish habitat and spawning, valley residents' drinking water supply, irrigation of valley farmlands, production of electricity, and a host of other concerns," summarized the *Mill City Independent Press*, "take precedence over the livelihood of Detroit and Idanha property owners and tenants."[91] And everyone came to believe that they had little power against these outside forces, as the *Mill City Independent Press* summarized: "The owners of the impacted businesses in Detroit have no say in this matter, and are mandated by location to have their yearly incomes eliminated or seriously diminished."[92] The area's reliance on tourism had made the area vulnerable to outside forces, which wielded their tremendous influence through the connections binding the canyon to the outside world.

As the North Santiam Canyon moved from the twentieth into the twenty-first century, a frustrated anger coalesced against outside forces that seemed increasingly distant and abstract. Yellow Ribbon Rallies, the legislative and rhetorical efforts of Communities for a Great Oregon, and the Save Our Lakes caravans all manifested and reinforced an us-versus-them reaction to and narrative about the influence of forces beyond local control. The local newspaper, which had traditionally served as the booster of business and connections to the outside world, reflected this transformation. The *Mill City Enterprise*'s subtitle had boasted of being published "On the Scenic North Santiam Highway—Gateway to the Heart of Nature's Empire." Its successor, the *Mill City Independent Press*, focused on being a "family based community publication dedicated to the North Santiam Canyon." For many people in that community, outsiders and their values seemed dangerous and outright confusing. After one of the US Army Corps of Engineers' public meetings in the spring of 2001, the *Mill City Independent Press* reported one person saying, "I'm not a very religious person, but my recollection of the biblical account of the foundation of the universe says that man shall have dominion over all other creatures large and small. So how can fish be more important than people?"[93] From that perspective, outsiders had abandoned traditional values and common sense, and they could not be trusted.

Nevertheless, in practice, the North Santiam Canyon remained committed to the various connections running through the area—the river attracting visitors to the Whitewater Festival, the corps' dam and reservoir that lured boaters, the roads that bore local companies' log trucks as well as the weight of 1935 Fords bound for a classic car festival, correspondence with legislators sympathetic to the timber industry, and the market connections that kept money and goods flowing in and out. Such connections inescapably bound the North Santiam Canyon to outside forces, even as local residents rebelled and identified themselves against such outsiders.

Epilogue

Speeding along State Highway 22 twenty years into the twenty-first century, visitors to the North Santiam Canyon can see signs of trouble through their car windows. A drive-through Subway fast-food restaurant in Mill City lures motorists away from sit-down eateries and local institutions Poppa Al's and Giovanni's across the highway. Drive-through coffee stands in Mehama, Gates, and east of Idanha tempt caffeine-addicted drivers who might otherwise stop and stay for a bit at Rosie's Mountain Coffee House, which the owners decided to put up for sale a few years ago. A Dollar General store sprouted up in Mill City in 2017, bringing with it low prices and a host of problems that are the hallmark of the bargain chain, including low wages, little fresh food, and undermining the local Mill City Market.[1] Passersby will also notice the proliferation of self- and mini-storage facilities along the highway—in Mehama, Mill City, Gates, and Idanha, with more under construction—where cheap land has become turnkey, unstaffed storage units for RVs and boats owned by Willamette Valley visitors. A traveler might be surprised with the amount of traffic on weekday mornings headed west and weekday evenings headed east, as the lower reaches of the area transform into bedroom communities for Salem. Such signs suggest challenges to permanence and power in the North Santiam Canyon.

The area also increasingly faces greater and more abstract challenges from forces well beyond the canyon and its residents' influence. Global warming, manifested as more frequent and severe droughts, wildfires, and lower and warmer water in the river and Detroit reservoir, increasingly threatens the North Santiam Canyon. In July 2017, lightning struck tinder-dry timber in the Mt. Jefferson Wilderness, igniting a wildfire that burned more than eleven thousand acres and cost $39 million to contain. The Whitewater Fire, as the US Forest Service named the blaze, burned hundreds of acres of private timberland, led to the closure of numerous backpacking trails, produced dangerous air-quality levels, and reduced tourism business that summer.[2] Two years earlier, in the summer of 2015, Oregon experienced a drought even worse than 2001, and, as in that

Coming just two years after the worst drought in Oregon's history and a toxic blue-green algae bloom, the 2017 Whitewater Fire in and around the Mt. Jefferson Wilderness highlighted the destructive effects of global warming on the North Santiam Canyon. Photograph from the National Wildfire Coordinating Group's InciWeb, accessed December 27, 2019, https://inciweb. nwcg.gov/incident/photograph/5420/79/69027.

fateful year, Detroit Lake did not fill and tourism businesses suffered. A wildfire that July did not help, either.

Global warming is causing other local problems, too. In May 2015, toxic blue-green algae, encouraged by warm water temperatures, bloomed in the reservoir, and the Oregon Health Authority warned against boating, waterskiing, fishing, and swimming—an obvious problem for tourism businesses in the area. Another and much longer-lasting bloom occurred in the spring and summer of 2018, and the Oregon Health Authority warned that climate change would lead to more: "that factors associated with global warming—hotter and drier conditions and a rapid snowmelt—could definitely increase conditions that cause algae blooms."[3] Global warming struck again in another way in 2018, when the US Army Corps of Engineers announced plans to build a three-hundred-foot water recirculation tower near Detroit Dam. This technological fix, the corps hoped, would lower the warm water temperatures caused by climate change that threatened endangered fish populations. Construction of the tower would require leaving the reservoir dry for at least a year and probably longer. Residents responded with understandable alarm, voicing their concerns at corps-organized public fora, emailing comments to the corps, and sounding off to the media. As Paul O'Donnell, owner of Mountain High Grocery in Detroit, told the *Statesman Journal*, "This scares the hell out of everybody. We could lose businesses in Detroit, and this will hit the rest of the Santiam Canyon hard as well."[4] As of this writing, the corps is exploring a different plan that would not require a two-year drawdown of the reservoir. But it is unfortunately clear that global warming will continue to affect the canyon—a cruel irony, given how much the area has come to depend on some of the very causes of global warming: the cars, RVs, logging trucks, and other greenhouse gas–producing vehicles streaming along Highway 22.

This is what the North Santiam Canyon looks like from car windows and media outlets: a place on the edge of dissolution and perhaps destruction. But a slightly more thoughtful drive through the region also reveals contrasting images that have developed. Businesses oriented toward passersby and recreational tourists appear throughout the canyon, from the new Pratum Co-Op Fuel gas station in Mehama to the eNRG Kayaking trucks and vans shuttling whitewater enthusiasts between Gates and Mill City. The twenty-first-century local timber industry appears along the highway, too: log trucks from Frank Lumber and Freres Lumber, Kelly Lumber Sales in Mill City, and Hardwood Components, a specialty hardwood mill and retailer in Mehama signposted by a constantly spinning faux sawmill blade. Other businesses point to a creative entrepreneurial spirit, including Greenhouses by Chad in Gates, where customers can order custom-made Douglas fir and cedar greenhouses, and Cartwright's Music Repair in Mill City, owned and operated by guitar virtuoso Ken Cartwright. Cartwright is also the station manager and program director at KYAC community radio, which since July 2013 "serves our Santiam Canyon residents including Mill City, Gates, Lyons, Mehama, the Little North Fork, Elkhorn, Stayton, Sublimity, surrounding and outlying areas and highway 22 from milepost 11 to milepost 47."[5] That distance gives motorists on Highway 22 about forty minutes of local radio and a sense of the creativity and resiliency of North Santiam Canyon residents.

Those with the time and interest to pull off the highway and explore a little more will find other examples of permanence and local power in the North Santiam Canyon. KYAC is a service of Santiam Hearts to Arts, a 501(c)(3) nonprofit whose mission is to "preserve, present and promote the fine and performing arts in the Santiam Canyon. We accomplish this by educating, informing and involving our diverse community."[6] Hearts to Arts also sponsors a community chorus group and arts and theater programs at local schools. Although the *Mill City Independent* closed in 2014, other community newsletters have emerged, including *Our Town* (covering events from Stayton in the Willamette Valley up to Mill City) and *Canyon Weekly*, which, as the paper's masthead explained, brings "News for our side of the mountain" (as of this writing, *Our Town* had recently purchased *Canyon Weekly*, and publication plans were unclear).[7] Even with the threat of toxic algae blooms and two years without a reservoir, there was some good news to report in 2018: after a four-year campaign to raise $400,000 needed to preserve the historic old railroad turned pedestrian bridge in Mill City, the group Save Our Bridge (SOB, another clever acronym, like SOL for Save Our Lake) landed an $8.1 million federal grant to restore the bridge and other infrastructure in Mill City, including new streets, sidewalks, lighting, and landscaping. The fundraising and grant indicated the enduring strength of the canyon's community and promised great things for the future, as Frances Thomas, a member of SOB, told *Our Town:* "We are delighted that the community has come together from the beginning with enthusiasm and support for this important project. Now this signature structure will serve the North Santiam Canyon for the next 100 years!"[8] In the restored railroad bridge, the persistence of a local news source, the creativity of a local arts nonprofit, and other ways, people in the North Santiam Canyon continue to explore ways of making home and community.

Seeing the resiliency and complexity of the North Santiam Canyon requires more than a fast trip in an air-conditioned car. Understanding this place and others like it in the West requires first and foremost a recognition that we may know *of* these places, but we do not really know much *about* them. We are literally passingly familiar, but actually knowing these places means getting out of the car, looking for the complexities of the past, and trying to make sense of them. This book hopes to help with that process, but there is so much more depth and breadth available in the places themselves, particularly in local historical groups like the North Santiam Historical Society and its Canyon Life Museum. Ultimately, though, the point of this book is simple: if you want to make sense of a place and the people who have lived and do live there, take that place and its people seriously. Treat them as actors, not objects. Taking that first step will move us toward a better understanding of the North Santiam Canyon and other peripheral places in the American West. Walking along—or at least not driving so fast—through and in these places, we'll see and learn some fascinating and surprising things about the region and the people that call it home.

Notes

INTRODUCTION

1 DeVoto, "The West," 364.
2 Pomeroy, *Pacific Slope*; Limerick, *Legacy of Conquest*; Worster, *Rivers of Empire*; White, *"It's Your Misfortune and None of My Own"*; Rothman, "Selling the Meaning of Place"; idem, *Devil's Bargains*; Langston, *Forest Dreams*.
3 Robbins, *Hard Times in Paradise*; idem, *Colony and Empire*. For Robbins's analysis applied at the scale of Oregon's history, see "Town and Country in Oregon." See also his *Landscapes of Conflict* and *Oregon*.
4 Robbins, "The 'Plundered Province,'" 595.
5 White, *Land Use, Environment, and Social Change*; Willingham, *Starting Over*; deBuys, *Enchantment and Exploitation*.
6 Leech, *The City That Ate Itself*.
7 Christensen, *Red Lodge and the Mythic West*.
8 Feldman, "View from Sand Island."
9 Willingham, *Starting Over*, 7-9.
10 Lengacher, "History of North Santiam Canyon"; Petersen, *Santiam Song*; Lisa Chalidze, Melody Munger, and Debbie Corning, "Niagara, Oregon"; Fleetwood, "Timeline—North Santiam Canyon." Other residents, current and former, have written about the North Santiam Canyon, including Rada, *Singing My Song*; Grafe, *Gates of the North Santiam*; and Ray Stout, "Mehama Story."
11 Some definitions of the North Santiam Canyon extend downstream to Stayton and beyond, to where the North Santiam River joins with the South Santiam River to become the Santiam River, but that area is both more proximate and similar to the Willamette Valley in its geography, climate, and economy than the North Santiam Canyon as defined here.

CHAPTER 1: MAKING HOMES, PROFITS, AND PATHS

1 Smithsonian Institution Columbia Basin Project River Basin Surveys, *Appraisal of the Archeological Resources*, 2.
2 Kelly, "Prehistoric Land-Use Patterns," 26; Peterson del Mar, *Oregon's Promise*, 14.
3 For a brief definition of this term and concept, see the *Oregon Encyclopedia*, s.v. "Glossary: Resettlement," accessed September 4, 2019, https://oregonencyclopedia.org/glossary/Resettlement. For application of the concept of

settler colonialism in the case of Oregon, see Jetté, *At the Hearth*; Whaley, *Oregon and the Collapse of Illahee*.

4 In addition to his publications, presentations, consultations, and other extensive work on native history in Oregon, David Lewis maintains the excellent *NDNHistory Research* blog, from which he shares new scholarship and research resources. Lewis's publications include his thesis, "Termination of the Confederated Tribes"; the article "Four Deaths"; and "Western Oregon Reservations," coauthored with Robert Kentta. For other scholarship on the Kalapuya, Molallla, and Warm Springs peoples, see, e.g., Beckham, *Indians of Western Oregon*; idem, *Oregon Indians*; Berg, *First Oregonians*; Mathias D. Bergmann, "'We Should Lose Much by Their Absence'"; Jacobs et al., *Kalapuya Texts*; Jetté, "'Beaver Are Numerous'"; Mackey, *The Kalapuyans*; Spores, "Too Small a Place."

5 Kelly, "Prehistoric Land-Use Patterns," 99.

6 For source maps and explanatory essays, see Lewis, *NDNHistory Research*.

7 Minto, "Number and Condition of the Native Race," 306. Scholarly research has since confirmed Alquema's figures; see Boyd, *Coming of the Spirit of Pestilence*, tables 15 and 16, pp. 323-24 and 238.

8 See Henry Zenk and Josh Levy, "Appendix A: Kalapuyan Treaty Groups Removed to Grand Ronde Reservation," in Mackey, *The Kalapuyans*; and Zenk, "Notes on Native American Place-Names."

9 For seasonal rounds, subsistence practices, and burning practices, see Boyd, *Indians, Fire, and the Land*, esp. "Strategies of Indian Burning in the Willamette Valley"; David G. Lewis, "Kalapuyans: Seasonal Lifeways, TEK, Anthropocene," *NDNHistory Research* (blog), November 8, 2016, https://ndnhistoryresearch.com/2016/11/08/kalapuyans-seasonal-lifeways-tek-anthropolocene/; Mackey, *The Kalapuyans*, 28, 43, 45-46; Jetté, *At the Hearth of the Crossed Races*, 18-19.

10 David Lewis argues that "ethnographic evidence from the Molalla suggests that they did not live within the high Cascades but instead along the foothills of the western section of the range." "Ethnographic Molalla Homelands in Historic Scholarship," *NDNHistory Research* (blog), October 21, 2018, https://ndnhistoryresearch.com/2018/10/21/the-ethnographic-molalla-land-claims/.

11 Boyd, *Coming of the Spirit of Pestilence*, 238-39.

12 David G. Lewis, "Molalla Tribal History," *NDNHistory Research* (blog), March 2, 2017. https://ndnhistoryresearch.com/molalla-ethnohistory/.

13 Jacobs et al., *Kalapuya Texts*, 41.

14 Kelly, "Prehistory Land-Use Patterns," 37-38.

15 David Lewis notes that "the Klamath trail continues to the west to end at the Santiam-Chemeketa village at Chemeketa Creek. The footprint of the trail was widened and paved to become State Street in Salem, Oregon." From correspondence with author, April 6, 2019. See also Lewis's, "Traditional Sharing of the Cascades Range by Tribes," *NDNHistory Research* (blog), November 12, 2018, https://ndnhistoryresearch.com/2018/11/12/traditional-sharing-of-the-cascades-range-by-tribes/.

16 David Lewis notes that "at least two battles involved the Klamath in the valley, the Abiqua battle and the battle of Battle Creek in the red Hill of South Salem." From correspondence with author, April 6, 2019. See also his "Battle Creek: The First Battle in the Willamette Valley," *NDNHistory Research* (blog), June 15, 2016, https://ndnhistoryresearch. com/2016/06/15/battle-creek-the-first-battle-in-the-willamette-valley/; idem, "The Battle of Abiqua, Second Battle of the Willamette Valley," *NDNHistory Research* (blog), December 30, 2017, https://ndnhistoryre- search.com/2017/12/30/ the-battle-of-abiqua-second-battle-of-the-willamette-valley/.

17 Gibson, *Cultural Resources Overview*, 8-9; Oregon Parks and Recreation Department, *Detroit Lake State Park Masterplan*, 7; Smithsonian Institution Columbia Basin Project River Basin Surveys, *Appraisal of the Archeological Resources*.

18 Jacobs et al., *Kalapuya Texts*, 28.

19 Mackey, *The Kalapuyans*, 78-79.

20 Kelly, "Prehistoric Land-Use Patterns," 65-66.

21 Mackey, *The Kalapuyans*, 79.

22 Qutoed in Jetté, *At the Hearth of the Crossed Races*, 29 and 36; see also Whaley, *Oregon and the Collapse of Illahee*, 39.

23 See Jetté, *At the Hearth of the Crossed Races,* 36 and 40-41.

24 "1850 Census, Silverton, Waldo Hills, Santiam Canyon Area, about 200 Homesteads" (1850), Canyon Life Museum, Mill City, OR.

25 Mackey, *The Kalapuyans*, 109 and 146.

26 The treaty negotiations, maps, and signed treaties are available in full in Mackey, *The Kalapuyans*, 98-167. See also "Documents Relating to the Negotiation of an Unratified Treaty." David Lewis has also written about the treaty negotiations; see, e.g., "The 1851 Treaty Commission Journal: Santiam Kalapuya Negotiations," *NDNHistory Research* (blog), November 14, 2017, https://ndnhistoryresearch.com/2017/11/14/the-1851-treaty- commission-journal-santiam-kalapuya-negotiations/; idem, *NDNHistory Research* (blog), "Rejection of the Nineteen 1851 Oregon Treaties," December 31, 2017, https://ndnhistoryresearch.com/2017/12/31/ rejection-of-the-nineteen-1851-oregon-treaties/.

27 The entire proceedings may have been moot from the beginning. Melinda Jetté has noted that Congress abolished the special Indian Treaty Commissions on February 27, 1851, two months before the Kalapuyans and Molallans traveled to Champoeg for the treaty negotiations; see *Oregon Encyclopedia*, s.v. "Kalapuya Treaty of 1855," accessed September 27, 2018, https://oregonencyclopedia.org/articles/kalapuya_treaty/#.W6zSWFJG2Ba.

28 Whaley, *Oregon and the Collapse of Illahee*, 185. For narrative and analysis of the treaty rejection, see 182-86. See also Jetté, *At the Hearth of the Crossed Races*, 195-96; Coan, "First Stage of the Federal Indian Policy."

29 Jetté, *At the Hearth of the Crossed Races*, 195.

30 Mackey, *The Kalpayans*, 167-71; "Ratified Treaty No. 282"; "Ratified Treaty No. 300"; David G. Lewis, "Temporary Reservation and Removal of the

Molalla Band of Indians 1855-1856," *NDNHistory Research* (blog), May 21, 2016, https://ndnhistoryresearch.com/2016/05/21/temporary-reservation-and-removal-of-the-molalla-band-of-indians-1855-1856/; idem, "When the Tribes Sold Everything: Oregon Tribal Treaty Payments," *NDNHistory Research* (blog), October 1, 2016, https://ndnhistoryresearch.com/2016/10/01/when-the-tribes-sold-everything-oregon-tribal-treaty-payments/; idem, "Treaty with the Molala, Negotiated December 21, 1855, Ratified March 8, 1859," *NDNHistory Research* (blog), January 16, 2018, https://ndnhistoryresearch.com/2018/01/16/treaty-with-the-molala-negotiated-december-21-1855-ratified-march-8-1859/.

31 Brent Merrill and Yvonne Hajda, "The Confederated Tribes of the Grand Ronde Community of Oregon," in Berg, *First Oregonians*, 120-45.

32 Correspondence with author, April 6, 2019.

33 Kelly, "Prehistoric Land-Use Patterns," 37-38.

34 Fleetwood, "Growing Up in Mill City."

35 Robbins, *Colony and Empire*, esp. Part 2; White, *"It's Your Misfortune and None of My Own,"* 243.

36 Fleetwood, "Timeline—North Santiam Canyon," 1.

37 Elliot, "Peter Skene Ogden Journals."

38 Minto, "From Youth to Age as an American," 157.

39 For histories relating the drama of the fur trade, see DeVoto, *Across the Wide Missouri*; Reid, *Contested Empire*; idem, *Forging a Fur Empire*.

40 Robbins, *Landscapes of Promise*, 56-57; Schwantes, *Pacific Northwest*, 74.

41 Robbins, *Landscapes of Promise*, 128-30; idem, *Colony and Empire*, 84-86; Burch, "Development of Metal Mining in Oregon"; Schwartz, *Rogue River Indian*; White, *"It's Your Misfortune and None of My Own,"* 265-67; Keith Bryant, "Entering the Global Economy," in Milner et al., *Oxford History of the American West*, 196-235; Limerick, *Legacy of Conquest*, 99-124.

42 Minto, "From Youth to Age as an American," 159-160.

43 Willis Grafe, *Gates of the North Santiam*, 32.

44 "Things in Oregon—From our own correspondent, Portland, Oregon, 25 June 1864," *The Daily Bulletin*, in Judge M.P. Deady Scrapbooks, #112, Oregon Historical Society, Portland.

45 The most complete history of mining in the area focuses on the Little North Fork: George, *Santiam Mining District*.

46 *Dayton Herald*, Friday 1897, in Judge M. P. Deady Scrapbooks, #112, Oregon Historical Society, Portland.

47 Fleetwood *Just a Few of Our Memories*, vol. 2, 12.

48 Grafe, *Gates of the North Santiam*, 32.

49 *Dayton Herald*, Friday 1897, in Judge M. P. Deady Scrapbooks, #112; p. 58 of Scrapbook 62, Oregon Historical Society, Portland.

50 "U.S. Census 1900," *North Santiam Historical Society Newsletter* (February/March 2005): 5-7.

51 "Diary of a Miner on the Santiam River, Oregon, 1863-1864," Manuscripts, Oregon Historical Society, Portland.

52 Fleetwood, *Just a Few of Our Memories*, vol. 2, 12; Cox, *Little North Santiam Mining District*; George, *Santiam Mining District*.

53 Minto, "Minto Pass."

54 Clark, *History of the Willamette Valley*.

55 Minto, "Minto Pass," 242.

56 Minto, "From Youth to Age as an American," 156-57.

57 Lowe, *John Minto*; *Oregon Encyclopedia*, s.v. "John Minto (1822-1915)," by William Lang, accessed November 14, 2018, https://oregonencyclopedia. org/articles/minto_john_1822_1915_/#.W-wqkSdG2BY; Minto, "OHQ 100 Years."

58 Galloway, "Tribute to John Minto."

59 "Interview with Jack Minto"; Lowe, *John Minto*, 77-78.

60 Fleetwood, "Timeline—North Santiam Canyon," 2.

61 *Mill City Logue*, January 17, 1929.

62 Throughout his life, Ephraim Henness vehemently defended his claim to the pass discovery. See *Salem Capitol Journal*, June 18, 1927; *Salem Oregon Statesman*, September 10, 1941; and *Mill City Enterprise*, April 28, 1949.

63 Bowen, *Willamette Valley*.

64 Fleetwood, "Timeline—North Santiam Canyon," 1; *Mill City Logue*, June 9, 1927; Will Potter, email correspondence with author, October 2005.

65 *Mill City Logue*, June 9, 1927.

66 Gadwa, "Autobiography."

67 US Census Bureau, *10th Census of Population Schedule*.

68 US Census Bureau, *10th Census of Population Schedule*.

69 Minnie Smith McCarty, quoted in Grafe, *Gates of the North Santiam*, 5-6.

70 Charles and Mary Hill Kelly, in Fleetwood, *Just a Few of Our Memories*, vol. 1, 4.

71 For brief surveys of the frontier myth, see Hine and Faragher, *Frontiers*, chap. 15, "The Myth of the Frontier"; White, *"It's Your Misfortune and None of My Own,"* 613-32; for a more in-depth study, see Slotkin, *Regeneration through Violence*; idem, *Fatal Environment*; idem, *Gunfighter Nation*.

72 Gadwa, "Autobiography."

73 Grafe, *Gates of the North Santiam*, 4.

74 Grafe, *Gates of the North Santiam*, 5.

75 Stout, "The Mehama Story."

76 "Farming in the Canyon," museum exhibit, Canyon Life Museum, Mill City, Oregon.

77 Fleetwood, "Timeline—North Santiam Canyon," 2-3; Lengacher, "History of the North Santiam Canyon."

78 Fleetwood, "Timeline—North Santiam Canyon," 2-3; Stout, "The Mehama Story."

79 Stout, "The Mehama Story," 7.

80 Edgar Williams & Co. and Marion County Historical Society, *Historical Atlas Map of Marion & Linn Counties*; "Survey Details—Township 9s, 3e," 1874, *General Land Office Records*, accessed November 23, 2019, https://glorecords.blm.gov/details/survey/default.aspx?dm_id=349424&sid=mvwt53fm.qod#surveyDetailsTabIndex=1.

81 "Thomas Brothers, Charles and William, Gates and Detroit, Compiled Information, Map" (n.d.), Canyon Life Museum, Mill City, OR.

CHAPTER 2: RAILROAD, FRAUD, AND COMPLICITY

1 For histories of the Oregon Pacific, see Scott, "Yaquina Railroad"; Clark et al., "T. Egenton Hogg"; Tonsfeldt, "History of the Oregon Pacific Railroad"; Fleetwood, "Successful Failure"; Gavin, *Empire of Dreams*.

2 "Oregon Pacific R.R. Co. Prospectus and Financial Circular," *Portland Morning Oregonian*, November 8, 1880.

3 White, *Railroaded*.

4 The phrase "mental territory" is from Morrissey, *Mental Territories*. For the fundamental changes brought by railroads, see Cronon, *Nature's Metropolis*.

5 Oregon Pacific Railroad Company, *Prospectus of the Oregon Pacific R.R. Co.*

6 Fleetwood, "Timeline—North Santiam Canyon," 2.

7 Quoted in Fleetwood, "Successful Failure," 4.

8 *West Shore*, October 19, 1889, 187. Many thanks to Greg Gordon for these notes.

9 Rauchway, *Murdering McKinley*, 162-63.

10 Scott, "Yaquina Railroad," 241.

11 Scott, "Yaquina Railroad," 229; Tanaka," First Person Who 'Owned' Mill City."

12 "Oregon Pacific R.R. Co. Prospectus," *Portland Morning Oregonian*, November 8, 1880.

13 Scott, "Yaquina Railroad," 241.

14 Grafe, *Gates of the North Santiam*, 38; Fleetwood, "Successful Failure," 5.

15 Limerick, "Property Values," in *Legacy of Conquest*, chap. 2. See also White, "Distributing the Land," in *"It's Your Misfortune and None of My Own,"* chap. 6.

16 "*Oregon Union/The Union Gazette/Corvallis Gazette*," Historic Oregon Newspapers, accessed July 18, 2018, https://oregonnews.uoregon.edu/history/uniongazette/.

17 Messing, "Public Lands, Politics, and Progressives." See also Kammer, "Land and Law in the Age of Enterprise."

18 The firsthand account of these trials is Puter and Stevens, *Looters of the Public Domain*. For more on the trials, see Messing, "Public Lands, Politics, and Progressives"; *Oregon Encyclopedia*, s.v. "Oregon Land Fraud Trials (1904-1910)," accessed March 9, 2016, http://www.oregonencyclopedia.org/

articles/oregon_land_fraud_trials_1904_1910_; *Oregon Encyclopedia*, s.v. "Stephen Puter (1857–?)," accessed May 31, 2018, https://oregonencyclo-pedia.org/articles/puter_stephen_1857_.

19 Puter and Stevens, *Looters of the Public Domain*, 47-48.

20 Puter and Stevens, *Looters of the Public Domain*, 46.

21 Puter and Stevens, *Looters of the Public Domain*, 46.

22 Langille et al., *Forest Conditions in the Cascade Range Forest Reserve Oregon*.

23 For the ways that such timber management laws were often created with the support and manipulation of the timber industry, see Clary, *Timber and the Forest Service*; Robbins, *Lumberjacks and Legislators*.

24 For more on C. A. Smith in Oregon, see Robbins, *Hard Times in Paradise*; *Oregon Encyclopedia*, s.v. "C. A. Smith Lumber Company," by William Robbins, accessed September 12, 2019, https://oregonencyclopedia.org/articles/c_a_smith_lumber_company/#.XXsRYiVG2go.

25 Puter, *Looters of the Public Domain*, 134.

26 Puter, *Looters of the Public Domain*, 50.

27 Puter, *Looters of the Public Domain*, 66.

28 Puter, *Looters of the Public Domain*, 136.

29 Hays, *Conservation and the Gospel of Efficiency*; Wiebe, *Search for Order*; Rodgers, "In Search of Progressivism"; Johnston, *Radical Middle Class*.

30 US Congress House Committee on Public Lands, *Oregon and California Land Grants*.

31 Scott, "Yaquina Railroad," 231, 237.

32 Grafe, *Gates of the North Santiam*, 38.

33 *Mill City Gazette*, May 8, 1891, reprinted in the *Mill City Logue*, September 2, 1926.

34 Gavin, *Empire of Dreams*, 148.

35 Fleetwood, "Timeline—North Santiam Canyon," 4.

36 Tonsfeldt, "History of the Oregon Pacific Railroad"; National Register of Historic Places, "Oregon Pacific Railroad Linear Historic District National Register of Historic Places Registration Form," Willamette National Forest and Deschutes National Forest, Blue River, OR, 1999.

37 Grafe, *Gates of the North Santiam*, 40.

38 Fleetwood, "Timeline—North Santiam Canyon," 5.

39 "Mehama House Hotel Register."

40 Grafe, *Gates of the North Santiam*, 65-70.

41 Fleetwood, "Successful Failure," 7.

42 J. A. W. Heidecke (Oregon City, Oregon), homestead certificate no. 4725, US Bureau of Land Management, "Land Patent Search," *General Land Office Records*, accessed June 18, 2018, http://glorecords.blm.gov/PatentSearch; "John A. William Heidecke (1857-1931)," Find a Grave Memorial, accessed June 21, 2018, https://www.findagrave.com/memo-rial/73798982/john-a._william-heidecke; "United States Census, 1900," database with images, *FamilySearch*, accessed December 18, 2019, https://

familysearch.org/ark:/61903/1:1:MSDN-KJL; Heidecke, *Breitenbush, Elkhorn, and Horeb Precincts.*

43 Puter, *Looters of the Public Domain*, 52.

44 Puter, *Looters of the Public Domain*, 55.

45 Puter, *Looters of the Public Domain*, 53-55.

46 Puter, *Looters of the Public Domain*, 154.

47 (Klamath Falls) *The Evening Herald*, January 8, 1932.

48 Land patents for Township 11 south, range 7 east, Willamette Meridian, Oregon, US Bureau of Land Management, "Land Patent Search," digital images, *General Land Office Records*, accessed June 18, 2018, https://glore-cords.blm.gov/search/.

49 Fleetwood, "Successful Failure."

50 Charles and Mary Kelly, "Train Memories," *Mill City Enterprise*, January 13, 1972.

51 "Oregon Central & Eastern Railroad Co. Time Table No. 1," in Gavin, *Empire of Dreams*, 260.

52 "Southern Pacific Timetable," July 4, 1915, Canyon Life Museum.

53 Fleetwood, "Successful Failure," 6.

54 Fleetwood, "Timeline—North Santiam Canyon," 5.

55 Dorris didn't run the paper for long, deciding to retire in October of that year and passing the paper on to O. A. Cheney, recently of Albany. See *Albany State Rights Democrat*, October 30, 1891.

56 *Mill City Logue*, September 2, 1926.

57 Lucy Lewis Scrapbook.

58 Ernst Lau, letter to North Santiam Historical Society, n.d., Canyon Life Museum, Mill City, Oregon.

59 *Mill City Gazette*, May 8, 1891.

CHAPTER 3: THE HAMMOND LUMBER COMPANY

1 Scott, *Weapons of the Weak*; idem, *Domination and the Arts of Resistance.*

2 For the history of A. B. Hammond, see Gordon, *When Money Grew on Trees*. See also Johnson, "Andrew B. Hammond," and Gage McKinney, "A. B. Hammond, West Coast Lumberman."

3 Johnson, "Andrew B. Hammond," 33.

4 Simultaneous to his purchase of the Oregon Pacific, Hammond bought another railroad, the Astoria and Columbia River Railroad. For more on that purchase and Hammond's influence on the Oregon coast (as well as information about the North Santiam Canyon), see Gordon, *When Money Grew on Trees*, chap. 10, and idem, "Economic Phoenix."

5 Fleetwood, "Timeline—North Santiam Canyon," 6.

6 Gordon, *When Money Grew on Trees*, chap. 9.

7 Minutes of the Board of Directors of the Santiam Lumbering Company, Hammond Lumber Company Files, vol. 27, Oregon Historical Society, Portland.

8 *Columbia River and Oregon Timberman*, June 1900, 17.

9   For timberland acquisitions and timber industry business strategies in the early twentieth century, see Brock, *Money Trees*, 25-30; Robbins, *Lumberjacks and Legislators*; Ficken, *Forested Land*; Robbins, *Hard Times in Paradise*; Cox, *Lumberman's Frontier*.

10 *Pacific Lumber Trade Journal*, October 1899, 18.

11 *Timberman*, September 1906, 34.

12 Gordon, *When Money Grew on Trees*, 199-218.

13 Hammond Lumber Company State of Timber and Land Accounts, 1913 to 1955, 3. Copy in author's possession.

14 "Tapping Cascade Timber," *Timberman*, June 1929.

15 Fleetwood, "Timeline—North Santiam Canyon," 9.

16 Curtis Cline in Fleetwood, *Just a Few of Our Memories*, vol. 2, 7.

17 *Mill City Logue*, October 21, 1926.

18 *Mill City Logue*, March 3, 1927, and June 30, 1927. See also Gordon, *When Money Grew on Trees*, 195.

19 "Logging with Skidders in the Cascade Mountains: Mill City Operations of Hammond Lumber Company," *Timberman*, July 1929, 44-45.

20 Hammond Lumber Company, Mill City, Oregon, appraisal by A. A. Semsen, August 22, 1929, Oregon Historical Society, Portland.

21 Holbrook, *Holy Old Mackinaw*; Steven Christopher Beda, "Landscapes of Solidarity"; Loomis, *Empire of Timber*. See also Prouty, *More Deadly than War!*

22 "Logging with Skidders," 44.

23 Lloyd M. Palmer, Map of Logging Camps, n.d., US Department of Agriculture, Forest Service, Canyon Life Museum, Mill City, OR.

24 *Directory of the Lumber Industry*.

25 Hammond Lumber Company, Mill City, Oregon, appraisal by A. A. Semsen, August 22, 1929, Oregon Historical Society, Portland.

26 *Mill City Logue*, November 4, 1926.

27 *Mill City Logue*, November 4, 1926; "United States Census, 1900," database with images, *FamilySearch*, accessed August 5, 2014, https://familysearch.org/; Oregon > Marion > ED 123 and Linn > ED 43, 44, citing *NARA Microfilm Publication T623* (Washington, DC: National Archives and Records Administration, n.d.); "United States Census, 1920," database with images, *FamilySearch*, accessed September 13, 2019, https://familysearch.org/; Oregon > Marion > ED 316, 332 and Linn > ED 296, citing *NARA Microfilm Publication T625* (Washington, DC: National Archives and Records Administration, n.d.).

28 *Columbia River and Oregon Timberman*, June 1900, 17; November 1903, 20; and March 1905, 20; *Timberman*, March 1916.

29 *Timberman*, March 1928, 24.

30 *Mill City Logue*, January 5, 1928, and March 8, 1928.

31 *Mill City Logue*, January 13, 1927.

32 Stanley Chance in Fleetwood, *Just a Few of Our Memories*, vol. 2, 43.

33 US Forest Service Detroit Ranger District, "Grazing Practice of Logged-Off Lands of the Hammond Lumber Company."

34 Curtis Cline in Fleetwood, *Just a Few of Our Memories*, vol. 2, 4.

35 Allen, *Company Town in the American West*; Carlson, *Company Towns*.

36 Otto Witt in Fleetwood, *Just a Few of Our Memories*, vol. 2, 17.

37 Morrow, "Note Book of C.C. Morrow."

38 William Bertram to Thomas LaDuke, "Hammond Job Offer," February 9, 1915, Canyon Life Museum, Mill City, OR.

39 Gertenrich, "Thomas Kay Woolen Mill," 105.

40 Robbins, *Colony and Empire*, esp. Part 2, "Forces of Transformation"; idem, *Hard Times in Paradise*.

41 *Timberman*, August 1911, 29; March 1923, 138; September 1928, 27-28; and October 1928, 24.

42 For examples of overproduction and railroad cars, see *Columbia River and Oregon Timberman*, September 1903, 9; November 1903, 11; *Timberman*, May 1907, 23.

43 Johnson, "Production of Lumber, Lath, and Shingles," table 2; National Bureau of Economic Research, "Index of Wholesale Prices of Lumber for United States.

44 *Timberman*, March 1916.

45 Quoted in Fleetwood, *Just a Few of Our Memories*, vol. 2, 10.

46 Stanley Chance in Fleetwood, *Just a Few of Our Memories*, vol. 2, 45.

47 Hays, *Conservation and the Gospel of Efficiency*; Clary, *Timber and the Forest Service*.

48 Ephraim Henness to John Minto, April 26, 1907. In the letter, Henness does not mention the controversy over the discovery of the pass, perhaps choosing to keep the matter separate from the more pressing issue of controlling the excesses of Hammond. For Minto's interest in forestry, see Cox, "Conservationist as Reactionary."

49 Rilla Schaeffer in Fleetwood, *Just a Few of Our Memories*, vol. 1, 13.

50 Leora Stevens in Fleetwood, *Just a Few of Our Memories*, vol. 1, 15.

51 Sylvia Gooch Stevenson, "Gooch History," in Fleetwood, *Just a Few of Our Memories*, vol. 2, pages 54-55.

52 For discussions of timber workers and their strategies of itinerancy, job changes, and longer-term employment, see Beda, "Landscapes of Solidarity"; Loomis, *Empire of Timber*.

53 Fleetwood, "Growing Up in Mill City."

54 *United [Grocers] Purity News*, March 1, 1929.

55 For the history of consumerism in the United States, see Cohen, *Making a New Deal*; Frank, *Purchasing Power*; Dumenil, *Modern Temper*; Cohen, *Consumers' Republic*.

56 Thomas Cronise Collection, MSS 2692, Oregon Historical Society, Portland.

57 The phrase "purchasing power" is from Dana Frank, who uses it in the much more politicized context of labor activism in Seattle in the early

twentieth century. The broader idea—exercising power through consumption—is, I think, useful in this less explicitly political context.

58 "Memories of Verne E. Hawkins," *North Santiam Canyon Historical Society Newsletter* (September/October/November 1996): 2.

59 *Mill City Logue*, April 14, 1927.

60 Charles and Mary Hill Kelly in Fleetwood, *Just a Few of Our Memories*, vol. 1, 6; Williams, *The Loggers*, 191.

61 *Mill City Logue*, May 14, 1933.

62 Frances Kazda Dolezal in Fleetwood, *Just a Few of Our Memories*, vol. 1.

63 Skocpol, "Civil Society in the United States."

64 Dumenil, *Modern Temper*, 4; Clawson, *Constructing Brotherhood*.

65 Fleetwood, "Timeline—North Santiam Canyon," 8, 13.

66 Emery and Emery, *Young Man's Benefit*, membership and lodges on table I.I, p. 23; comparison to other societies on p. 3.

67 "Constitution and By-Laws of Mill City Lodge, No. 144, I.O.O.F.," February 16, 1900, Mill City Lodges IOOF, Canyon Life Museum, Mill City, OR.

68 Emery and Emery, *Young Man's Benefit*, 24.

69 Quoted in Fleetwood, *Just a Few of Our Memories*, vol. 1, 15.

70 *Mill City Logue*, September 26, 1926.

71 "1900 and 1920 Census Notes Re: Occupations and Place of Birth," Canyon Life Museum, Mill City, Oregon.

72 Hammond Company Files, vol. 29, payroll files, Oregon Historical Society, Portland.

73 "United States Census, 1930," database with images, *FamilySearch*, accessed December 10, 2015, https://familysearch.org/ark:/61903/3:1:33SQ-GRC8-SXC?cc=1810731&wc=QZF7-96Z%3A648804701%2C649697601%2C649 721401%2C1589282428; Oregon > Linn > Mill City > ED 28 > image 10 of 18, citing *NARA Microfilm Publication T626* (Washington, DC: National Archives and Records Administration, 2002).

74 Quoted in Fleetwood, *Just a Few of Our Memories*, vol. 2.

75 Quoted in Fleetwood, *Just a Few of Our Memories*, vol. 2.

76 Rilla Schaeffer, in Fleetwood, *Just a Few of Our Memories, Volume I*, page 13.

77 "United States Census, 1920," database with images, *FamilySearch*, accessed September 13, 2019, https://familysearch.org/ark:/61903/3:1:33S7-9RNT-Y6D?cc=1488411&wc=QZJB-FBD%3A1036471901%2C1036668101%2C 1038356401%2C1589335791; Oregon > Marion > Breitenbush > ED 316, citing *NARA Microfilm Publication T625* (Washington, DC: National Archives and Records Administration, n.d.).

78 "1900 and 1920 Census Notes Re: Occupations and Place of Birth," Canyon Life Museum, Mill City, OR.

79 Armitage and Jameson, *Women's West*; Johnson, *Roaring Camp*; White, *"It's Your Misfortune and None of My Own,"* 277–78.

80 For the size, scope, and impact of immigration, see Nugent, *Crossings*; Rauchway, *Blessed among Nations*.

81 Fleetwood, *Just a Few of Our Memories*, vol. 2, 47.

82 Jacobson, *Whiteness of a Different Color*. For nativism and immigration, see also Bennett, *Party of Fear*; Nugent, *Crossings*; Jacobson, *Barbarian Virtues*; Higham, *Strangers in the Land*; Daniels, *Guarding the Golden Door*.

83 US Census Bureau, *14th Census of Population Schedule, 1920*.

84 Podrabsky, "Mill City Czech Immigrants."

85 *Mill City Logue*, April 3, 1929.

86 *Mill City Logue*, November 11, 1926.

87 "Constitution and By-Laws of Mill City Lodge."

88 For the "second Klan," see Jackson, *Ku Klux Klan in the City*; MacLean, *Behind the Mask of Chivalry*; Gordon, *Second Coming of the KKK*.

89 Johnson, "Anti-Japanese Legislation in Oregon." For recruitment through the Masons, see Dumenil, *Modern Temper*, 238. For numbers of Klaverns, see Eckard Toy, "Robe and Gown: The Ku Klux Klan in Eugene, Oregon, during the 1920s," in Lay, *Invisible Empire in the West*, 162.

90 *Mill City Logue*, December 8, 1927.

91 For immigration restriction legislation, see Daniels, *Guarding the Golden Door*.

92 Gordon, *When Money Grew on Trees*, 348.

93 Gordon, *When Money Grew on Trees*, 276 (profits), 4 (California holdings), and chap. 11, "Assembling an Empire."

94 Gordon, *When Money Grew on Trees*, 385.

CHAPTER 4: THE GREAT DEPRESSION

1 Robbins, *Hard Times in Paradise*. For the situation in Oregon more generally, see idem, "Surviving the Great Depression," and Munro, "Seventy-Fifth Anniversary of the New Deal." For the Great Depression and New Deal in the West, see Lowitt, *New Deal and the West*.

2 *Mill City Logue*, December 12, 1929.

3 *Mill City Logue*, October 31, 1929.

4 *Mill City Logue*, February 26, 1931.

5 *Mill City Logue*, May 3, 1928. For declines in the timber market during this period, see Johnson, "Production of Lumber, Lath, and Shingles"; Moravets, *Lumber Production in Oregon and Washington*; Robbins, *Hard Times in Paradise*, 78-79.

6 *Mill City Logue*, August 6, 1931; Walt Leisy in Fleetwood, *Just a Few of Our Memories*, vol. 2, 39.

7 Lea, "Report on the Hammond Lumber Company," 31-32.

8 *Four L Lumber News*, July 1, 1935, 27.

9 Kelly, "Autobiography."

10 *Mill City Logue*, October 1, 1931.

11 Stanley Chance in Fleetwood, *Just a Few of Our Memories*, vol. 2, 43.

12 *Mill City Logue*, December 8, 1932.

13 "Southern Pacific Employee (Freight) Timetables."

14 Fisher, "Through the Thirties."

15 *Mill City Logue*, August 26, 1926.

16 *Mill City Logue*, February 9, 1933.

17 *Mill City Logue*, May 25, 1933.

18 *Mill City Logue*, September 2, 1926.

19 Tom La Duke, "Gentleman of the Road," in Fleetwood, *Just a Few of Our Memories*, vol. 2.

20 Henry Bock, "A Memory of Gates during the Depression Era," in Fleetwood, *Just a Few of our Memories*, vol. 2.

21 Fisher, "Through the Thirties," 3.

22 Henry Bock, "Chittum Bark Trail," *North Santiam Historical Society Newsletter* (July/August/September 2003): 4.

23 Stanley Chance in Fleetwood, *Just a Few of Our Memories*, vol. 2, 42.

24 Munro, "Seventy-Fifth Anniversary of the New Deal," 306-7; Maher, *Nature's New Deal*.

25 Fleetwood, "Timeline—North Santiam Canyon," 14.

26 Walter E. Seamster, "From Memory," *North Santiam Historical Society Newsletter* (January/February 2002): 3.

27 Clipping from CCC Publication *The Review*, February 15, 1940; "Santiam Pass Ski Lodge," *Restore Oregon* (blog), accessed November 19, 2018, https://restoreoregon.org/most-endangered-places-2018/santiam-pass-ski-lodge/.

28 Seamster, "From Memory."

29 Seamster, "From Memory," 9.

30 *Mill City Logue*, July 16, 1931.

31 Oregon State Highway Division, *Historical Highway Projects*.

32 Fisher, "Through the Thirties," 10.

33 Rogers, "Clyde Rogers Family."

34 Fisher, "Through the Thirties," 6.

35 Steiner, "Regionalism in the Great Depression"; Webb, "By the Sweat of the Brow"; White, "Poor Men on Poor Lands."

36 Glen E. Shelton, "I Remember," *North Santiam Historical Society Newsletter* (February/March 1995): 3.

37 Fisher, "Through the Thirties," 4.

38 Fleetwood, "Growing Up in Mill City."

39 Walt Leisy in Fleetwood, *Just a Few of Our Memories*, vol. 2, 39.

40 Grafe, "Short History of Gates."

41 *Mill City Logue*, June 30, 1932.

42 Toman and Griffen, "Toman Family Memories."

43 Fleetwood, "Growing Up in Mill City."

44 Fisher, "Through the Thirties," 15.

45 Young Family, "Dream of the Scott Young Family."

46 Dorothy J. (Young) Newman, interview by Sue McMillan, February 21, 2008.

47 Kelly, "Autobiography."

48 Salem *Capital Journal*, April 24, 1937; Otto Witt in Fleetwood, *Just a Few of Our Memories*, vol. 1, 17; *Mill City Enterprise*, March 10, 1949; *Timberman*, February 1936, 85.

49 Petersen, *Santiam Song*, 42-43.

50 Fleetwood, "Timeline—North Santiam Canyon," 14.

51 Petersen, *Santiam Song*, 59.

52 McRae, "Journey Home."

53 Walt Leisy in Fleetwood, *Just a Few of Our Memories*, vol. 2, 39.

54 Grafe, *Gates of the North Santiam*, 15.

CHAPTER 5: THE HIGHWAY AND THE DAM

1 Wells, *Car Country*; Gutfreund, *Twentieth-Century Sprawl*.

2 Robbins, *Landscapes of Conflict*, chap. 2; idem, "Willamette Valley Project of Oregon."

3 Worster, *Rivers of Empire*; White, *Organic Machine*; Reisner, *Cadillac Desert*.

4 Wells, *Car Country*.

5 Oregon State Highway Division, *Highway Historical Projects*.

6 Stanley Chance in Fleetwood, *Just a Few of Our Memories*, vol. 2, 44.

7 Tom Fisher, "Through the Thirties," 9.

8 Lowell Fleetwood in Fleetwood, *Just a Few of Our Memories*, vol. 2, 15.

9 Oregon State Highway Division, *Highway Historical Projects*; *Mill City Logue*, December 18, 1930.

10 *Oregon Statesman* and *Capital Journal*, December 12, 1930.

11 US Department of Agriculture, Forest Service, Willamette National Forest, *North Santiam Recreation Guide*. For more on the Skyline Trail, see Barker, "Oregon Skyline Trail."

12 Ed Thurston, "Hoodoo Ski Bowl Short History," June 9, 1959, Canyon Life Museum, Mill City, OR.

13 Cook, "From Hot Springs to Heritage."

14 Minto, "From Youth to Age as an American," 158.

15 Chapman, "Forest Service Summer Homes at Breitenbush."

16 F. W. Ross, "Breitenbush Hot Springs: First Class Hotel," *Daily Capital Journal* (Salem, OR), August 22, 1902, 3, quoted in Cook, "From Hot Springs to Heritage," 63.

17 Van Winkle, "Waters of the Breitenbush Hot Springs."

18 *Breitenbush Hot Springs, Oregon*, investment prospectus brochure, n.d., "Detroit" Box, North Santiam Canyon Historical Society, Mill City, OR.

19 *Mill City Logue*, July 4, 1929.

20 *Mill City Logue*, December 18, 1930.

21 *Mill City Enterprise*, December 30, 1948.

22 *Mill City Enterprise*, February 9, 1950.

23 *Mill City Logue*, October 21, 1926.

24 *Mill City Enterprise*, February 9, 1950.

25 Stafford, *Diary*, October 20, 1945.

26 *Mill City Logue*, February 27, 1930.

27 Oregon State Highway Division, *Historical Highway Projects*.

28 *Mill City Enterprise*, December 30, 1948.

29 For a thoughtful and thorough institutional history of river development in Oregon, see Willingham, *Army Engineers and the Development of Oregon*. For "hydraulic society," see Donald Worster, *Rivers of Empire*; for "organic machine," see White, *Organic Machine*.

30 Some notable exceptions: Barber, *Death of Celilo Falls*; Loo, "People in the Way"; idem, "Disturbing the Peace."

31 The approach of this section and this chapter more broadly developed from an earlier article; see Reinhardt, "Drowned Towns in the Cold War West."

32 "Logging With Skidders In The Cascade Mountains," *The Timberman* (July 1929): 44-45; Curtis Cline in Fleetwood, *Just a Few of Our Memories*, vol. 2, 8.

33 Melody Munger, correspondence with author, May 27, 2019.

34 Drawson, "Letter to the Editor."

35 Willingham, *Army Engineers and the Development of Oregon*, 107.

36 Stevens, *Reservoirs for Navigation and Flood Control*, 37.

37 Robbins, "Willamette Valley Project of Oregon"; White, *Organic Machine;* Eve Vogel, "Columbia River's Region."

38 Flood Control Act of 1936, Pub. L. No. 74-738.

39 Willamette River Basin, Oregon, H. Doc. 544, 75th Cong., 3rd Sess. (1938).

40 Fisher, "Through the Thirties," 21.

41 US Army Corps of Engineers, Portland District, *Review Report on Columbia River and Tributaries*, 1.

42 See Robbins, "Willamette Valley Project of Oregon."

43 US Army Corps of Engineers, Portland District, *Review of Survey Report Willamette River and Tributaries Oregon*, 367.

44 US Army Corps of Engineers, Portland District, *Review of Survey Report Willamette River and Tributaries Oregon*, 396.

45 *Mill City Enterprise*, February 9, 1948.

46 *Mill City Enterprise*, June 11, 1953.

47 *Mill City Enterprise*, September 15, 1949.

48 US Army Corps of Engineers, Portland District, *Review of Survey Report Willamette River and Tributaries Oregon*.

49 *Mill City Enterprise*, December 30, 1948.

50 *Mill City Enterprise*, June 4, 1953.

51 "Tompkins, Robert L. Pay Stub from Detroit," 1950, Oregon Historical Society, Portland; US Department of Labor, "Occupational Wage Survey for Portland, Oregon, June 1951," 12; "History of Federal Minimum Wage

Rates under the Fair Labor Standards Act, 1938-2009," US Department of Labor, accessed August 23, 2019, https://www.dol.gov/whd/minwage/chart.htm#.UNuMXXeDmSo.

52 *Mill City Enterprise*, March 10, 1948.

53 *Mill City Enterprise*, April 7, 1949

54 *Mill City Enterprise*, October 13, 1949

55 *Mill City Enterprise*, March 10, 1949.

56 *Mill City Enterprise*, June 7, 1949.

57 US Army Corps of Engineers, "Real Estate Planning Report."

58 US Army Corps of Engineers, "Detroit Project Job Construction Manual."

59 US Army Corps of Engineers, Portland District, *Review of Survey Report Willamette River and Tributaries Oregon*.

60 "Realty Deals Portend Building Rise," *Mill City Enterprise*, August 11, 1949.

61 "Cedar Tavern & Cedars Restaurant and Lounge, 1949–1999 / Three Generations of Ownership by the Layman Family," ca. 1999, Detroit File, North Santiam Historical Society, Mill City, OR.

62 "Passing of Detroit Brings Both Cheers and Moans," *Oregonian* (Portland), May 21, 1952.

63 Col. T. H. Lipscomb to residents of Detroit, June 18, 1952, NARA— Portland District.

64 Detroit Construction Manual, 29.

65 Letter from Col. O. E. Walsh, district engineer, May 13, 1949, NARA RG 77, US Army Corps of Engineers, Portland District, Portland, OR.

66 Lipscomb to division engineer, North Pacific Division, April 22, 1952, NARA—Portland District and United States v. Cochran, No. 6642 (unpublished case, D. Or. November 14, 1952).

67 United States v. John W. Outerson et al., US District Court, Portland, OR, July 12, 1949.

68 "Passing of Detroit Brings Both Cheers and Moans," *Oregonian* (Portland), May 21, 1952.

69 US Army Corps of Engineers, *Columbia River and Tributaries*.

70 "Correspondence with David Orr in Detroit," 1938, National Archives and Records Administration, Pacific-Alaska Region, Seattle, WA.

71 "Detroit Order OK'd," *Mill City Enterprise*, July 21, 1949.

72 Dottie Young oral history and "Idanha," March 5, 1959, Canyon Life Museum, Mill City, OR.

73 *Mill City Enterprise*, September 15, 1949.

74 *Mill City Enterprise*, December 15, 1949.

75 *Mill City Enterprise*, June 9, 1949.

76 Col. D. S. Burns to division engineer, North Pacific Division, December 21, 1949, NARA—Portland District; Lipscomb to Ivan Oakes, December 14, 1951, NARA—Portland District.

77 Platted map, Marion County Assessor's Office, Salem, OR; "Rising Detroit Dam on North Santiam Forces Mass Evacuation of Entire Community," *Capital Journal* (Salem, OR), May 25, 1952.

78 "Hammond Addition to Detroit" plat, vol. 16, p. 22, Marion County Clerk, Salem, OR; Deed records from sales of tracts in Hammond Addition by Hammond Lumber Company, Marion County Clerk, Salem, OR; Petition to incorporate the City of Detroit, May 15, 1952, Marion County Clerk, Salem, OR.

79 Dottie Young oral history.

80 "Rising Detroit Dam on North Santiam Forces Mass Evacuation of Entire Community," *Capital Journal* (Salem, OR), May 25, 1952; Hammond Addition to Detroit plat, vol. 16, p. 22, Marion County Clerk, Salem, OR; Hammond Addition deed records, Marion County Clerk, Salem, OR; US Army Corps of Engineers, "Tract Register for Detroit Lake-Big Cliff."

81 "A Day for Reflection," *Mill City Enterprise*, May 29, 1952.

82 "Cedar Tavern & Cedars Restaurant and Lounge, 1949–1999 / Three Generations of Ownership by the Layman Family," ca. 1999, Detroit File, North Santiam Historical Society, Mill City, OR.

83 Mrs. S. T. Moore, "Detroit Had Dramatic Year in '52," *Mill City Enterprise*, January 8, 1953.

84 "Minutes of Meeting: Arrangements Committee for Dedication of Detroit Dam," April 6, 1953, Canyon Life Museum, Mill City, OR.

85 "Detroit Dam Dedication Ceremony Brochure," June 10, 1953, Canyon Life Museum, Mill City, OR.

86 *Mill City Enterprise*, June 11, 1953.

CHAPTER 6: BECOMING A TIMBER COMMUNITY

1 For an insightful study on the development of, membership in, and identity of "timber communities," see Carroll, *Community and the Northwestern Logger*.

2 Rajala, *Clearcutting the Pacific Rain Forest*; Robbins, *Hard Times in Paradise*, chap. 9.

3 *Mill City Enterprise*, June 7, 1949.

4 Oregon State Highway Division, *Historical Highway Projects*.

5 *Mill City Enterprise*, January 22, 1953.

6 US Department of Agriculture, Forest Service, Willamette National Forest, "Forest Road Mileage Summary."

7 See esp. Hirt, *Conspiracy of Optimism*; Robbins, *Landscapes of Conflict*, section III.

8 Rakestraw and Rakestraw, *History of the Willamette National Forest*, 201-3.

9 US Department of Agriculture, Forest Service, Detroit Ranger District, "Harvest by Decade."

10 *Mill City Enterprise*, January 22, 1953; February 12, 1953; and February 26, 1953.

11 Anonymous interviewee in "A Human Geographic Issue Management System for Natural Resource Managers: The Mill City / Lyons Community Resource Unit," James Kent Associates, accessed December 23, 2019, http://www.jkagroup.com/methods/willamette/chapterfour.htm; "More Sawdust in the Valley," letter to North Santiam Historical Society, 1996, Canyon Life Museum, Mill City, OR.

12 *Mill City Enterprise*, September 3, 1953.

13 *Mill City Enterprise*, January 9, 1964; May 30, 1963.

14 US Department of Agriculture, Forest Service, Willamette National Forest, "Timber Cut and Sold Worksheet."

15 Prudham, *Knock on Wood*. For logging technology, see Rajala, *Clearcutting the Pacific Rain Forest.*

16 *Mill City Enterprise*, May 26, 1949.

17 *Statesman Journal*, February 27, 1949; *Mill City Enterprise*, March 31, 1949.

18 *Capital Journal*, May 28, 1949; *Albany Democrat-Herald*, June 22, 1949.

19 *Mill City Enterprise*, September 1, 1955.

20 *Mill City Enterprise*, March 29, 1951.

21 *Mill City Enterprise*, November 25, 1948; "Producer Price Index by Commodity for Lumber and Wood Products," Federal Reserve Bank of St. Louis, accessed September 9, 2019, https://fred.stlouisfed.org/series/WPU08.

22 *Mill City Enterprise*, February 10, 1948.

23 *Mill City Enterprise*, June 30, 1949.

24 *Mill City Enterprise*, May 10, 1956.

25 *Mill City Enterprise*, May 10, 1956.

26 John L. Walker, "Simpson: A Century of Growth and Future Prospects. The S.J. Hall Lecture in Industrial Forestry," University of California, Berkeley, College of Natural Resources, accessed November 26, 2019, https://nature.berkeley.edu/site/lectures/sjhall/1990.php. For Simpson history, see Spector, *Family Trees.*

27 *Mill City Enterprise*, October 23, 1957; and December 20, 1957.

28 "Producer Price Index by Commodity for Lumber and Wood Products: Plywood," Federal Reserve Bank of St. Louis, accessed September 9, 2019, https://fred.stlouisfed.org/series/WPU083.

29 *Mill City Enterprise*, June 8, 1960.

30 *Mill City Enterprise*, August 29, 1960.

31 *Mill City Enterprise*, August 3, 1967; "Producer Price Index by Commodity for Lumber and Wood Products: Plywood."

32 US Census Bureau, *19th Census of Population Schedule, 1980, Summary Tape File 3A, Oregon, Marion and Linn Counties, Mill City CCD,* University of Oregon Knight Library, Eugene, Oregon (Washington, D.C.: National Archives), microfiche.

33 For Hammond labor relations, see Gordon, *When Money Grew on Trees*, chaps. 16-18. For timber workers and class conflict in the Pacific Northwest, see Beda, "Landscapes of Solidarity," Lipin, *Workers and the*

Wild, Loomis, *Empire of Timber*, and Robbins, *Hard Times in Paradise*, chap. 10.

34 Hammond Lumber Company Files, Oregon Historical Society, Box 20.

35 John Jackson, "Politics and the Milkman in Detroit," in Fleetwood, *Just a Few of Our Memories*, vol. 1, 41.

36 The instructive term "countervailing" comes from Eric Rauchway, who explains and uses the term most concisely in *The Great Depression and the New Deal*.

37 Stafford, *Diary*, October 3, 1942, and June 16, 1944.

38 *Mill City Enterprise*, July 28, 1949.

39 For organized labor's postwar approach to combining antagonism with accommodation and compromise in industrial relations, see Dubofsky and Dulles, *Labor in America*, chaps. 19-20.

40 "Labor Agreement, Detroit Dam Project," April 8, 1949, Morrison-Knudsen Labor Relations, 1947-1962, MSS 22 Box 4, Folder "Projects; Dams, Detroit Dam," Boise State University Library Special Collections, Boise, ID.

41 International Woodworkers of America, "Records, 1936-1987," Box 199/244, "Expired Contracts: 3-246, Oakridge Trucking – 3-261, Georgia Pacific," Folder EXP. CONT'S—3-25 (F,L); 3-2561 (C), University of Oregon Special Collections, Corvallis.

42 US Department of Labor, "Industry Wage Survey: West Coast Sawmilling, June 1964," *Bulletin of the US Bureau of Labor Statistics* 1455 (June 1964): 20, https://fraser.stlouisfed.org/title/4637/item/498051.

43 Stafford, *Diary*.

44 *Mill City Enterprise*, May 11, 1950.

45 *Mill City Enterprise*, July 28, 1954.

46 For the IWA, see Beda, "Landscapes of Solidarity," and Lembcke and Tattam, *One Union in Wood*.

47 *Mill City Enterprise*, December 15, 1988.

48 *Mill City Enterprise*, October 12, 1967.

49 Petersen, *Santiam Song*, chap. 2, sections 14-17.

50 Quoted in Petersen, *Santiam Song*, 37.

51 United States v. Champion International Corp., Young & Morgan, Inc., Bugaboo Timber Co., Freres Lumber Co., Inc., Freres Veneer Co., and Frank Lumber Co., Inc., L. James Bagley, Vernon R. Morgan, Robert T. Freres, and A. J. Frank, 557 F.2nd 1270 (9th Cir. 1977), https://law.justia.com/cases/federal/appellate-courts/F2/557/1270/272936/.

52 *Mill City Enterprise*, September 23, 1965.

53 *Mill City Enterprise*, May 9, 1968.

54 *Mill City Enterprise*, September 26, 1968; September 4, 1969.

55 *Mill City Enterprise*, September 4, 1969.

56 *Mill City Enterprise*, October 2, 1969.

57 Quoted in Petersen, *Santiam Song*, 46.

58 *Willamette Week* (Portland, OR), July 28, 1975.

59 *Willamette Week*, July 28, 1975.

60 *Mill City Enterprise*, May 27, 1976.

61 *Mill City Enterprise*, September 29, 1977.

62 Detroit City Council minutes, November 9, 1977, City Recorder's Office, Detroit, OR.

63 *Mill City Enterprise*, October 12, 1967.

64 "Cheating on Sales of Timber Costing Millions Every Year," *Oregonian*, November 17, 1991; "Federal Judge Erases Names on Indictment," *Oregonian*, January 2, 1992; "Federal Timber Conspiracy Trial of Retired Scaler Goes to Jury," *Oregonian*, July 8, 1992; "Log Scaler Guilty of Timber Sales Scam," *Oregonian*, July 16, 1992.

65 *Statesman Journal* (Salem, OR), October 20, 1993.

66 *Mill City Enterprise*, June 16, 1988.

67 Ron Oberg, "NS Plywood, Workers at Odds over Pay," *Stayton Mail*, June 29, 1988.

CHAPTER 7: ENVIRONMENTALISM AND TOURISM

1 Gottlieb, *Forcing the Spring*; Hays, *Beauty, Health, and Permanence*; idem, *History of Environmental Politics*; Rome, *Bulldozer in the Countryside*; Rothman, *Greening of a Nation?*; Sellers, *Crabgrass Crucible*.

2 Lengacher, History of the North Santiam Canyon; Kelly, "Prehistoric Land-Use Patterns," 116.

3 *Mill City Logue*, July 4, 1929.

4 Worster, *Nature's Economy*; Marx, *Machine in the Garden*; Marsh, *Man and Nature*; Nash, *Wilderness and the American Mind*.

5 *Mill City Enterprise*, January 7, 1960.

6 "Park in Cool Cascades Is Only Forty Miles From Salem," *Oregon Statesman*, June 15, 1961; "Niagara," Marion County Oregon, accessed December 26, 2018, https://www.co.marion.or.us/PW/Parks/descriptions/Pages/niagara.aspx.

7 For the history of this project, see Robbins, *Landscapes of Conflict*, 232-37.

8 *Mill City Enterprise*, March 29, 1956.

9 *Mill City Enterprise*, January 14 and March 10, 1960.

10 Harvey, *Symbol of Wilderness*; Sutter, *Driven Wild*; Harvey, *Wilderness Forever*.

11 Marsh, *Drawing the Lines in the* Forest, chap. 3; Rakestraw and Rakestraw, *History of the Willamette National Forest*, 109.

12 Marsh, *Drawing the Lines in the Forest*, 69.

13 *Mill City Enterprise*, January 26, 1967.

14 *Mill City Enterprise*, September 26, 1968.

15 Kevin Marsh's *Drawing Lines in the Forest* explores fights over old-growth forests in the Pacific Northwest in the decades after World War II, and Paul Hirt's *Conspiracy of Optimism* portrays decades of intensive timber extraction encouraged by the US Forest Service, even as conservation and preservation demands increased. Those broader origins are reflected on in brief in

Marcot et al., *Of Spotted Owls, Old Growth, and New Policies*, and in other histories and contemporary accounts of the spotted owl controversy, including Spies and Duncan, *Old Growth in a New World*; Booth, *Valuing Nature*; Durbin, *Tree Huggers*; Dietrich, *Final Forest*; Carroll, *Community and the Northwestern Logger*; Satterfield, *Anatomy of a Conflict*. For reflection on this history and its legacy, see Loomis and Edgington, "Lives under the Canopy."

16 Hirt, *Conspiracy of Optimism*.

17 Dennis Frank, interview with author, 2006.

18 US Department of Agriculture, Forest Service, Willamette National Forest, "Timber Cut and Sold Worksheet."

19 Dennis Frank, interview with author, 2006.

20 A comprehensive history about Opal Creek has yet to be written, but journalist Zach Urness has provided a concise history in "The Fight That Saved Opal Creek's Ancient Forest," *Statesman Journal*, September 24, 2016, https://www.statesmanjournal.com/story/news/2016/09/24/opal-creek-hike-logging-three-pools-little-north-santiam-river/90384728/. *Showdown at Opal Creek*, a contemporary account by journalist David Seidemann, is interesting and engaging.

21 Hirt, *Conspiracy of Optimism*; Prudham, *Knock on Wood*, esp. chap. 6, "Timber and Town." William Robbins notes that "During the booming national-forest harvests of the 1980s (and before the spotted-owl rulings), nearly 200 sawmills closed in Oregon and Washington, and forest-products employment dropped by 25,000 workers" (*Landscapes of Conflict*, 210). For more about the complex origins and evolution of timber industry and forest problems, see Nancy Langston, *Forest Dreams, Forest Nightmares*; Rajala, *Clearcutting the Pacific Rain Forest;* and Robbins, *Landscapes of Conflict*, 205-10.

22 For a history of the Yellow Ribbon Rallies and the associated Yellow Ribbon Campaign, see Medford, "Lumber, Community, and the Anti-Environmentalist." The rallies and the Yellow Ribbon Campaign are also noted in Dumont, "Demise of Community and Ecology in the Pacific Northwest."

23 *Mill City Enterprise*, September 1, 1988.

24 *Mill City Enterprise*, April 19, 1989.

25 "Legislators Chide Lyons Mill for Paying Employees at Rally," *Statesman Journal*, February 25, 1989; "Timber Rally Leads to a Truck-Drivin' Log Jam for Traffic," *Oregonian*, April 14, 1990.

26 Myles McMillan, interview with author, 2006.

27 CGO newsletter, March 1992; Liz VanLeeuwen Spotted Owl Collection.

28 Dan Postrel, "Group Will Fight Environmental Moves," *Statesman Journal*, November 12, 1991.

29 CGO newsletter, August 1992; Liz VanLeeuwen Spotted Owl Collection.

30 CGO newsletter, March 1991; Liz VanLeeuwen Spotted Owl Collection.

31 CGO newsletter, May 1992; Liz VanLeeuwen Spotted Owl Collection.

32 CGO newsletter, August 1992; Liz VanLeeuwen Spotted Owl Collection.

33 CGO newsletter, December 1991; Liz VanLeeuwen Spotted Owl Collection.

34 *Mill City Enterprise*, January 12, 1989.

35 *Mill City Enterprise*, February 2, 1989.

36 CGO newsletter, May 1992, July 1991, November 1991.

37 CGO newsletter, March 1992; Liz VanLeeuwen Spotted Owl Collection.

38 For the changing role and approach of scientists in the US Forest Service as seen through the old-growth debates and the Northwest Forest Plan, see Wellock, "Dickey Bird Scientists Take Charge." For a sampling of reports and retrospective analyses from the agencies and individuals involved in creating and implementing the Northwest Forest Plan, see Christensen et al., "Northwest Forest Plan"; Haynes and Perez, "Northwest Forest Plan Research Synthesis"; Stankey et al., "Adaptive Management and the Northwest Forest Plan"; Thomas et al., "Northwest Forest Plan."

39 Dan Postrel, "Timber Workers Assess Their Future," *Statesman Journal*, July 2, 1993.

40 Petersen, *Santiam Song*, chap. 3, pp. 5 and 39.

41 Petersen, *Santiam Song*, 39, 68, 69.

42 Ted Freres, interview with author, 2006.

43 "A Human Geographic Issue Management System for Natural Resource Managers in the Willamette Valley, Oregon," Social Ecology and the JKA Group, accessed November 20, 2019, http://www.jkagroup.com/methods/willamette-index/index.htm.

44 *Mill City Enterprise*, July 27, 1989.

45 Oregon Parks and Recreation Department, *Detroit Lake State Park Visitor Counts, 1965-2003*.

46 US Department of Agriculture, Forest Service, Detroit Ranger District, "North Santiam Complex Revenue Summary, 1996-2000."

47 *Mill City Enterprise*, July 22, 1954.

48 *Mill City Enterprise*, September 27, 1956.

49 *Mill City Enterprise*, March 25, 1954.

50 Oregon Secretary of State Corporation Division, *Active and Inactive Business Name City Search*.

51 Christensen, *Red Lodge and the Mythic West*; Rothman, *Devil's Bargains*. See also Philpott, *Vacationland*, Pierce, "Winds of Change."

52 *Mill City Enterprise*, May 2, 1963.

53 *Mill City Enterprise*, January 20, 1994.

54 Detroit City Council Minutes, April 9, 1985.

55 "Monthly Total Precipitation, Detroit Dam, Oregon (35292): Period of Monthly Climate Summary," Western Regional Climate Center, accessed August 25, 2007, http://www.wrcc.dri.edu/cgi-bin/cliMAIN.pl?or2292.

56 "The Great Western Drought of 1977," *Time*, March 7, 1977.

57 "Detroit Reservoir Nearly Full," *Mill City Enterprise*, May 26, 1977.

58 "Monthly Total Precipitation, Detroit Dam."

59 "Summer Fun Could Evaporate," *Oregonian*, March 12, 2001.

60 *Mill City Independent Press*, February 14, 2001; March 7, 2001; March 21, 2001.

61 "Record Low Water Levels at Detroit Lake Has Locals Worried," *Mill City Independent Press*, February 14, 2001.

62 Oregon Parks and Recreation Department, *Detroit Lake State Park Visitor Counts, 1965-2003*; US Department of Agriculture, Forest Service, Detroit Ranger District, "North Santiam Complex Revenue Summary, 1996-2000."

63 Stephanie Knowlton, "Farmers, Business Owners, Boaters Fight for Water," *Salem Statesman Journal*, September 23, 2001.

64 The US Army Corps of Engineers' press releases from 2001 emphasize the extraordinary conditions of that rain year. See "U.S. Army Corps of Engineers struggles to manage limited water supply," March 5, 2001; "Meetings to tell about Willamette water situation," April 17, 2001; "Corps of Engineers to increase water releases to protect fish," April 26, 2001, available at "News Releases—Portland District—US Army Corps of Engineers," accessed December 23, 2019, https://web.archive.org/web/20090115203212/https://www.nwp.usace.army.mil/pa/news/home.asp?y=2001.

65 "Detroit Business Group Change Focus after Recent Corps of Engineers Meeting," *Mill City Independent Press*, May 2, 2001.

66 Col. Randall Butler, Commander, US Army Corps of Engineers Northwest Project, "Memorandum for the Record." memorandum,

67 US Census Bureau, *Characteristics of the Population*; U.S. Census Bureau, "Census 2000 Summary File 1, Total Population," for Salem City, accessed December 20, 2019, https://factfinder.census.gov/bkmk/table/1.0/en/DEC/00_SF1/P001/1600000US4164900.

68 For the City of Salem's use of water from the North Santiam River, see Mauldin, *Sweet Mountain Water*.

69 US Army Corps of Engineers, *Columbia River and Tributaries*, 239.

70 Col. Randall Butler, Commander, US Army Corps of Engineers Northwest Project, "Memorandum for the Record."

71 National Oceanic and Atmospheric Administration, "Endangered and Threatened Species."

72 These figures are for Big Cliff Dam, the "regulating dam" one mile downstream from Detroit Dam and the final Army Corps of Engineers release point for water from Detroit Reservoir. Data queried from "Big Cliff Dam and Lake," US Army Corps of Engineers, accessed December 23, 2019, http://www.nwd-wc.usace.army.mil/dd/common/projects/www/bcl.html.

73 Col. Randall Butler, Commander, US Army Corps of Engineers Northwest Project, "Memorandum for the Record," 3.

74 Pope, *Nuclear Implosions*.

75 Wallis, *Evaluation of the North Santiam River Salmon Hatcheries*.

76 Willingham, *Army Engineers and the Development of Oregon*, 201.

77 *Mill City Enterprise*, September 8, 1977, and October 15, 1977.

78 *H.R. Doc. No. 531*, 81st Cong., 2nd sess. (1948), 1.

79 *H.R. Doc. No. 544*, 75th Cong., 3rd sess. (1938), 91.

80 Dan Itel, "Boaters Protest Low Detroit Lake," *Statesman Journal*, June 10, 2001.

81 *Mill City Independent Press*, March 21, 2001.

82 *Mill City Independent Press*, May 23, 2001.

83 Letter from Mike Swaim to Pam Hill, June 1, 2001, in author's possession.

84 *Mill City Independent Press*, May 16, 2001.

85 *Mill City Independent Press*, May 23, 2001.

86 *Mill City Independent Press*, June 13, 2001.

87 *Mill City Independent Press*, July 25, 2001.

88 Heidi Helwig, Public Relations Officer, U.S. Army Corps of Engineers, Portland District, interview by KATU-2 Evening News, Portland, Oregon, April 13, 2005, http://www.katu.com/salem/story.asp?ID=76454.

89 "Federal Lakes Recreation—Pilot Lake Demonstrations," US Department of the Interior, accessed April 24, 2004, https://web.archive.org/web/20031231025820/http://www.doi.gov/flr/list_of_lakes.html .

90 Stephanie Knowlton, "Farmers, Business Owners, Boaters Fight for Water," *Statesman Journal*, September 23, 2001.

91 *Mill City Independent Press*, March 7, 2001.

92 *Mill City Independent Press*, May 2, 2001.

93 *Mill City Independent Press*, March 21, 2001.

EPILOGUE

1 Chris McGreal, "Where Even Walmart Won't Go: How Dollar General Took Over Rural America," *Guardian*, August 13, 2018.

2 Zach Urness, "Canyon Fire Brings Up Questions," *Statesman Journal*, December 27, 2017.

3 Salem Statesman Journal, "Did Climate Trigger Toxic Algae Bloom Hurting Salem's Water?," OregonLive.com, June 7, 2018, https://www.oregonlive.com/pacific-northwest-news/index.ssf/2018/06/did_climate_trigger_toxic_alga.html.

4 Zach Urness, "Empty Lake to Save Fish?," *Statesman Journal*, January 14, 2018, https://statesmanjournal.newspapers.com/image/366834437/.

5 "About Us," KYAC 94.9 FM Radio, accessed January 8, 2019, http://www.kyacfm.org/about-us.

6 "About Us," Santiam Hearts to Arts (H2A) website, accessed January 8, 2019, http://www.santiamh2a.org/about-us.

7 "Local News," *Canyon Weekly*, accessed January 8, 2019, http://www.theCanyonweekly.com/category/local-news/; *Our Town Santiam*, May 1, 2019, https://issuu.com/mappublications/docs/ots_05012019/3.

8 "Historic Railroad Bridge Receives Major Department of Transportation Grant," *Our Town Santiam*, accessed January 8, 2019, http://ourtownlive.com/ourtownsantiam/?p=3346.

Bibliography

Primary Sources

GOVERNMENT DOCUMENTS

Butler, Col. Randall, Commander, US Army Corps of Engineers Northwest Project. "Memorandum for the Record. Subject: Willamette Reservoir Operations for 2001 — Decision Process Documentation." May 29, 2001. Copy in author's possession. Provided by Matt Rea, Willamette Basin Coordinator, US Army Corps of Engineers, April 14, 2004.

Detroit City Council Minutes. City Recorder's Office, Detroit, OR.

"Documents Relating to the Negotiation of an Unratified Treaty of April 19, 1851, with the Kalapuya and Molala Indians." April 19, 1851. National Archives and Records Administration, Washington, DC. http://digicoll. library.wisc.edu/cgi-bin/History/History-idx?type=header&id=History. Unrat1851no14.

Heidecke, John W. *Breitenbush, Elkhorn, and Horeb Precincts, Marion, Oregon, United States, Citing Enumeration District (ED) 123, Sheet 6B, Family 149.* NARA microfilm publication T623. Washington, DC: National Archives and Records Administration, 1972. [FHL microfilm 1,241,349.]

Langille, H. D., Fred Plummer, Arthur Dodwell, Theodore Rixon, and John Leiberg. "Forest Conditions in the Cascade Range Forest Reserve Oregon." Professional Paper 9. Department of the Interior US Geological Survey, Washington, DC, 1903.

National Oceanic and Atmospheric Administration. "Endangered and Threatened Species: Threatened Status for Three Chinook Salmon Evolutionarily Significant Units in Washington and Oregon, and Endangered Status of One Chinook Salmon ESU in Washington." *Federal Register* 64, no. 56 (March 24, 1999): 14308.

Oregon Parks and Recreation Department. *Detroit Lake State Park Masterplan.* Salem: Oregon Parks and Recreation Department, 2002.

——. "Detroit Lake State Park Visitor Counts, 1965-2003." Database report. Copy in author's possession. Generated by Tom Hughes, Oregon Parks and Recreation Department (OPRD) Revenue Economist, and Frank Howard, OPRD Public Information Officer, Salem, May 2004.

Oregon Secretary of State Corporation Division. "Active and Inactive Business Name City Search on Mehama, Lyons, Mill City, Gates, Detroit and Idanha, 1990-2000." Database report. Copy in author's possession.

Generated by Business Registry Division, Oregon Secretary of State, Salem, April 29, 2005.

Oregon State Highway Division. *Historical Highway Projects, North Santiam Highway*. Salem: Oregon State Highway Division, June 1977.

Stevens, J. C. *Reservoirs for Navigation and Flood Control on Willamette River, Oregon*. Portland, OR: Stevens & Koon, Consulting Engineers, May 10, 1935.

US Army Corps of Engineers, Portland District. "Real Estate Planning Report Covering Proposed Acquisition of Lands, Detroit Dam, Marion and Linn Counties Oregon." August 30, 1946. Real Estate Division, Portland District, US Army Corps of Engineers, Portland, OR.

——. *Columbia River and Tributaries*, vol. 4, Appendix J, Part II. Portland, OR: US Army Corps of Engineers, 1948.

——. "Detroit Project Job Construction Manual" [ca. 1948]. Detroit Dam Project Codes 601 and 602. Portland District Civil Works Project Files, US Army Corps of Engineers, RG 77, National Archives and Records Administration, Pacific–Alaska Region, Seattle.

——. *Review of Survey Report Willamette River and Tributaries Oregon, Appendix I—Public Hearings*, vol. 3, *Public Hearing held at Salem, Oregon, April 25, 1947*. Portland, OR: US Army Corps of Engineers, 1948.

——. *Review Report on Columbia River and Tributaries*, vol. 1, Appendix J. Portland, OR: US Army Corps of Engineers, 1951.

——. "Final Project Ownership Map, Detroit Reservoir." 1957. Real Estate Division, Portland District, US Army Corps of Engineers, Portland, OR. Copy in author's possession.

US Bureau of Land Management. General Land Office Records. Accessed November 22, 2019. https://glorecords.blm.gov.

US Census Bureau. *10th Census of Population Schedule, 1880, Oregon, Marion and Linn Counties, Fox Valley and Mehama Precincts*. Salem: Oregon State Archives. Washington, DC: National Archives, 1881. Microfilm.

——. "United States Census, 1900." Database with images. *FamilySearch*. Accessed June 14, 2016. http://FamilySearch.org. [Citing NARA microfilm publication T623. Washington, DC: National Archives and Records Administration, n.d.]

——. *14th Census of Population Schedule, 1920, Oregon, Marion and Linn Counties, Mill City Precinct*. Salem: Oregon State Archives. Washington, DC: National Archives, 1921. Microfilm.

——. *19th Census of Population Schedule, 1980, Summary Tape File 3A, Oregon, Marion and Linn Counties, Mill City CCD*. Eugene: University of Oregon Knight Library. Washington, DC: National Archives, 1981. Microfiche.

——. *Characteristics of the Population: Number of Inhabitants, Oregon*. PC80<H>1-A39. Washington, DC: US Census Bureau, 1981. http://www2.census.gov/prod2/decennial/documents/1980a_orABC-01.pdf.

———. "Characteristics of the Population: Total Population, Salem City, Oregon." Census 2000 Summary File. US Census Bureau American Fact Finder. Accessed December 20, 2019. https://factfinder.census.gov/bkmk/table/1.0/en/DEC/00_SF1/P001/1600000US4164900.

US Congress House Committee on Public Lands. *Oregon and California Land Grants: Hearings Before the Committee on Public Lands, House of Representatives, 64th Congress, 1st Session.* Washington, DC: US Government Printing Office, 1916.

US Department of Agriculture, Forest Service, Detroit Ranger District. "Harvest by Decade." Memorandum, n.d. Copy in author's possession. Provided by Rod Stewart, District Ranger, Detroit District, Willamette National Forest, April 15, 2004.

———. "North Santiam Complex Revenue Summary, 1996-2000." Memorandum, n.d. Copy in author's possession. Provided by Rod Stewart, district ranger, Detroit District, Willamette National Forest, April 15, 2004.

US Department of Agriculture, Forest Service, Willamette National Forest. *North Santiam Recreation Guide.* Blue River, OR: US Department of Agriculture, Forest Service, Willamette National Forest, 1936. In author's possession. Courtesy of Cara Kelly, US Forest Service archaeologist.

———. "Timber Cut and Sold Worksheet, District Sale Detail, Detroit District, 1984-1988." Microfiche, n.d. Willamette National Forest Supervisor's Office, Eugene, OR.

———. "Forest Road Mileage Summary." Database report, n.d. Copy in author's possession. Generated by Palmer Utterback, transportation engineer, Forest Service Region Six Supervisor's Office, Eugene, OR, April 20, 2005.

———. *Hogg's Railroad: Transformation of a Dream.* Mill City, OR: Canyon Life Museum.

US Department of the Interior. "Federal Lakes Recreation—Pilot Lake Demonstrations." Accessed April 25, 2004. https://web.archive.org/web/20031231025820/http://www.doi.gov/flr/list_of_lakes.html.

US Department of Labor. "Occupational Wage Survey: Portland, Oregon, June 1951." *Bulletin of the US Bureau of Labor Statistics* 1042 (June 1951).

———. "Industry Wage Survey: West Coast Sawmilling, June 1964." *Bulletin of the US Bureau of Labor Statistics* 1455 (June 1964): 20, https://fraser.stlouisfed.org/title/4637/item/498051.

ORAL HISTORIES / PERSONAL RECOLLECTIONS

Eliot, T. C., ed. "The Peter Skene Ogden Journals." *Quarterly of the Oregon Historical Society* 11 (1910): 201-22.

Fisher, Tom. "Through the Thirties: Detroit Oregon, As I Remember." Written recollection, n.d. Oral History Collection, Canyon Life Museum, Mill City, OR.

Fleetwood, Evangelyn, ed. *Just a Few of Our Memories.* Vol. 1, *Revised, Enlarged and Illustrated.* 2nd ed. Mill City, OR: North Santiam Historical Society, 1998.

————. *Just a Few of Our Memories.* Vol. 2, *Mill City Oregon, 1888-1988.* Mill City, OR: North Santiam Historical Society, 1988.

Fleetwood, Lowell. "Growing Up in Mill City." Lecture presented at a meeting of North Santiam Historical Society, Mill City, OR, February 3, 1994. Oral History Collection, Canyon Life Museum, Mill City, OR.

Gadwa, William Isaac. "Autobiography, 1874-1945." *Oregon Historical Quarterly* 80 (1979): 269-85.

"Interview with Jack Minto, Son of John Minto." Marion County Historical Society Radio History Series, October 31, 1961. Transcript photocopy. Marion County Historical Society, Salem, OR.

Kelly, Carl. "Autobiography of Carl Hall Kelly Jr.," n.d. In author's possession.

Lau, Ernst. Letter to North Santiam Historical Society, n.d. Canyon Life Museum, Mill City, OR.

McRae, John. "Journey Home . . . A Local Man Returns to a Much Harder Time." *Friendswood (TX) Journal*, April 18, 2001. Copy at Canyon Life Museum, Mill City, OR.

Podrabsky, Arey. "Mill City Czech Immigrants." Letter to North Santiam Historical Society, n.d.. Canyon Life Museum, Mill City, OR.

Rogers, Clyde M. "The Clyde Rogers Family." Letter to North Santiam Historical Society, n.d.. Canyon Life Museum, Mill City, OR.

Stafford, Carmen Elaine. *Diary, 1941-1950.* Copy in author's possession. Courtesy of Melody Munger, North Santiam Historical Society, Mill City, OR.

Toman, Albert W., and Mildred Toman Griffen. "Toman Family Memories." Letter to North Santiam Historical Society, n.d. Oral History Collection, Canyon Life Museum, Mill City, OR.

"Tompkins, Robert L. Pay Stub from Detroit," 1950. Oregon Historical Society, Portland.

Young Family. "The Dream of the Scott Young Family." Personal family recollection, n.d. Oral History Collection, Canyon Life Museum, Mill City, OR.

MISCELLANEOUS

Chalidze, Lisa, Melody Munger, and Debbie Corning. "Niagara, Oregon: Autobiography of a Place," n.d. Unpublished partial manuscript in author's possession.

"Diary of a Miner on the Santiam River, Oregon, 1863-1864. Coll 8. Oregon Historical Society Research Library, Portland, OR.

Directory of the Lumber Industry (Pacific Coast). Portland, OR: Timberman Publishers, 1926. [Reprinted in *North Santiam Historical Society Newsletter* (July/August 1999): 4.]

Edgar Williams & Co. and Marion County Historical Society. *Historical Atlas Map of Marion & Linn Counties, Oregon, 1878.* Salem, OR: Marion County Historical Society, 1976. [Reprinted 2004.]

Hammond Lumber Company Files. Oregon Historical Society, Portland.

Henness, Ephraim, to John Minto, April 26, 1907. Oregon Historical Society, Portland. Photocopy on file at Canyon Life Museum, Mill City, OR.

Gibson, Eric. *Cultural Resources Overview and Reconnaissance Investigation for the Mill City Diversion Project, North Santiam River, Oregon*. Eugene, OR: Professional Analysts, 1983.

Grafe, Willis. "A Short History of Gates." Lecture presented at a meeting of North Santiam Historical Society, Mill City, Oregon, March 7, 2002. Oral History Collection, Canyon Life Museum, Mill City, OR.

International Woodworkers of America. Box 199/244, "Expired Contracts: 3<H>246, Oakridge Trucking – 3<H>261, Georgia Pacific," Folder EXP. CONT'S—3<H>25 (F,L); 3<H>2561 (C). University of Oregon Special Collections, Corvallis.

Johnson, Herman M. "Production of Lumber, Lath, and Shingles in Washington and Oregon 1869-1936." *PNW Old Series Research Notes* 24 (1938): 1-12.

Judge M. P. Deady Scrapbooks. Oregon Historical Society, Portland.

Lea, R. W. "A Report on the Hammond Lumber Company and Affiliated Companies," June 5, 1935. Charles H. McLeod Papers, K. Ross Toole Archives, University of Montana, Missoula.

Lengacher, John. "Untitled Manuscript History of North Santiam Canyon," circa 1994. Canyon Life Museum, Mill City, OR.

Liz VanLeeuwen Spotted Owl Collection, 1973-2004 (Bulk 1983-1998). 1983, Box 4 AC 03.02.03.10, Folder "CBO - Mill City, 1991-1992." Oregon State University Library Special Collections and Archives, Corvallis.

"Logging with Skidders in the Cascade Mountains: Mill City Operations of Hammond Lumber Company." *Timberman* (July 1929): 44-45.

Lucy Lewis Scrapbook. MSS Lewis. Oregon State University Libraries Special Collections and Archives, Corvallis.

"Mehama House Hotel Register [Manuscript], 1893-1903." Manuscripts, Oregon Historical Society, Portland.

Morrison-Knudsen Labor Relations. 1947-1962, MSS 22 Box 4, Folder "Projects; Dams, Detroit Dam." Boise State University Library Special Collections, Boise, ID.

Morrow, C .C. "Note Book of C.C. Morrow, Mill City, Oregon." 1919. Willamette Heritage Center, Salem, OR.

National Bureau of Economic Research. "Index of Wholesale Prices of Lumber for United States." Federal Reserve Bank of St. Louis. Accessed September 9, 2019. https://fred.stlouisfed.org/series/M0464AUSM336NNBR.

Puter, S. A. D., and Horace Stevens. *Looters of the Public Domain*. Portland, OR: Portland Printing House, 1908.

"Ratified Treaty No. 282, Documents Relating to the Negotiation of the Treaty of January 22, 1855, with the Kalapuya and Other Confederated Bands of Indians of the Willamette Valley." January 22, 1855. University of Wisconsin–Madison Libraries, Digital History Collection, http://digicoll.library.wisc.edu/cgi-bin/History/History-idx?type=header&id=History. IT1855no282.

"Ratified Treaty No. 300, Documents Relating to the Negotiation of the Treaty of December 21, 1855, with the Molala Indians." December 21, 1855. University of Wisconsin–Madison Libraries, Digital History Collection, http://digicoll.library.wisc.edu/cgi-bin/History/History-idx?type=header&id=History.IT1855no300.

Smithsonian Institution Columbia Basin Project River Basin Surveys. *Appraisal of the Archeological Resources of Twelve Reservoirs in the Willamette Valley, Oregon.* Portland, OR: US Army Corps of Engineers, Portland District, Technical Library, 1949.

"Southern Pacific Employee (Freight) Timetables, Brooklyn Subdivision." Photocopies courtesy of Bill Hyde, president, Pacific Northwest Chapter of the National Railway Historical Society, Portland, OR.

US Forest Service Detroit Ranger District. "Grazing Practice of Logged-Off Lands of the Hammond Lumber Company." Detroit, OR: US Forest Service Detroit Ranger District, 1920.

Van Winkle, Walton. "Waters of the Breitenbush Hot Springs, Oregon." *Journal of Industrial and Engineering Chemistry* 5, no. 4 (April 1, 1913): 300–301.

Secondary Sources

Allen, James B. *The Company Town in the American West.* Norman: University of Oklahoma Press, 1966.

Armitage, Susan H., and Elizabeth Jameson. *The Women's West.* Norman: University of Oklahoma Press, 1987.

Barber, Katrine. *Death of Celilo Falls.* Seattle: University of Washington Press, 2005.

Barker, Stuart. "The Oregon Skyline Trail: Evolving Attitudes toward Nature Tourism." *Oregon Historical Quarterly* 120, no. 1 (Spring 2019): 46–73.

Beckham, Stephen Dow. *The Indians of Western Oregon: This Land Was Theirs.* Coos Bay, OR: Arago Books, 1977.

———. *Oregon Indians: Voices from Two Centuries.* Corvallis: Oregon State University Press, 2006.

Beda, Steven Christopher. "Landscapes of Solidarity: Timber Workers and the Making of Place in the Pacific Northwest, 1900-1964." PhD thesis, University of Washington, 2015.

Bennett, David Harry. *The Party of Fear: From Nativist Movements to the New Right in American History.* Chapel Hill: University of North Carolina Press, 1988.

Berg, Laura, ed. *The First Oregonians.* 2nd ed. Portland: Oregon Council for the Humanities, 2007.

Bergmann, Mathias D. " 'We Should Lose Much by Their Absence': The Centrality of Chinookans and Kalapuyans to Life in Frontier Oregon." *Oregon Historical Quarterly* 109, no. 1 (2008): 34–59.

Booth, Douglas E. *Valuing Nature: The Decline and Preservation of Old-Growth Forests.* Lanham, MD: Rowman & Littlefield, 1994.

Bowen, William A. *The Willamette Valley: Migration and Settlement on the Oregon Frontier.* Seattle: University of Washington Press, 1978.

Boyd, Robert. *The Coming of the Spirit of Pestilence: Introduced Infectious Diseases and Population Decline among Northwest Coast Indians, 1774-1874.* Seattle: University of Washington Press, 1999.

———, ed. *Indians, Fire, and the Land in the Pacific Northwest.* Corvallis: Oregon State University Press, 1999.

Brock, Emily K. *Money Trees: The Douglas Fir and American Forestry, 1900-1944.* Corvallis: Oregon State University Press, 2015.

Burch, Albert. "Development of Metal Mining in Oregon." *Oregon Historical Quarterly* 43, no. 2 (1942): 105–28.

Carlson, Linda. *Company Towns of the Pacific Northwest.* Seattle: University of Washington Press, 2003.

Carroll, Matthew S. *Community and the Northwestern Logger: Continuities and Changes in the Era of the Spotted Owl.* Milton, UK: Routledge, 2019.

Chapman, Lloyd. "The Forest Service Summer Homes at Breitenbush," 1997. Unpublished manuscript. Canyon Life Museum, Mill City, OR.

Christensen, Bonnie. *Red Lodge and the Mythic West: Coal Miners to Cowboys.* Lawrence: University Press of Kansas, 2002.

Christensen, Harriet H., Terry L. Raettig, and Paul Sommers. *Northwest Forest Plan: Outcomes and Lessons Learned from the Northwest Economic Adjustment Initiative, Proceedings of a Forum, July 29-30, 1997.* PNW-GTR-484. Portland, OR: US Department of Agriculture Forest Service, Pacific Northwest Research Station, 1999.

Clark, Cleon. *History of the Willamette Valley and Cascade Mountain Wagon Road.* Bend, OR: Deschutes County Historical Society, 1987.

Clark, Keith, G. F. Pearson, and H. K. Davenport. "T. Egenton Hogg—A Footnote." *Oregon Historical Quarterly* 84, no. 3 (1983): 300–307.

Clary, David. *Timber and the Forest Service.* Lawrence: University Press of Kansas, 1986.

Clawson, Mary Ann. *Constructing Brotherhood: Class, Gender, and Fraternalism.* Princeton, NJ: Princeton University Press, 1989.

Coan, C. F. "The First Stage of the Federal Indian Policy in the Pacific Northwest, 1849-1852." *Quarterly of the Oregon Historical Society* 22, no. 1 (1921): 46–89.

Cohen, Lizabeth. *Making a New Deal: Industrial Workers in Chicago, 1919-1939.* Cambridge: Cambridge University Press, 1990.

———. *A Consumers' Republic: The Politics of Mass Consumption in Postwar America.* New York: Alfred A. Knopf, 2003.

Cook, Travis. "From Hot Springs to Heritage: A Cultural History of the Breitenbush Hot Springs." *Willamette Valley Voices: Connecting Generations* 2, no. 2 (Summer 2013): 53–79.

Cox, James B. *Little North Santiam Mining District: Cultural Resource Inventory Report.* Eugene, OR: US Department of Agriculture, Forest Service, Willamette National Forest, 1985.

Cox, Thomas R. "The Conservationist as Reactionary: John Minto and American Forest Policy." *Pacific Northwest Quarterly* 74, no. 4 (1983): 146–53.

——. *The Lumberman's Frontier: Three Centuries of Land Use, Society, and Change in America's Forests.* Corvallis: Oregon State University Press, 2010.

Cronon, William. *Nature's Metropolis: Chicago and the Great West.* New York: W. W. Norton, 1991.

Daniels, Roger. *Guarding the Golden Door: American Immigration Policy and Immigrants since 1882.* New York: Farrar, Straus & Giroux, 2005.

deBuys, William. *Enchantment and Exploitation: The Life and Hard Times of a New Mexico Mountain Range.* Rev. and expanded ed. Albuquerque: University of New Mexico Press, 2015.

DeVoto, Bernard. "The West: A Plundered Province." *Harper's Magazine* 169 (1934): 355–64.

——. *Across the Wide Missouri.* Boston: Houghton Mifflin, 1964.

Dietrich, William. *The Final Forest: The Battle for the Last Great Trees of the Pacific Northwest.* New York: Simon & Schuster, 1992.

Drawson, Maynard C. "Letter to the Editor: 'Niagara' and 'China Dam.'" *Oregon Historical Quarterly* 71, no. 4 (1970): 349–57.

Dubofsky, Melvyn, and Foster Rhea Dulles. *Labor in America: A History.* 7th ed. Wheeling, IL: Harlan Davidson, 2004.

Dumenil, Lynn. *The Modern Temper: American Culture and Society in the 1920s.* New York: Hill and Wang, 1995.

Dumont, Clayton W. "The Demise of Community and Ecology in the Pacific Northwest: Historical Roots of the Ancient Forest Conflict." *Sociological Perspectives* 39, no. 2 (1996): 277–300.

Durbin, Kathie. *Tree Huggers: Victory, Defeat and Renewal in the Northwest Ancient Forest Campaign.* Seattle, WA: Mountaineers, 1996.

Emery, George Neil, and John Charles Herbert Emery. *A Young Man's Benefit: The Independent Order of Odd Fellows and Sickness Insurance in the United States and Canada, 1860-1929.* Montreal: McGill-Queen's University Press, 1999.

Feldman, James. "The View from Sand Island: Reconsidering the Peripheral Economy, 1880–1940." *Western Historical Quarterly* 35, no. 3 (August 1, 2004): 285–307.

Ficken, Robert. *The Forested Land: A History of Lumbering in Western Washington.* Seattle: University of Washington Press, 1987.

Fleetwood, Evangelyn. "A Successful Failure: The Oregon Pacific Railroad." *Historic Marion* 40, no. 3 (Fall 2002): 1–8.

——. "Timeline—North Santiam Canyon." 2005. Canyon Life Museum, Mill City, OR.

Frank, Dana. *Purchasing Power: Consumer Organizing, Gender, and the Seattle Labor Movement, 1919-1929.* New York: Cambridge University Press, 1994.

Galloway, William. "A Tribute to John Minto." *Quarterly of the Oregon Historical Society* 17, no. 1 (1916): 44–46.

Gavin, Scott M. *Empire of Dreams: The Story of the Oregon Pacific, Oregon's Most Controversial Railroad.* Toledo, OR: Yaquina Pacific Railroad Historical Society, 2016.

George, Anthony G. *The Santiam Mining District of the Oregon Cascades: A Cultural Property Inventory and Historical Survey / Prepared for Shiny Rock Mining Corporation.* Salem, OR: Solo Press, 1985.

Gertenrich, Caryl. "The Thomas Kay Woolen Mill in Salem, Oregon 1900-1959." MS thesis, Oregon State University, 1977.

Gordon, Greg. "Economic Phoenix: How A. B. Hammond Used the Depression of 1893 and a Pair of Defunct Oregon Railroads to Build a Lumber Empire." *Oregon Historical Quarterly* 109, no. 4 (Winter 2008): 598–621.

———. *When Money Grew on Trees: A. B. Hammond and the Age of the Timber Baron.* Norman: University of Oklahoma Press, 2014.

Gordon, Linda. *Second Coming of the KKK: The Ku Klux Klan of the 1920s and the American Political Tradition.* New York: Liveright, 2018.

Gottlieb, Robert. *Forcing the Spring: The Transformation of the American Environmental Movement.* Washington, DC: Island Press, 1994.

Grafe, Willis. *Gates of the North Santiam.* Woodburn, OR: privately printed, 1989.

Gutfreund, Owen D. *Twentieth-Century Sprawl: Highways and the Reshaping of the American Landscape.* Oxford: Oxford University Press, 2005.

Harvey, Mark. *A Symbol of Wilderness: Echo Park and the American Conservation Movement.* Seattle: University of Washington Press, 2000.

———. *Wilderness Forever: Howard Zahniser and the Path to the Wilderness Act.* Seattle: University of Washington Press, 2007.

Haynes, Richard, and Gloria Perez. *Northwest Forest Plan Research Synthesis.* PNW-GTR-498. Portland, OR: US Department of Agriculture Forest Service, Pacific Northwest Research Station, January 2000.

Hays, Samuel P. *Conservation and the Gospel of Efficiency: The Progressive Conservation Movement, 1890-1920.* Cambridge, MA: Harvard University Press, 1959.

———. *Beauty, Health, and Permanence: Environmental Politics in the United States, 1955-1985.* New York: Cambridge University Press, 1987.

———. *A History of Environmental Politics since 1945.* Pittsburgh: University of Pittsburgh Press, 2000.

Higham, John. *Strangers in the Land: Patterns of American Nativism, 1860-1925.* New Brunswick, NJ: Rutgers University Press, 2002.

Hine, Robert V., and John Mack Faragher. *Frontiers: A Short History of the American West.* Lamar Series in Western History. New Haven, CT: Yale University Press, 2007.

Hirt, Paul W. *A Conspiracy of Optimism: Management of the National Forests since World War Two.* Lincoln: University of Nebraska Press, 1996.

Holbrook, Stewart H. *Holy Old Mackinaw: A Natural History of the American Lumberjack.* New York: Macmillan, 1938.

Jackson, Kenneth. *The Ku Klux Klan in the City, 1915-1930.* New York: Oxford University Press, 1967.

Jacobs, Melville, Albert Samuel Gatschet, and Leo Joachim Frachtenberg. *Kalapuya Texts.* Seattle: University of Washington Press, 1945.

Jacobson, Matthew Frye. *Whiteness of a Different Color: European Immigrants and the Alchemy of Race.* Cambridge, MA: Harvard University Press, 1999.

———. *Barbarian Virtues: The United States Encounters Foreign Peoples at Home and Abroad, 1876-1917.* New York: Hill and Wang, 2001.

Jetté, Melinda Marie. " 'Beaver Are Numerous, but the Natives . . . Will Not Hunt Them': Native-Fur Trader Relations in the Willamette Valley, 1812-1814." *Pacific Northwest Quarterly* 98, no. 1 (2006): 3–17.

———. "Dislodging Oregon's History from Its Mythical Mooring: Reflections on Death and the Settling and Unsettling of Oregon." *Oregon Historical Quarterly* 115, no. 3 (2014): 444–47.

———. *At the Hearth of the Crossed Races: A French-Indian Community in Nineteenth-Century Oregon, 1812-1859.* Corvallis: Oregon State University Press, 2015.

Johnson, Dale. "Andrew B. Hammond: Education of a Capitalist on the Montana Frontier." PhD diss., University of Montana, 1976.

Johnson, Daniel P. "Anti-Japanese Legislation in Oregon, 1917-1923." *Oregon Historical Quarterly* 97, no. 2 (1996): 176–210.

Johnson, Susan Lee. *Roaring Camp: The Social World of the California Gold Rush.* New York: W. W. Norton, 2001.

Johnston, Robert D. *The Radical Middle Class: Populist Democracy and the Question of Capitalism in Progressive Era Portland, Oregon.* Princeton, NJ: Princeton University Press, 2006.

Kammer, Sean M. "Land and Law in the Age of Enterprise: A Legal History of Railroad Land Grants in the Pacific Northwest, 1864-1916." PhD diss., University of Nebraska–Lincoln, 2015.

Kelly, Cara McCulley. "Prehistoric Land-Use Patterns in the North Santiam Subbasin on the Western Slopes of the Oregon Cascade Range." M.A. thesis, Oregon State University, 2002.

Langston, Nancy. *Forest Dreams, Forest Nightmares: The Paradox of Old Growth in the Inland West.* Seattle: University of Washington Press, 1996.

Lay, Shawn. *The Invisible Empire in the West: Toward a New Historical Appraisal of the Ku Klux Klan of the 1920s.* Urbana: University of Illinois Press, 1992.

Leech, Brian James. *The City That Ate Itself: Butte, Montana and Its Expanding Berkeley Pit.* Reno: University of Nevada Press, 2018.

Lembcke, Jerry, and William M. Tattam. *One Union in Wood.* New York: International Publishers, 1984.

Lewis, David G. *NDNHistory Research: Indigenous, Public and Critical Essays* (blog). http://ndnhistoryresearch.wordpress.com.

———. "Termination of the Confederated Tribes of the Grand Ronde Community of Oregon: Politics, Community, Identity." PhD thesis, University of Oregon, 2009.

———. "Four Deaths: The Near Destruction of Western Oregon Tribes and Native Lifeways, Removal to the Reservation, and Erasure from History." *Oregon Historical Quarterly* 115, no. 3 (2014): 414–37.

Lewis, David G., and Robert Kentta. "Western Oregon Reservations: Two Perspectives on Place." *Oregon Historical Quarterly* 111, no. 4 (2010): 476–85.

Limerick, Patricia Nelson. *The Legacy of Conquest*. New York: W. W. Norton, 1987.

Lipin, Lawrence M. *Workers and the Wild: Conservation, Consumerism, and Labor in Oregon, 1910-30*. Urbana: University of Illinois Press, 2007.

Loo, Tina. "People in the Way: Modernity, Environment, and Society on British Columbia's Arrow Lakes." *BC Studies* 142 and 143 (2004): 161–91.

———. "Disturbing the Peace: Environmental Change and the Scales of Justice on a Northern River." *Environmental History* 12, no. 4 (2007): 895–919.

Loomis, Erik. *Empire of Timber: Labor Unions and the Pacific Northwest Forests*. New York: Cambridge University Press, 2016.

Loomis, Erik, and Ryan Edgington. "Lives under the Canopy: Spotted Owls and Loggers in Western Forests." *Natural Resources Journal* 52 (2012): 99–134.

Lowe, Beverly. *John Minto: Man of Courage, 1822-1915*. Salem, OR: Kingston Price, 1980.

Lowitt, Richard. *The New Deal and the West*. Bloomington: Indiana University Press, 1984.

Mackey, Harold. *The Kalapuyans: A Sourcebook on the Indians of the Willamette Valley*. 2nd ed. Salem, OR: Mission Mill Museum Association; Grande Ronde, OR: Confederated Tribes of Grand Ronde, 2004.

MacLean, Nancy. *Behind the Mask of Chivalry: The Making of the Second Ku Klux Klan*. New York: Oxford University Press, 1994.

Maher, Neil M. *Nature's New Deal: The Civilian Conservation Corps and the Roots of the American Environmental Movement*. New York: Oxford University Press, 2007.

Marcot, Bruce G., Jack Ward Thomas, US Interagency Scientific Committee, Pacific Northwest Research Station. *Of Spotted Owls, Old Growth, and New Policies: A History since the Interagency Scientific Committee Report*. Portland, OR: US Department of Agriculture, Forest Service, Pacific Northwest Research Station, 1997.

Marsh, George Perkins. *Man and Nature; Or, Physical Geography as Modified by Human Action*. Seattle: University of Washington Press, 2003.

Marsh, Kevin. *Drawing Lines in the Forest: Creating Wilderness Areas in the Pacific Northwest*. Seattle: University of Washington Press, 2007.

Marx, Leo. *The Machine in the Garden: Technology and the Pastoral Ideal in America*. New York: Oxford University Press, 2000.

Mauldin, Frank. *Sweet Mountain Water: The Story of Salem, Oregon's Struggle to Tap Mt. Jefferson Water and Protect the North Santiam River*. Salem, OR: Oak Savanna, 2004.

McKinney, Gage. "A. B. Hammond, West Coast Lumberman." *Journal of Forest History* 28, no. 4 (1984): 196–203.

Medford, Elizabeth. "Lumber, Community, and the Anti-Environmentalist Movement: Environmentalists Cannot See the Wood for the Trees." MA thesis, University of Oregon, 2005.

Messing, John. "Public Lands, Politics, and Progressives: The Oregon Land Fraud Trials, 1903-1910." *Pacific Historical Review* 35, no. 1 (1966): 35–66.

Milner, Clyde A., Carol O'Connor, and Martha Sandweiss, eds. *The Oxford History of the American West*. New York: Oxford University Press, 1994.

Minto, John. "The Number and Condition of the Native Race in Oregon When First Seen by White Men." *Quarterly of the Oregon Historical Society* 1, no. 3 (1900): 296–315.

———. "Minto Pass: Its History, and an Indian Tradition." *Quarterly of the Oregon Historical Society* 4, no. 3 (1903): 241–50. https://www.jstor.org/stable/20609580.

———. "From Youth to Age as an American." *Quarterly of the Oregon Historical Society* 9, no. 2 (1908): 127–72.

———. "OHQ 100 Years: From Youth to Age as an American: John Minto in the Willamette Valley." *Oregon Historical Quarterly* 101, no. 2 (2000): 237–45.

Moravets, F. L. *Lumber Production in Oregon and Washington, 1869-1948*. Portland, OR: Pacific Northwest Forest and Range Experiment Station, Division of Forest Economics, 1949.

Morrissey, Katherine G. *Mental Territories: Mapping the Inland Empire*. Ithaca, NY: Cornell University Press, 1997.

Munro, Sarah Baker. "The Seventy-Fifth Anniversary of the New Deal: Oregon's Legacy." *Oregon Historical Quarterly* 109, no. 2 (2008): 304–11.

Nash, Roderick Frazier. *Wilderness and the American Mind*. 5th ed. New Haven, CT: Yale University Press, 2014.

Nugent, Walter. *Crossings: The Great Transatlantic Migrations, 1870-1914*. Bloomington: Indiana University Press, 1992.

Oregon Pacific Railroad Company. *Prospectus of the Oregon Pacific R.R. Co.* New York: J. B. Beers, 1880.

Petersen, Jim. *Santiam Song*. Mill City, OR: Freres Lumber, 2018.

Peterson del Mar, David. *Oregon's Promise: An Interpretive History*. Corvallis: Oregon State University Press, 2003.

Philpott, William. *Vactionland: Tourism and Environment in the Colorado High Country*. Seattle: University of Washington Press, 2014.

Pierce, Jason. "The Winds of Change: The Decline of Extractive Industries and the Rise of Tourism in Hood River County, Oregon." *Oregon Historical Quarterly* 108, no. 3 (2007): 410–31.

Pomeroy, Earl. *The Pacific Slope: A History of California, Oregon, Washington, Idaho, Utah, and Nevada.* Seattle: University of Washington Press, 1965.

Pope, Daniel. *Nuclear Implosions: The Rise and Fall of the Washington Public Power Supply System.* New York: Cambridge University Press, 2008.

Prouty, Andrew Mason. *More Deadly Than War! Pacific Coast Logging, 1827-1981.* New York: Garland, 1985.

Prudham, W. Scott. *Knock on Wood: Nature as Commodity in Douglas Fir Country.* New York: Routledge, 2005.

Rada, Edward L. *Singing My Song: Growing Up in a Lumber Town Mill City, Oregon 1916-1939.* Bloomington, IN: AuthorHouse, 2009.

Rajala, Richard. *Clearcutting the Pacific Rain Forest: Production, Science, and Regulation.* Vancouver: University of British Columbia Press, 1998.

Rakestraw, Lawrence, and Mary Rakestraw. *History of the Willamette National Forest.* Eugene, OR: US Department of Agriculture, Forest Service, Willamette National Forest, 1991.

Rauchway, Eric. *Murdering McKinley: The Making of Theodore Roosevelt's America.* New York: Hill and Wang, 2003.

———. *Blessed among Nations: How the World Made America.* Reprint. New York: Hill and Wang, 2007.

———. *The Great Depression and the New Deal: A Very Short Introduction.* Oxford University Press, 2008.

Reid, John Phillip. *Contested Empire: Peter Skene Ogden and the Snake River Expeditions.* Norman: University of Oklahoma Press, 2002.

———. *Forging a Fur Empire: Expeditions in the Snake River Country, 1809-1824.* Norman, OK: Arthur H. Clark, 2011.

Reinhardt, Bob H. "Drowned Towns in the Cold War West: Small Communities and Federal Water Projects." *Western Historical Quarterly* 42, no. 2 (May 1, 2011): 149–72.

Reisner, Marc. *Cadillac Desert: The American West and Its Disappearing Water.* Rev. ed. New York: Penguin, 1993.

Robbins, William G. "The Willamette Valley Project of Oregon: A Study in the Political Economy of Water Resource Development." *Pacific Historical Review* 47, no. 4 (1978): 585–605.

———. *Lumberjacks and Legislators: Political Economy of the U.S. Lumber Industry, 1890-1941.* College Station: Texas A&M University Press, 1982.

———. "The 'Plundered Province' Thesis and the Recent Historiography of the American West." *Pacific Historical Review* 55, no. 4 (1986): 577–97.

———. *Colony and Empire: The Capitalist Transformation of the American West.* Lawrence: University Press of Kansas, 1994.

———. *Landscapes of Promise: The Oregon Story, 1800-1940.* Seattle: University of Washington Press, 1997.

———. *Landscapes of Conflict: The Oregon Story, 1940-2000.* Seattle: University of Washington Press, 2004.

———. *Oregon: This Storied Land.* Portland: Oregon Historical Society Press, 2005.

——. *Hard Times in Paradise: Coos Bay, Oregon*. Rev. ed. Seattle: University of Washington Press, 2006.

——. "Surviving the Great Depression: The New Deal in Oregon." *Oregon Historical Quarterly* 109, no. 2 (2008): 311–17.

——. "Town and Country in Oregon: A Conflicted Legacy." *Oregon Historical Quarterly* 110, no. 1 (2009): 52–73.

Rodgers, Daniel T. "In Search of Progressivism." *Reviews in American History* 10, no. 4 (December 1982): 113–32.

Rome, Adam. *The Bulldozer in the Countryside: Suburban Sprawl and the Rise of American Environmentalism*. Cambridge: Cambridge University Press, 2001.

Rothman, Hal K. "Selling the Meaning of Place: Entrepreneurship, Tourism, and Community Transformation in the Twentieth-Century American West." *Pacific Historical Review* 65, no. 4 (November 1996): 525–57.

——. *Devil's Bargains: Tourism in the Twentieth-Century American West*. Lawrence: University Press of Kansas, 1998.

——. *The Greening of a Nation? Environmentalism in the United States since 1945*. Belmont, CA: Wadsworth/Thomson Learning, 1998.

Satterfield, Terre. *Anatomy of a Conflict: Identity, Knowledge, and Emotion in Old-Growth Forests*. Vancouver: University of British Columbia Press, 2002.

Schwantes, Carlos A. *The Pacific Northwest: An Interpretive History*. Lincoln: University of Nebraska Press, 1996.

Schwartz, E. A. *The Rogue River Indian War and Its Aftermath, 1850-1980*. Norman: University of Oklahoma Press, 1997.

Scott, James C. *Weapons of the Weak: Everyday Forms of Peasant Resistance*. New Haven, CT: Yale University Press, 1985.

——. *Domination and the Arts of Resistance: Hidden Transcripts*. New Haven, CT: Yale University Press, 1990.

Scott, Leslie M. "The Yaquina Railroad: The Tale of a Great Fiasco." *Oregon Historical Quarterly* 16, no. 3 (1915): 228–45.

——. "Indian Diseases as Aids to Pacific Northwest Settlement." *Oregon Historical Quarterly* 29, no. 2 (1928): 144–61.

Seideman, David. *Showdown at Opal Creek: The Battle for America's Last Wilderness*. New York: Carroll & Graf, 1993.

Sellers, Christopher C. *Crabgrass Crucible: Suburban Nature and the Rise of Environmentalism in Twentieth-Century America*. Chapel Hill: University of North Carolina Press, 2012.

Skocpol, Theda. "Civil Society in the United States." In *The Oxford Handbook of Civil Society*, 109–21. New York: Oxford University Press, 2011.

Slotkin, Richard. *Regeneration through Violence: The Mythology of the American Frontier, 1600-1860*. Middletown, CT: Wesleyan University Press, 1973.

——. *The Fatal Environment: The Myth of the Frontier in the Age of Industrialization, 1800-1890*. 1st ed. New York: Atheneum, 1985.

——. *Gunfighter Nation: The Myth of the Frontier in Twentieth-Century America*. Norman: University of Oklahoma Press, 1998.

Spector, Robert. *Family Trees: Simpson's Centennial Story*. Bellevue, WA: Documentary Book Publishers, 1990.

Spies, Thomas A., and Sally L. Duncan. *Old Growth in a New World: A Pacific Northwest Icon Reexamined*. Washington, DC: Island Press, 2009.

Spores, Ronald. "Too Small a Place: The Removal of the Willamette Valley Indians, 1850-1856." *American Indian Quarterly* 17, no. 2 (1993): 171–91.

Stankey, George H., et al. "Adaptive Management and the Northwest Forest Plan: Rhetoric and Reality." *Journal of Forestry* 101, no. 1 (February 2003): 40–46.

Steiner, Michael C. "Regionalism in the Great Depression." *Geographical Review* 73, no. 4 (1983): 430–46.

Stout, Ray. "The Mehama Story." *Marion County History* 10 (1969–71): 17–27.

Sutter, Paul. *Driven Wild: How the Fight against Automobiles Launched the Modern Wilderness Movement*. Seattle: University of Washington Press, 2002.

Tanaka, Stefan. "The First Person Who 'Owned' Mill City." *North Santiam Historical Society News* 15, no. 2 (August 2, 2013): 2.

Thomas, Jack Ward, Jerry F. Franklin, John Gordon, and K. Norman Johnson. "The Northwest Forest Plan: Origins, Components, Implementation Experience, and Suggestions for Change." *Conservation Biology* 20, no. 2 (April 2006): 277–87.

Tonsfeldt, Ward. *History of the Oregon Pacific Railroad in the Cascade Mountains 1886-1889*. R6-WILL-010<H>07. US Department of Agriculture, Forest Service, Willamette National Forest, 1998.

Vogel, Eve. "The Columbia River's Region: Politics, Place and Environment in the Pacific Northwest, 1933–Present." PhD thesis, University of Oregon, 2007. https://scholarsbank.uoregon.edu/xmlui/handle/1794/6280.

Wallis, Joe. *An Evaluation of the North Santiam River Salmon Hatcheries*. Clackamas: Oregon Fish Commission Research Laboratory, 1963.

Webb, Pamela. "By the Sweat of the Brow: The Back-to-the-Land Movement in Depression Arkansas." *Arkansas Historical Quarterly* 42, no. 4 (1983): 332–45.

Wellock, Thomas. "The Dickey Bird Scientists Take Charge: Science, Policy, and the Spotted Owl." *Environmental History* 15, no. 3 (2010): 381–414.

Wells, Christopher W. *Car Country: An Environmental History*. Seattle: University of Washington Press, 2014.

Whaley, Gray H. *Oregon and the Collapse of Illahee: U.S. Empire and the Transformation of an Indigenous World, 1792-1859*. Chapel Hill: University of North Carolina Press, 2010.

White, Richard. "Poor Men on Poor Lands: The Back-to-the-Land Movement of the Early Twentieth Century: A Case Study." *Pacific Historical Review* 49, no. 1 (1980): 105–31.

——. *Land Use, Environment, and Social Change: The Shaping of Island County, Washington*. Paperback ed. Seattle: University of Washington Press, 1992.

——. *"It's Your Misfortune and None of My Own": A New History of the American West*. Norman: University of Oklahoma Press, 1993.

——. *The Organic Machine: The Remaking of the Columbia River*. New York: Hill and Wang, 1996.

——. *Railroaded: The Transcontinentals and the Making of Modern America*. New York: W. W. Norton, 2012.

Wiebe, Robert H. *The Search for Order, 1877-1920*. New York: Hill and Wang, 1967.

Williams, Richard Lippincott. *The Loggers*. Alexandria, VA: Time-Life Books, 1981.

Willingham, William. *Army Engineers and the Development of Oregon: A History of the Portland District, U.S. Army Corps of Engineers*. Washington, DC: US Army Corps of Engineers, 1983.

——. *Starting Over: Community Building on the Eastern Oregon Frontier*. Portland: Oregon Historical Society Press, 2005.

Worster, Donald. *Rivers of Empire: Water, Aridity, and the Growth of the American West*. Oxford University Press, 1992.

——. *Nature's Economy: A History of Ecological Ideas*. 2nd ed. New York: Cambridge University Press, 1994.

Zenk, Henry. "Notes on Native American Place-Names of the Willamette Valley Region." *Oregon Historical Quarterly* 109, no. 1 (2008): 6–33.

Index